LAW AND SOCIAL ORDER IN THE UNITED STATES

LAW AND SOCIAL ORDER
IN THE UNITED STATES

BY JAMES WILLARD HURST

Cornell University Press   ITHACA AND LONDON

First published 1977 by Cornell University Press.
Published in the United Kingdom by Cornell University Press Ltd., 2–4 Brook Street, London W1Y 1AA.

International Standard Book Number 0–8014–1063–0
Library of Congress Catalog Card Number 76–28015
Printed in the United States of America by York Composition Co., Inc.
Librarians: Library of Congress cataloging information appears on the last page of the book.

Preface

This volume seeks to outline some key subject-matter divisions of United States legal history, considered for the insights it can offer into the general history of the country.

Part One identifies some distinctive dimensions of legal history as a field of study. I begin here because the meaning of legal history as a field derives from the presence of law in society as a particular institution, possessing its own forms of organized power and its own ways of operating. Chapter I is the most general in scope; though it does not purport to sketch all significant topics in the country's legal history, it uses particular examples to give a sense of the broad potential range of the subject, particularly viewed as social history of the law. Chapter II deals with the core of legal history. It outlines the development of the major types of authority wielded by the principal agencies of law, on the hypothesis that the kinds of authorized working capacities these agencies hold have been more important than their formal structure in determining their impact on public policy.

Part Two presents two specially important examples of the law in interplay with other institutions and currents of values. Chapters III and IV build on the proposition that this culture highly prized active, creative will. In their efforts to exert will on their situations, individuals have confronted challenges both from the physical and biological environment and from the social environment. Chapter III deals with public-policy responses to the challenge of the physical and biological setting, exploring relations between law and science and technology. Chapter IV focuses on

5

law's efforts to shape, serve, and adapt to two social institutions of great influence—the market and the big business corporation.

My purpose is to sketch subjects that promise useful development. These essays thus do not purport to tell a full story of what they touch. Elaborate documentation would not be appropriate; the footnotes simply offer material illustrative or suggestive of the propositions in the text. Moreover, the amount of work that has been done in United States legal history is still too limited to allow a full discussion of many topics. This volume ventures too often into unexplored or thinly explored territory to make full mapping possible. I have put down propositions that I believe valid on the basis of what I know, but I am conscious that I do not know enough of many things.

A skeptic may ask whether such a confession of limitations does not deprive this book of warrant for being. The question is fair, but its answer derives from the general state of the field. None of us at this stage knows very much about the history of law in the society. Resources devoted to studying the history of law have been highly inadequate to the reach of the subject into the life of the United States. But it is likely that commitments have been limited in good part because we have not sufficiently surveyed the potential subject matter of the field to raise challenges that might elicit more resources.

I am particularly conscious of two areas of omission. I have chosen to emphasize the social history of law—law in relation to other social institutions and to general currents of ideas and inertia in the society. This emphasis scants, though it does not ignore, study of the meaning of legal order to individual life—to individual privacy and creative will, to the stresses social living puts on individual thinking and feeling, to individual experience of the opportunities and constraints attending different phases of life's course, from youth, to maturity, to old age. Second, this focus on the social aspect of legal history pushes out of the central spotlight the history of law told in terms of such familiar doctrinal headings as property, tort, and contract. Each of these is an area of the law's impingement on life that deserves the historian's attention. Public policy as a dimension of the individual's life course warrants study because in this aspect it relates to a universal factor; we all experience life alone as well as together. Public policy as embodied in the law's own doctrinal patterns warrants study because such categories manifest much of the law's reality as a distinct institution. These doctrinal headings embody functional contributions that law makes to such general social concerns as fostering production and exchange of goods and services or handling the costs of accidents; they also encompass much of law's vested professional interests and its contributions to social inertia. I have subordinated such elements in these essays not because I regard them as unimportant, but simply because I have sought to present in rather brief form a general point of view toward legal history.

I am grateful to Cornell University for the invitation to deliver the Carl L. Becker Lectures in April 1976, from which these essays derive. My thanks go also to Michael Kammen of Cornell's Department of History, to Roger Cramton of the Cornell Law School, and to their colleagues, for providing a most hospitable setting for the lectures.

Themes developed in this book grow out of a long-term program of work in the social history of law in the United States. Over some years I have been indebted for support in this effort to the Social Science Research Council, the Rockefeller Foundation, the administration of the University of Wisconsin, and the trustees of the William F. Vilas Trust Estate, under whose auspices I hold a chair as Vilas Professor of Law at the University of Wisconsin. Of course, the book does not purport to speak for any of these agencies; I take sole responsibility for what I write.

JAMES WILLARD HURST

Madison, Wisconsin

Contents

Contents

Analytical Table of Contents

THE RANGE
AND THE CENTER
OF LEGAL HISTORY

CHAPTER I

The Range of United States Legal History

At first sight, study of the legal history of the United States is a specialized inquiry, dealing with only one dimension of complex events. Yet it is an unusual specialty, for the events of which the law was a part range over most of the country's experience. One can more readily separate out from other aspects of the society the history of the family, or the church, or the school than he can the history of law. That this was a law-minded, law-using people, whose affairs were touched by legal processes at many points, is a basic fact that quickly enforces itself on one who examines legal elements in the life of the United States.[1] Legal history is a way of studying the general history of the country's character and development.

Basic also is the fact that people generally have used law in a narrowly practical way. Typically they were concerned with law more as an instrument for desired immediate results than as a statement of carefully legitimated, long-range values. This is not to say that law did not express and to some extent establish significant hierarchies of values; even in its everyday practicality much of law's business consisted of assigning and enforcing priorities among people's wants and needs. In so down-to-earth a matter as setting the terms on which man might build dams in Wisconsin forest country for waterpower or to control the volume of water for carrying logs, statutes dealt with value priorities; the legislature preferred waterpower over agriculture to the extent that it allowed the dam builder to flood upstream land, subject to procedures for fair compensation; it preferred trans-

1. Tocqueville, 1:247–253, 272–280.

port over waterpower to the extent that it required the dam builder to provide slides for the passage of rafted logs. But a characteristic of the culture was that these value priorities emerged only by implication from the particulars of hundreds of dam franchise statutes; the nineteenth-century legislature provided no explicit code to align competing stream uses, no legislative committee produced a reasoned statement of the premises underlying the procession of special dam franchise statutes, and —most significant—legislators made no explicit judgments relating stream use to the general pace and range of Wisconsin's economic development.[2]

This narrowly practical character of the uses of law cautions us against equating legal history with legal philosophy. Philosophy deals with the potential, history with the actual uses of law. Philosophy thus can provide a critique of events, revealing the limitations of public policy in sharper relief than might otherwise appear. But the values that people wrote into law and more or less implemented through law did not add up to a neatly balanced, conceptually complete pattern of human interests. Consider again, in this light, public policy affecting bulk transport and the growth of Wisconsin's lumber industry. In an ideally complete pattern of social values, law should embody concern for the long-term as well as the short-term productivity of the economy. From the long-term view, social interest called for holding the pace and methods of exploiting the Wisconsin forest within limits consistent with keeping the forest a continuing, sustained-yield resource. As matters worked out through the nineteenth century, public policy included little effective expression of this value. For example, lawmakers bent all their efforts to facilitating development of the streams, and later the railways, to move maximum output of the forest to Midwest markets, heedless of what this tempo spelled for the good order of the economy two or three generations hence.[3]

2. Hurst (4), 205–206, 220–225.
3. Id., 37, 41–47, 95–107, 112–116, 124, 135, 206–207, 220, 254, 261, 470–471, 502, 542, 588.

That uses of law reach broadly through the life of the country without also embodying a comparably broad philosophy of these uses creates problems for telling the history of law. What went on is such a mixture of calculation and lack of calculation as to defy neat relation. There can be no single point of view from which all United States legal history falls into a coherent sequence. Rather, the subject must be turned this way and that, to catch different but relevant aspects of a complex reality.

Legal Processes as the Core of Legal History

There is a legal history of the United States because law existed as a distinct, massive institution, acting on and being acted on by other currents of life. Thus legal history properly begins with the story of legal agencies and their immediate products.

In deciding what to include as "law" I do not find it profitable to distinguish "law" from "government" or from "policy." The heart of the matter is that we formed organizations for collective action characterized by their own distinctive bases of legitimacy —some legitimated by popular election, some by prescribed forms of appointment—by their distinctive structures, and by possession of a legitimate monopoly of force. These agencies worked through their own procedures—for example, passing statutes to tax or to spend public money, or deciding cases or controversies within legally established standards of rules. The presence of politically organized power is the special feature, with all the relations and practices that spring directly from its exercise. In order to see law in its relations to the society as a whole, one must appraise all formal and informal aspects of politically organized power—observe the functions of all legal agencies (legislative, executive, administrative, or judicial) and take account of the interplay of such agencies with voters and nonvoters, lobbyists and interest groups, politicians and political parties. This definition overruns traditional boundaries dividing study of law from study of political history, political science, and sociology. But these boundaries are partly the products of accidents of academic history and partly the expression of practical divisions of labor; they are not fixed by categorical differences among the facts of behavior that give rise to our concern with legal history. There has been a tendency to identify legal history with the history of courts and court-made doctrine. This identification in turn sometimes has carried the implication that legal history proper deals only with fixed or relatively certain value criteria, as compared with values still emerging out of interest-group controversy or out of tentative gropings toward new formulations of interest. But the distinctive fact is that the society used certain agencies and processes based on politically organized power to bring interests over some threshold of social awareness and to provide accepted procedures for identifying, debating, and determining priorities among interests. It was no less the function of law to bring public policy into being than to apply already existing policy; legal history should run wherever these functions ran, simply because, however settled or unsettled, the product of these processes was in substantial part the product of legal operations.[4]

The principal impact of law on the country's history was made by the activity of four kinds of formal legal agencies—the electorate, legislatures, courts, and executive or administrative offices. One could add to this list the processes of formal constitution making. But, important as were constitution makers, for the present purpose we can put them aside. Their most enduring contributions show in the operations of the other agencies. Indeed, most constitution making proceeded through legislative bodies; there was but one federal Constitutional Convention, and though there were several hundred state constitutional conventions, they added up to relatively little structural innovation in the legal order, and in large part they did more clumsily work that should have been left to legislation.

4. Hurst (3), 137–151, 182–214.

From the outset of our legal history the electorate was a distinct lawmaking agency because law always limited those eligible to participate in creating the structure of legal order. Normally the body of voters exerted only a background or framework-setting influence and did not supply the principal movement in public policy; law, as Mr. Justice Holmes crisply observed, could not all be made in town meeting.[5] But the extent and working character of the electorate affected the working character of the more specialized agencies. Thus what law did to define the body of voters was a significant aspect of legal history.

Law normally defined voters as individuals, not as members of functional groups or as members of class or caste. There were important qualifications on this proposition, about which swirled some of the most bitter issues of the social balance of power, as law denied voter status at one time or another to Indians, slaves, freed blacks, women, and aliens. The over-all direction of policy, however, with roots reaching back to the Parliamentary Revolution in England, was to enlarge the electorate; there were long, hard-fought delaying battles over this trend, but never a reversal of direction in formal policy.[6] Of course, formal policy was never the whole story, and there were informal reversals of formal broadening of the suffrage—by legal subterfuge, by violence against rights given by the Thirteenth and Fifteenth Amendments, and by recurrent dilution of votes by malapportionment and gerrymandering of legislative districts.[7]

Public policy also included concern for the legal and practical independence of the electorate. Voters were limited by their ignorance; in offset, the law fostered public and private education and asserted protection for free speech, free press, and

5. Bi-Metallic Investment Co. v. State Board of Equalization, 239 U.S. 441, 445 (1951).

6. Cf. Harper v. Virginia State Board of Elections, 383 U.S. 663, 670 (1966); Kramer v. Union Free School District, 395 U.S. 621 (1969). See also, Campbell et al., Chap. 11; Key, Chap. 17, especially 526–530.

7. Hacker and Zahler (2), 95–97, 501; Key, 531–541, 552–568; Merriam, 1507–1511; Morison and Commager, 2:20, 378; Williams, 249–250.

peaceful assembly. Voters were limited by fear. Against fear of political abuse, the Consitution erected barriers to bills of attainder or loose charges of treason, and from the late nineteenth century on statutes provided for the secrecy of the ballot box. The secret ballot was also a protection against fear of private power, as was legislation against discrimination in employment on account of voting, against such private armies as the Ku Klux Klan, and against the power of private money in election campaigns.[8] Realistic appraisal of law's contributions and defaults affecting the working quality of the electorate posed as sophisticated a challenge as any confronting the legal historian. But the challenge needed to be met, for the presence of the electorate introduced a factor of legitimate contingency into all other holding of public power that was basic to the constitutional ideal of responsible government.[9]

Important as it was, the body of voters was a force that stood always in the background of the more continuously active agencies of law. As to the more active agencies, legal history confronts two principal themes—one, the division of labor among departments of lawmaking; the other, the division of labor according to scale or reach of authority, involving both federalism and the allocation of responsibilities between state and local government.

Departmental division of labor, in turn, involves two themes, one less marked by change and movement than the other. First is history of the formal structure of the legislative, judicial, executive, and administrative arms of government, both national and state. Second is history of the lawful powers or capacities of these branches, which, more than formal structure, gave working meaning to legislative, executive-administrative, and judicial processes. This second subject I reserve to the next chapter. Here let

8. Padover, 649 (Jefferson, *Notes on Virginia*, Query XIII), 668 (Query XIV); Mann, 1:592–593.

9. See Yick Wo v. Hopkins, 118 U.S. 356, 370 (1886); Reynolds v. Sims, 377 U.S. 533, 562 (1964).

me take brief note of some aspects of the structural development of the principal branches.

The formal structure of agencies showed less change than did the patterns of agency powers. From the outset of national life the two-chamber legislature was the norm. Originally there was some inclination to set up one of the two chambers on terms that would make it specially representative of a functional, economic interest—that of the landed or commercial-agricultural party. But the currents of Jacksonian equality swept away that distinction by the 1830's, and thenceforth there was considerable ambiguity as to the functional significance of two chambers, beyond generating friction and delay in lawmaking.[10] By mid-twentieth century some greater rationale had entered the two-house division. By then the staple pattern was that one house should have members of longer terms and broader constituencies than the other; these features tended to make the two houses responsive to somewhat different political and interest-group pressures, thus affording at least the opportunity for different policies than might come from a single chamber. In the background of both houses since the 1830's was the fundamental factor that both normally were composed of legislators from geographically and not functionally defined constituencies, each of which elected one representative. This basic feature provided a more open field for the maneuver of particular interests, but also tended to give politicians more scope to play interests against each other, and so contributed a degree of practical independence for the political process. This relative openness and independence created the distinctive sense in which the legislative branch was the most "representative" of the major legal agencies. The practical outcomes in public policy form large themes of consensus and difference in the society.[11] One other feature of legislative structure deserves emphasis. Bicameralism and the single-member,

10. Hurst (1), 44.
11. American Political Science Association, 17, 35–40, 47–50, 59; Walker, 160–167.

geographically defined constituency were stable elements for some 150 years. The role of the legislative committee changed more. Originally committees were ad hoc, select bodies, charged only with specific matters. Henry Clay's leadership of the House of Representatives set a significant new pattern, with broad establishment of standing committees. From the late nineteenth century on, both in Congress and in the states, standing committees mounted in importance, to become the principal work places of legislatures and to develop traditions of jurisdictional autonomy and ties to particular executive offices that threatened the capacity of their parent chambers to remain masters of policy making. The growth of practical power concentrated in committees was the most striking structural change in the legislative branch after mid-nineteenth century.[12]

Once policy makers established salient characteristics of judicial structure, these features tended to endure with a stubbornness special to that branch. Most of the work of courts concerned highly focused disputes or matters of administration of lively interest only to the immediate parties, conducted within a highly technical frame of procedure known only to lawyers; in this setting it was not surprising that general opinion, or even legislative interest, rarely was alert to problems of judicial organization and procedure. The historic moral was clear: policy makers should take care what structural provisions they made for judicial process because of the extreme difficulty in mustering the requisite political momentum to change what once was set.[13] Among various problem areas of judicial structure, let me note three: selection and tenure, localism, and exaggeration of the appellate function.

The model set by the first states, soon bulwarked by the provision for federal courts, was that judges be appointed. But by mid-nineteenth century the surge of Jacksonian equality had

12. Fenno (1), Chaps. 1, 10, and (2), xiii, 276–278, 280, 289; Truman, 330–331, 369–387; Woodrow Wilson, 56, 60, 70, 78.
13. Hurst (1), 88, 91, 95, 111, 120; Jacob, 142–146; Harry W. Jones (1), 3, 6; Winters and Allard, 147, 151, 155.

established the trend that in most states judges were elected. There is not convincing evidence that the difference between appointment and election made significant differences in the performance of state appellate courts. But by the twentieth century, election of trial court judges clearly did not work well in an increasingly urban, metropolitan setting; voters were indifferent and ill-informed, and election tended simply to blur responsibility for the quality of the bench. By the second half of the twentieth century several states were experimenting with a mixed system, under which a judge was appointed to sit for a number of years and then run for election on his record; if the voters removed him, the appointing process would provide his successor. The change seemed a promising one, but it was a slow, uphill battle against a century-old populist tradition.[14]

Two other matters of policy tradition affecting court organization had closely related effects. From early days when transportation was difficult and even dangerous, the country inherited a tradition that trial courts should be located close to the people whose disputes they might handle and that each trial court was responsible simply for the business of its locality. Again, urbanization brought acute problems. Substantial disproportions arose in the volume of business brought to trial courts in different areas, but the tradition of localism meant that each trial judge operated in isolation from his fellows, regardless of how thin or thick the docket of his court. The problem affected both state and federal trial courts. A pool of judicial manpower was needed, subject to some over-all administrative management that would put judges in sufficient number where business demanded them. The first steps to unify state courts were taken on a municipal level about the 1920's, and a Judicial Conference of the United States was set up in 1922 to begin some coordination of federal court manpower. Congress created an administrative office for the federal courts in 1939 and provided also for federal conferences organized by circuits. By mid-century some states had begun to

14. Haynes, 85–101; Hurst (1), 122–123, 134.

set up offices to coordinate judicial manpower on a statewide basis. But the localist bias was deep-rooted, and the movement toward pooled trial court resources was faltering and slow.[15] The situation was more difficult because national and state legislative tradition opposed generous provision for trial court facilities. From nineteenth-century experience the country inherited a strong bias toward exalting the importance of appellate courts while neglecting the lower courts, a bias derived largely from the lagging development of legislative lawmaking. A growing country needed law to service a growing economy in decades when state legislatures lacked experience to meet the need. The result over the span from about 1810 to 1890 was to cast on state appellate courts a large burden of providing common (judge-made) law, especially to service the needs of the market for a law of contract, property, and security instruments. Hence policy makers learned to exalt the role of appellate judges as lawmakers, to the neglect of staffing the trial courts and providing them with needed auxiliary facilities. This trend continued into mid-twentieth century with disastrous consequences for overburdened trial courts of metropolitan areas, bringing the trial process close to breakdown in many areas.[16]

During the twentieth century the structure of executive and administrative agencies underwent much more drastic change than affected legislatures or courts. Before then the only area of major growth was in the independent status of the office of chief executive. The federal Constitution created the potential of a strong presidency by giving the President an independent elected basis. This independence was strengthened by informal political practice when the rise of national political parties in effect took the selection of the President away from the electoral college and gave the President a claim to a national constituency, thus arming him powerfully to assert a new position of policy leadership. Early state constitutions, reflecting distrust of executive power

15. Hurst (1), 92–96, 114–115; Jacob, 140–142.
16. Hurst (1), 93, 177, 189, 269; Harry W. Jones (1), 5, 6, and (2), 124, 126, 128, 130.

inherited from the Revolution, had made the governor subject to the legislature. But state constitution makers soon changed this position and provided the governor with his own title directly from the voters as well as giving him the veto.[17] Most of the significant changes in the position of the chief executive in the nation and in the states occurred, however, by practical development of the authority wielded by the office, rather than by structural change; the next chapter takes further note of this. The principal structural changes in the executive and administrative establishments came by legislation, with the proliferation of offices during and after the last quarter of the nineteenth century as national and state governments enlarged their service and regulatory roles. Of particular importance was the creative decade from about 1905 to 1915, which saw the rapid rise of independent administrative agencies—notably a strengthened Interstate Commerce Commission and the new Federal Reserve System and Federal Trade Commission on the national scene and new state agencies concerned with factory safety, workmen's compensation, and public utility regulation. Concurrently executive departments in the national government expanded. All of these developments had in common a lack of provision for effective oversight or coordination of policy either by legislators or chief executives. By mid-twentieth century some measures had been taken to introduce more oversight of executive departments through the Federal Bureau of the Budget (later the Office of Management and Budget) and through state departments of administration assisting to implement centralized executive budgets. This change, however, left the problem of checking and coordinating the performance of independent administrative agencies, which—sometimes in alliance with particular legislative committees—tended to operate as separate baronies.[18]

Problems of determining the proper scale of government activ-

17. Hurst (1), 235, 236, 383, 400–404; Koenig, Chaps. 2, 7.
18. Marver Bernstein, 35–47, 71–73, 164–168, 176–179, 253–258, 286–287; Hurst (1), 419–421, 424–425, 428; Kohlmeier, 266–286; Smithies, Chaps. IV, V.

ity have bulked large in United States legal history. Issues of federalism were primary. After the Civil War ratified the establishment of an indissoluble national union, critical structural change rested on four constitutional amendments. The three post-Civil War amendments barred the states' capacity to create property in human beings and nationalized protection of broadly defined civil rights, including the right to vote. The substance of these changes was largely destroyed for some eighty years by loss of heart in Congress and by the political bargain of 1877, withdrawing federal enforcement of the newly declared rights. But the civil rights legislation of the 1960's and judicial activity under both old and new civil rights laws emphasized the potential of the Civil War amendments to redistribute roles between the national and the state governments.[19] The fourth constitutional amendment to alter federal structure was the sixteenth. In broadly empowering the national government to lay and collect income taxes, the Sixteenth Amendment carried the potential of a drastic shift to the central government of authority to allocate economic resources by law and to affect the terms on which much private business proceeded.[20] Of equally high importance to federal distribution of powers over the economy was the power wielded by the Supreme Court, dating from the days of John Marshall, to define the scope of the commerce clause of the Constitution, both as a source of judicial limitation on state laws trenching upon a national free-trade market and as a source of judicial expansion of the definition of what commerce Congress might regulate. In both its negative and its affirmative aspects, the commerce clause at the hands of the Court became a major base for moving power toward the center in the federal system.[21]

States had a counterpart to problems of federalism in the apportionment of service and regulatory functions between state and local governments. Save for home-rule provisions put into

19. Frantz, 1353; McLaughlin, 724–727.
20. Blum and Kalven, 29–35; Groves, 153, 158, 188–190, 202–206; Hacker and Zahler (2), 128, 264; Paul, 97–99, 677–679, 685–694.
21. Frankfurter, passim; Stern, 1335.

state constitutions in the twentieth century, this area was governed by statute law; by and large the domains of local government existed at the pleasure of state government. Within statutory frames, there appeared here an analogue to the movement toward the center in the national scene. In the nineteenth century local government did most of the service and police work of the states; this pattern was natural in decades of poor transport and communications, limited revenues, and want of a tradition of expert public administration. As the twentieth century brought increased demands on the states for services and for regulation, attendant on a more interdependent way of life, need was felt for funds that only state taxes could supply and for more central administration or supervision to deal with conditions of more than merely local concern. Local government continued to provide an important dimension of legal order, but legal history must now reckon with the force of apparatus, funding, and oversight that came from the state capital.[22]

Comparative Contributions of Major Legal Agencies to Lawmaking

The general course of public policy from 1776 to 1976 shows some patterns formed by the relative contributions of the major legal agencies. The formal outputs of the agencies show their own intersecting curves of activity. Tracing these is a useful way to find some of the outlines of the country's legal history.

One can plot a curve of statute law that begins at a modest and yet substantial level, rises considerably from the 1830's to the 1880's, then shows a marked increase of pitch and takes off into an ascending line, which in the 1970's shows no sign of turning down. Before 1880 the bulk of this statutory contribution consisted of provision of organizations for public and private collective action (charters of local government units, creation of federal and state bureaus or agencies, charters of philanthropic

22. Sharkansky, 42, 76–77; Woody, 1294, 1298–1299, 1302–1303, 1306, 1314–1315, 1317–1319, 1321.

associations and of business corporations) and franchises encouraging types of private economic ventures barred by the common law to the generality (franchises to dam or bridge or improve navigable waters, to establish rights of way for turnpikes, canals, or railroads, to operate banks, insurance companies, or water supply companies). Some regulation of private and official conduct was built into these organizational statutes—for example, defining jurisdictional lines of government units or setting standards of reasonable rates and services for public utilities. But to this point legislation included a relatively small amount of regulation restricting exercise of official or private will; the dominant note in the statute books before 1890 was to enable action, not to restrict it. Familiar types of crimes against person or property were defined, but most existing regulatory legislation concerned private dealings in the market (the Statute of Frauds, usury laws, recording acts). In these aspects the statute law of the country's first century reflected the preoccupation with settlement and the mustering of resources for economic growth, primarily in market-measured terms.[23]

From the 1880's, but most markedly from the take-off decade of 1905–1915, the regulatory component of statute law became much more prominent and added considerably to the volume of legislation, a shift of emphasis that brought a new type of statute law concerning organized relationships. The focus changed from enabling organized action to injecting more public management or supervision of affairs and providing more sustained, specialized means of defining and enforcing public policy. Symbolic of this turn of affairs were the statutes creating the modern federal and state administrative apparatus; typical was the shift from factory safety laws that simply commanded employers to provide safe work places to laws implemented by provision for administrative rule making and inspection. A major exception was the law of the modern business corporation. Here legislatures respon-

23. Hurst (5), 17–18, 21–22, 30, 46, 56; Stimson, passim.

sive to the demands of business promoters broadened enabling rather than regulatory legislation, in effect allowing corporate management to write charters in their own terms, enlarging the powers of managers at the expense of the position of investors. But at the same time this interest in a new style of corporation law swelled the volume of legislation. At the beginning of the last quarter of the twentieth century, the curve of statute law continues to mount; the long-term course of public policy has been to make legislation the framework and principal body cf the law.[24]

United States legal history began with distrust of and hence deliberate restriction of executive power and with only rudimentary administrative machinery. Thus as we chart the principal types of lawmaking, the exercise of judicial power provides the next lines of our graph. Courts contributed to the content of public policy mainly in three forms: by judge-made creation of substantive policy (the common law), by judicial review of the constitutionality of legislative and executive (and, later, administrative) action, and by judicial interpretation of statutes and of administrative legislation made under statutory delegation. Well into the last quarter of the nineteenth century legislative processes—especially in the states—were crude. Legislators worked with little experience and little precedent to guide their jobs; sessions were short; legislators were part-time amateurs at public policy making; only slowly did a standing committee system develop (and more slowly still a supporting machinery of skilled draftsmen, researchers, and consultants) to bring more specialized care to the creation of statute law. But the country was in bustling growth after the 1820's. A growing population, expanding trade, industry, and finance, the introduction of machine-production processes hazardous to life and limb, a lively trade in land titles—all these generated the need for standards and rules of law to adjust relationships and resolve conflicts. Legislatures

24. Fine, 353–369; Freund, 20–31, 83–102, 109–112, 117–120, 123, 130–143; Hurst (5), 61–62, 69–76.

lacked the confidence and the drive to respond adequately to this demand for law. Most of the demand rose out of one-to-one or small-group-to-individual relationships that could be brought to issue within the confines of lawsuits in which particular litigants confronted each other. Thus between about 1810 (when significant publication of court opinions began) and the 1880's the demand for law was met by a steadily mounting curve of appellate court output.[25]

This is the classic time in the United States of the appearance of the common law of contracts, property, torts, domestic relations, mortgages, suretyship, commercial instruments, the familiar crimes against person or property. It was a heady period for judges. Though they might claim modestly that they were merely declaring law that already existed in some undefined realm of principle, three generations of judges learned pride of position as prime lawmakers. For reasons related to the relative powers or legal capacities of courts and legislatures, the curve of common-law production began to turn down by the 1890's and has declined continually through the twentieth century. By mid-twentieth century new common law had become a small, marginal part of the flow of policy making. Courts continued to apply and refine the nineteenth-century common-law inheritance, but in increasing measure statute law took over even in what had been the common-law fields. Judgemade law probably would never wholly disappear, for the infinite diversity of affairs continued to churn up situations for which statute law did not provide. But by the 1920's it was plain that the bulk of lawmaking was by legislation or by executive or administrative action under statutory delegation.[26]

From the beginning of the nation courts successfully asserted their title to refuse authority to legislation they found to offend provisions of the federal or state constitutions. From time to time the cry was raised that this was usurped power, but the charge never carried the day. The curve of the judicial review function

25. Hurst (1), 185–189; Pound (2), Chap. VI.
26. Friedman (1), Chap. V, (3), 465–468; Llewellyn, 5, 36–41, 63–74.

began at a low level, rose in volume and importance about mid-nineteenth century, took off substantially in the last quarter of the nineteenth century, and peaked in the 1920's and early 1930's. This ascending curve mainly reflected judges' handling of challenges to legislation that regulated morals or behavior in the market—legislation on liquor control, regulation of hours and conditions of labor, rudimentary protection of consumers against fraud, or threats to health or safety. The curve of judges' creation of restrictive constitutional doctrine turned down sharply from the late 1930's. The United States Supreme Court, pace setter of judicial review, then began to apply a strong presumption of constitutionality in protection of economic regulatory legislation. But, unlike the curve of common-lawmaking, the judicial review graph did not descend to marginal significance. From the late 1940's on, courts confronted an unprecedented volume of claims on behalf of individual civil liberties, rising out of cold war tensions, the more sharply felt pressures of a mass society on individuals, and fresh demands of blacks that they obtain some of the fair sharing so long deferred under the Civil War amendments. The Supreme Court began to enlarge definitions of the substantive protections of the Bill of Rights concerning free speech and association, the rights of those accused of crime, access to the ballot, fair representation in legislatures, equality under law without arbitrary distinctions drawn according to race, sex, religion, or national origin. In these areas the justices were cautious in announcing outright reversal of the ordinary presumption of constitutionality that they were now vigorously applying in support of economic regulatory statutes, but they began to mark out preferred values and to identify suspect classifications. Thus in substance the justices put a heavy burden of persuasion on the proponent of legislation that on its face or in demonstrated effort trenched upon Bill-of-Rights values deemed specially linked to values of human personality. In this respect, in the third quarter of the twentieth century, the judicial review curve turned up significantly.[27]

27. With Powell v. Pennsylvania, 127 U.S. 678 (1888), and Williamson

The vigorous growth of statute law and substantive administrative law after 1900 brought a third line of judicial authority. However carefully drawn, statutes and administrative rules could not anticipate all difficult issues of application thrown up by the infinite diversity of affairs. As legislation and administrative rules bulked larger in the whole body of law, judges began to make their major contribution through interpretation of statutes and rules. Some such business came to courts in earlier years, of course, but, relatively, interpretation loomed in the twentieth century as judges' principal contribution to lawmaking. It was a less overt type of judicial lawmaking than had gone on in the nineteenth-century generations of fashioning a great body of common law. Both in doctrine and in practice modern judges acted as agents of other lawmakers, within policies primarily marked out by legislators or administrators. Despite this subordinate role the courts still made substantial policy contributions, as they did, for example, under the Sherman (antitrust) Act. This curve of judicial activity, unlike that for common law, followed the upward curve of legislative and administrative activity, with no sign of diminution.[28]

Our chart will show no great contribution to the body of law from executive offices or administrative agencies until the 1890's. In part this fact reflects the high distrust of executive power with which our legal tradition began; in part it reflects a relatively simple, inexperienced legal order with no conviction of need to invest resources heavily in administration. We can plot major executive-administrative contributions from the decade 1905–1915, which first saw the grant of substantial rule-making, rule-enforcement, and adjudicative powers to executive offices and

---

v. Lee Optical of Oklahoma, 348 U.S. 483 (1955) (presumption of constitutionality of economic regulations), compare Schneider v. State, 308 U.S. 147 (1939), Joseph Burstyn, Inc. v. Wilson, 343 U.S. 495 (1952), Kramer v. Union Free School District, 395 U.S. 621 (1969), and McLaughlin v. Florida, 379 U.S. 184 (1964) (preferred values).

28. Horack, 41–49, 53–56; Hurst (1), 185–188.

independent administrative agencies. The apparent exception of the Interstate Commerce Commission, created in 1887, is really no exception; that body did not acquire authority of great impact until Theodore Roosevelt maneuvered through Congress in 1906 a first step toward the grant of broad rate-making powers. From the early twentieth century the curve of substantive administrative law mounted as sharply in policy significance as did the curve of legislation, reflecting the growing delegation of powers by legislators to administrators. Indeed, by mid-twentieth century the curve for administrative legislation perhaps topped that for statute law; by the 1950's lawyers with business clients and individuals with demands on the increasing service functions of government had to turn more to administrative rule books than to statute books to locate the legal frame of reference for their affairs.[29]

When we chart lines of activity of the major legal agencies we find that, with differences in times of onset and in pace, the lines all show increased action, with the one exception of the sharply reduced creation of common law. Two basic points of legal history are implicit in the over-all pattern. One is the steady trend, most marked after the 1870's, to enlarge resort to law, especially in reference to the economy. The second reflects the distinctive capabilities of different types of legal process. It was not accidental that the making of common law flourished in decades of relatively limited use of legislative and executive power; lawmaking by litigation was most capable of handling problems left primarily to private will, but lacked capacity to meet issues that called for raising and spending public money and for creating new forms of organized, collective action. With our time chart to provide a general frame of reference, the next chapter will consider salient features of the working personalities of the principal legal agencies, derived from the different types of authority the agencies processed.

29. Marver Bernstein, Chaps. 1, 2; Kenneth C. Davis, 7–9, 15–17, 34–44, 56–57, 65–68, 72; Joseph P. Harris, 31–35; Landis (3), Chap. I.

The Need for a Social History of Law

Appraisal of the structure and capacities of legal agencies and of their relative contributions to the body of public policy provide the core of United States legal history. But this is only a beginning. Realistic legal history must be a social history, pursuing law into whatever relations it has had to the whole course of the society. There are reasons deep in the human enterprise, as well as particular to the United States, why this should be so.

First are facts of record. From 1776 to 1976 there was so much interplay between law and other-than-legal institutions and values that we ignore reality if we try to treat law as a self-contained area in social life. This is not to deny that, as is common in human institutions, law tended to develop its own vested interests, so that those wielding legal power were regularly in danger of treating their familiar jurisdictions, procedures, and perquisites as ends in themselves. Legal doctrine offers many instances of such institutional myopia. The concepts of "property" or "freedom of contract," for example, were invoked in the late nineteenth century as if they explained reasons why due process of law barred statutory regulations of economic transactions, instead of simply stating the conclusion the judges desired, that the legislature might not do what it wanted to do. On a more positive side, legal tradition and practice tended to define and foster some humane values distinctive to the law, such as the ideals of procedural due process and the equal protection of the laws. But both the negative and the affirmative products of the law were only part of the record, which included a much broader range of back-and-forth contacts between legal and other social institutions. For example, we need to see the full dimensions of the assertion and later erosion of substantive due process of law as a limit on economic regulatory legislation; to grasp this change, we must relate both the statutes and judges' reaction to them to tensions between nineteenth-century exaltation of entrepreneurial will in the market and the gathering sense after the 1890's of the need to adjust gains and costs flowing from the use of expanded science and technology.[30]

A second argument for treating the history of law as the legal history of society rests on some hard facts of the human situation, given particular urgency in the cultural circumstances of the United States. In all societies individuals confront stubborn facts enforcing scarcity of life satisfactions. They must deal with impersonal, uncaring physical and biological limits and threats to their life energies. They must deal with limits set to individual or group will by inescapable contacts with wills of other individuals and groups and by the more impersonal pressures derived from living among larger populations. Probably the legal history of any society in which law emerges as a fairly distinct institution consists largely in uses of law to deal with the scarcity of life satisfactions. But in the time and setting of the United States such relations of law to the general conditions of individual and social life took on a particular sweep and urgency. For here the people mustered an uncommon energy of will to adapt to scarcity imposed by physical, biological, and social facts, or—more audaciously—to try to change the limiting facts. The accidents of timing settled this country in the surging tide of middle-class supremacy. The heart of the middle-class outlook was a high premium on the active will, on striving and improvising to adapt circumstances to a restless demand to increase the range of human satisfactions, particularly by acting on the economic dimension of life. Confronting a continent that was largely unopened and undeveloped, challenged constantly by the frustrating sense of gaps between potential accomplishment and limited means for exerting leverage on the natural and social situation, individuals were moved to prize collective means to increase their ability to affect the course of their lives in society. They found in law one prime area for experiment in increasing their

30. Bikle, 6–9, 11–16, 18–19, 21–22; Pound (3), 1:350–358.

collective capacity, and thus they wove law intricately into the fabric of their social experience.[31]

There were ambiguities in the middle-class pattern of values, as these applied to law. Because our highly individualistic culture prized the active private will, the tendency was to protect it against public encroachment. Yet these individuals wanted above all else to make their wills effective on circumstances. Their pragmatic readiness to seek effective outlets for will inclined them to use collective effort where that promised greatest effect. Law offered one of the most promising instruments of collective effort. These attitudes made it difficult to draw neat definitions of "conservative" and "liberal" positions regarding use of the powers of the state. The ambiguities emerge in a notable essay of 1883 by William Graham Sumner, an arch spokesman for the virtues of free contract and against the deficiencies of active state policy. Sumner sought to draw a line of principle between "natural" ills to which life subjects all individuals and which should be met only by sturdy private will, and ills derived from the imperfections of social institutions, for which social action was appropriate. The line did not stand out clearly in the record of public policy. One natural ill was certainly the barriers that physical space put on human exchange and communication. But public policy showed little hesitation in promoting turnpikes, canals, and railroads to overcome space. Disease threatened all individuals, but as knowledge spread of preventive measures, the law of public health and sanitation steadily grew. On the other hand, the imperfections of civil institutions included problems arising out of unequal bargaining position, yet Sumner exalted the rationality of freedom of contract against efforts by law to care for persons in dependent positions. In this light, it appeared that the "natural" ills that Sumner wanted the law to leave alone were primarily limitations or deficiencies of effective private will. Yet the trend of public policy was against him, as in such fields

31. Crèvecoeur, 52–56, 75–78; Curti, 644–650; Hurst (2), 7, 17, 37, 44, 59–70; Tocqueville, 2:43, 106, 109, 136, 155–157.

as industrial accident, factory safety, and consumer protection the law broadened its concern for individuals in disadvantageous social positions. When we set Sumner's effort to define a limiting principle on state action against the record, it appears that at bottom what we most prized was effective use of will on circumstances, with no dogmatic barrier against will mustered through legal action.[32] If we probe deeper for some limiting principle, we may more likely find it in Alexander Hamilton. Hamilton was ready to make affirmative and energetic use of law to advance the economy, as by bounties or a protective tariff to foster the growth of machine-based factory production. But implicit in his policy was a limitation, that the power of the state be used where it promised multiplier rather than merely additive results, as by the prodigious increases in productivity offered by the machine.[33] However we resolve the problems of principle between Hamilton and Sumner, the basic fact remains that the country was prepared to use law in aid of active will to an extent that implicated legal history with the general currents of life in the society.

To these aspects of the social record, we should add a factor peculiarly tied to law, which makes a third argument for a social history of law. By inheritance from the Parliamentary Revolution, as well as from our own break with England, politics in the United States included a stubbornly persistent demand that all organized power be accountable to others than the immediate powerholders for the quality of the ends and means of using power. This was the ideal of constitutionalism, which originated as a demand for limitations on government power. But its underlying principle could be and was extended to require that responsibility also be enforced on private power, particularly as the forms of private power developed to more prominence; the extension was symbolized not only by expansion of the law of tort and crimes, but also by the Sherman Act. The constitutional ideal

32. Sumner, 2:720–721; cf. Dicey, Lecture VIII; Freund, 20–32, 81–84, 91–102, 109–134.
33. Alexander Hamilton, 4:87, 89.

thus inherently involved law in all other institutions or social patterns that involved phenomena of power and thus broadens the reach of legal history into social history.[34]

Finally, law existed in a social context, involving other-than-legal institutions (the family, the church, science, and technology) and other-than-legal value patterns (the idea of individuality or the prizing of a rising standard of living). Among these various factors, law typically had only limited effect, though its marginal contributions to social experience were often of high importance to the whole outcome of affairs. Roscoe Pound pointed to this aspect when he emphasized the importance of studying the limits of effective legal action—in itself a major theme for legal history.[35] We can see the marginality of law in two aspects. On the one hand, where law was a substantial moving cause in events, its impact usually seems to have been felt where other social factors were moving toward or supported the same outcome. Thus, after the initial turmoil of the late 1930's, federal statutory protection of union organization and collective bargaining was effective because by then the high division of labor in modern industry was generating pressures of management self-interest, as well as general social interest, in promoting labor peace. There had been a bad record of violence and disturbance in labor relations since the 1870's, but the times had to ripen for effective legal intervention.[36] In the second place, often the law affected society simply in a supporting role, by defining, legitimizing, and standardizing patterns of behavior that were shaped by other factors originating outside of or apart from any legal process. Thus feudal land tenure never took hold in this country, and the fee simple became the norm of landholding, not by constitutional or statutory provisions declaring freehold tenure the norm, but because the vast land areas of the country and the social facts of restless settlement in the surge of the commercial and industrial revolutions made it impossible for any tightly

34. Cf. Hurst (5), 63, 75, 82, 83, 153.
35. Pound (3), 3:353–373.
36. Marver Bernstein, Chaps. 7, 10, 11; Dulles, Chaps. VII, X, XV.

centered powerholders to monopolize land titles in perpetuity.[37]

To some extent we made the marginality of law a matter of principle. As I noted, the policy record allows us to draw no dogmatic line barring resort to action by the state to affect circumstances. But substantive due process did include the notion that public power should be used only for a public purpose and not for private advantage. The law of crimes and the First Amendment protection of free speech and free exercise of religion included the distinction between idea and overt act, and—except for the dangerous reach of charges of conspiracy—confined the law to dealing simply with overt action that could be deemed antisocial. Equity developed the policy that government should not intervene in the internal affairs of lawful private associations, save to see to fair enforcement of their own procedures and standards. In such various ways public policy expressed the judgment that in some realms of social life the law should act only at the margin. Again, the effect is to direct attention to legal history as social history, rather than as the history of a self-contained institution.[38]

Institutions, Ideas, and Inertia

The record shows that almost any major area of the history of public policy in the United States has involved three dimensions of social experience. Typically law has been concerned with (1) the establishment and maintenance of social institutions, along with (2) the formulation and application of integrating ideas to bring values into some ordered pattern, and (3) has felt the impress of general drift or inertia in social affairs and has been used in varying degree to offset such inertia. If we inquire as to law's functions in the society, analysis in the face of otherwise confus-

37. Christman, 289–304; Marshall Harris, 116, 298, 362–366, 373–378, 390, 400.

38. Cf. Ballard v. United States, 322 U.S. 78 (1944); Joseph Burstyn, Inc. v. Wilson, 343 U.S. 495 (1952); John F. Jelke Co. v. Emery, 193 Wis. 311, 214 N.W. 369 (1927).

ing detail will be advanced by recalling that these dimensions are likely to be present in any given policy situation.

Institutions. Effective will to shape social experience called for sustained, shared, or at least interlocked behavior in the service of particular shared or related goals. These patterns of behavior constitute social institutions, whose existence determines much of the content of life in society. Law itself is an institution, as are the family, the church, publicly and privately organized education and philanthropy, science and technology, and the market. In this society there was no closed catalogue of institutions; the diverse energies of the society produced new ones from time to time, and old ones declined or disappeared. Railroad bureaucracies supplanted organized stagecoach lines. The mass-circulation newspaper supplanted the output of the small printer, and the newspapers confronted highly organized competition in the emergence of great radio and television empires. Wherever we encounter substantial, continued, organized activity with means structured to pursue shared goals, we deal with behavior that at some stage of consequence can be called institutional.

Law was concerned with other-than-legal institutions on two principal counts. We relied on law as an instrument of social order. But the resources that could be mobilized through law alone always were limited, even in the affluent twentieth century; law, as noted earlier, was typically a marginal factor in social order, though its marginal impact was often critically important to the whole outcome of affairs. Public policy thus showed concern for the existence and functioning of other-than-legal institutions because it had to rely largely on these to achieve over-all social cohesion. Education, Thomas Jefferson observed, was important for the life values it could help instill in future citizens; the bases of social order would be laid substantially in the schoolroom. The church declared its prime work to be the care of individual souls, but its precepts and admonitions supplemented the policeman and the magistrate in keeping sober responsibility among the people.[39] A second, more negative aspect was that law

39. Padover, 667–669; West Virginia State Board of Education v. Bar-

claimed for itself the legitimate monopoly of force in the society. Almost any substantial, sustained, organized center of activity might become a competitor with the state in exercising direct or indirect compulsion on individuals' wills. Hence, even under a regime of the most liberal general incorporation acts, the state continued to insist that its grant was necessary to the existence of legally recognized entity capacity in private associations. Hence, too, as big business corporations emerged to institutional status in the twentieth century, government pumped new vigor into flagging antitrust laws, as means to exert some external check on new centers of social as well as economic power.[40]

Law dealt with other social institutions in two ways. To some extent it legitimated them as accepted parts of the whole social pattern. More broadly, it helped to supply functional requisites of their existence.

Law's legitimation of institutions was typically after the fact. The family, the market, science, and technology did not exist by legal fiat, but as products of complex behavior originating outside the forms of law. In such instances law legitimated the institutions not by creating them, but by lending them its protection once they existed. The continuing interaction of buyers and sellers created a market; law recognized the social validity of the market by protecting its regular dealings against intrusion of force or fraud. The continued relations of men and women and the care of children created families; the law recognized the social validity of the family by providing regular forms of marriage, by limiting divorce, and by providing remedies against third persons who interfered with the family relation, as well as by providing property, tax, and inheritance laws that fastened family control of wealth and income. The church provided an analogous, but somewhat different situation. In the English inheritance, the law created a state church and legitimated it not only by positive protection but by laying disabilities on those who would not

nette, 319 U.S. 624 (1943); Walz v. Tax Commission of the City of New York, 397 U.S. 664 (1970).

40. Hofstadter, 194, 229–233; Hurst (5), 115, 116, 119–121.

adhere to it. The First Amendment provided, however, that the federal government might not establish any church. Several states carried over from the colonial period traditions of legal support for an established church. But the diversity and fluidity of population in this country militated against continuance of such practices, and by mid-nineteenth century state laws had divorced the states from discriminatory favor for any particular denomination. In the twentieth century the Supreme Court capped this development by ruling that the due-process clause of the Fourteenth Amendment incorporated the First Amendment ban on establishment and its guarantee of the free exercise of religion. Churches existed thus by reason of shared religious convictions of their communicants, and not by act of law.[41]

In some borderline cases the law may be estimated to exert a more positive influence in creating institutions, such as in grants of incorporation. Only the legislature could confer legal-entity status on a group of individuals. The corporate form of organization cannot be identified as clearly indispensable to institutional existence; unincorporated private associations carried on many philanthropic undertakings, and some large business enterprises were conducted as limited partnerships or unincorporated joint-stock associations. But the corporate form offered such substantial advantages in continuity and internal discipline that in practice it became the staple for many kinds of collective action. Private academies, libraries, and colleges came to exist under special statutory charters. Philanthropic foundations normally functioned under grants of incorporation. Weightiest of all grew to be the great business corporations. By mid-twentieth century several score of these held assets and administered affairs and flows of funds that gave them as much economic force as was held by most states, and they functioned with the continuity and bureaucratized direction characteristic of other social institutions. The corporate form of organization gave advantages for mustering

41. Howe, 73, 82, 106, 108, 155, 156; cf. School District of Abington Township, Pa. v. Schempp, 374 U.S. 203 (1963).

large assets under concentrated management power and thus involved the law deeply in the institutional life of such entities as the American Telephone and Telegraph Company, General Motors, or General Electric. The continued activity under federal antitrust laws and the development from the 1930's on of a new body of federal law regulating many aspects of corporate finance in effect acknowledged how deeply law was implicated in and responsible for big corporate business as part of the country's institutional structure.[42]

Most of law's relations to other social institutions involved lending support by helping to provide instruments or procedures functional to their operations. To the market law supplied the law of contract, property, and security instruments. In the background stood the processes of courts, when bargaining relations broke down, to apportion gains and losses and to provide a minimum base for supporting the expectations on which bargain depended.[43]

To the family law contributed definitions of the relative rights of wife and husband in family economic assets and the right of parents to govern the conduct of their children, as well as rules governing liability of family members to third persons in contract and tort. Beyond these bounds nineteenth-century law generally left the family an undisturbed autonomy. But in a more fluid, interdependent twentieth century, law much more deeply affected, and on the whole tended to narrow, the functions of the family. Compulsory school laws took away a good deal of the control parents earlier had exercised over children. The Supreme Court qualified this development by ruling that, consistent with the Fourteenth Amendment, the state might not claim a monopoly of education; due process of law guaranteed parents the right to send their children to private schools of the parents' choice,

42. Chayes, 25; Heilbroner (1), 11–13, 18–19, 21–22; Hurst (5), 119–123; Kaysen and Turner, Chap. I; Rostow (2), 46.
43. Hurst (2), 8, 11, 12, 13, 14, 22, 44–51, 90–93, (3), 5, 47, 52, 54, 79, 99, 186–191, 297–300.

as long as the schools met minimum, secular educational standards set by law. In the nineteenth century the economic and health security of the family normally was left to the resources of each family group, supplemented by private charity or by grudging public relief. In a high division-of-labor, urban-impersonal twentieth-century society, general opinion found it unacceptable to leave the family totally to its own resources. Unemployment insurance, old age and survivors' payments, public financing of health care, and aid to families with dependent children developed to spread over the society burdens formerly shouldered by the individual family unit. As law extended its functional supports, it also extended its bureaucracy into family relationships and to that extent reduced the social autonomy of the family institution.[44]

It was not deemed inconsistent with constitutional and statutory policy against an establishment of religion for the law to render some supporting services to churches generally. Public money might not pay the salaries of clergy or finance the building of churches, but the police protected the peaceable assembly of religious groups as well as secular ones, the street department would repair the way on which churches stood, and the fire department would put out a blaze in a church building as in any other. No serious problem arose in such instances where churches simply shared benefits held in common with secular society. More questionable, but sanctioned by public policy practice which ran concurrent in time with the policy on separation of church and state, was tax exemption of church property. Here was a major economic contribution by the general society to church groups, which were relieved of sharing the overhead costs of the services and protections that religious associations enjoyed along with secular ones. In analogous fashion, the Supreme Court ruled that states might enact Sunday-closing laws against business

44. Ogburn and Tibbitts, 661–663, 672–673, 676–677, 694–695, 703–704, 707; Williams, 41–46, 55–61; cf. Pierce v. Society of Sisters, 268 U.S. 510 (1925); Steward Machine Co. v. Davis, 301 U.S. 548 (1937) and Helvering v. Davis, id., 619 (1937).

activity, without offending First Amendment values. The strict logic of separation policy would have invalidated both tax exemption and Sunday laws. In substance the Court's acceptance of these legal supports of church activity recognized that the principles of separation of state and church and the free exercise of religion were matters of somewhat flexible standards and not of tight rules and that a prevailing consensus in the society valued the existence of churches for their contributions to secular order.[45]

Education eventually became much more deeply involved with the law than did the family or the church. But through the mid-nineteenth century, provision of schooling was left largely to private initiative; the law's principal contribution for some decades was to provide incorporation for private educational institutions. Part of the faith of Jacksonian egalitarianism, however, was the belief that every child was entitled to education; from this impetus public schooling spread steadily in the late nineteenth century. At first local governments shouldered the load mainly, but in the twentieth century this area of policy was specially marked by the trend to centralize functions at state capitals. By mid-twentieth century statutes contained a complex, highly technical array of provisions dealing with the financing of education, the licensing of teachers, and the content of curricula. Public support of education, at first limited to the grammar schools, moved heavily by the 1920's into support of high schools and state universities. Private academies dwindled in number, but privately endowed colleges and universities, favored by tax exemptions, continued to provide some competitive alternatives to public schools. The importance of maintaining some diversity between public and private education grew as the society tended to enlarge the responsibilities it thrust on the public schools, and to standardize its demands.[46]

45. Zorach v. Clauson, 343 U.S. 306 (1952); McGowan v. Maryland, 366 U.S. 420 (1961); Walz v. Tax Commission of the City of New York, 397 U.S. 664 (1970).

46. Bancroft, 1:368; Mann, 1:589; Morison and Commager, 1:511–518, 2:304–307, 310–312.

Two somewhat inconsistent pressures created special tensions for public education. On the one hand, this rather narrowly pragmatic society asked that the schools teach practical skills, particularly those useful to the functioning of the market. On the other hand, the society asked that the schools take on an increasing part of the burden of inducting young people into prevailing middle-class ideologies concerning politics, citizenship, and social responsibility in general. Asked to provide both technical and value-laden accomplishments, the schools were pressured to do more than public budgets usually provided the means to do well. Tensions were accentuated because at the same time, over much of the society, the family and the church seemed to do less than they once had done in transmitting social norms to the young. The problems for the morale of the educational enterprise were the greater because twentieth-century laws substantially extended the years of required schooling. Again, there were disturbing value tensions in the background; extended schooling appeared to reflect the inability of the job market to absorb the young as much as it did concern for educational values as such, and rebellious young people sensed this fact. Again, the problems might have been met, or much reduced, had school budgets and public opinion provided means to meet the challenges with vigor and imagination. But, substantial as was the public financing of education, the society did not seem really prepared to invest assets or courage equal to the expectations it had of its school systems.[47]

In the late twentieth century one sign of the increased tension under which education operated has been the law's heightened concern with school discipline. Issues were evaded for many years under the question-begging formula that education was a privilege and not a right. But as the reach of the state extended into details of individual living—not only in education, but also in provision of public services and care of dependent persons—the Supreme Court found the right-privilege distinction unreal. Even

47. Lerner, 732–738; Lynd and Lynd (1) 196–199, (2) 204, 219–226, 234–241; Williams, 270–271, 273–276, 285–287, 292–294.

if there were not an initial claim of right to certain state-provided facilities, once those facilities were made available, human stakes in fair and equal administration of them were high. As applied to education, from the 1950's on this recognition of the extended impact of the law on individuals' lives has led the Court to rule that students, including those not yet of age, are entitled to procedural due process of law and the equal protection of the laws as they are affected by school discipline. This line of decisions was important in itself, but it was even more important for what it symbolized, of needed response to the reach of the modern bureaucratic state into individual life.[48]

Legal history needs to come to terms with the fact that legal processes had more involvement with some institutions than with others. Though its impact was likely to be marginal in most aspects of other-than-legal institutions, law had more effect on the market than on the family or the church, for example. There was probably no one reason behind these differential impacts of legal processes. One factor may have been the extent to which transactions fell into separate episodes on the one hand or within sustained relations on the other. The more fragmented were individuals' dealings, the more likely they were to resort to law. Thus even within the market, individuals went to law less when they were involved in business relations, the profit of which lay in sustained patterns of dealing, than when they dealt only in single bargains.[49] Another factor was the relative importance the culture attached to different sectors of life. Law had much to do with religious observance in England in centuries when people were actively concerned not only for their salvation but for the implications of church power in national and international politics. In the United States, from the late eighteenth century on, law was less involved in religion in a society whose devotion went more and more to increasing material wealth, and in which threats of international power politics had become separated

48. Tinker v. Des Moines Independent Community School District, 393 U.S. 503 (1969).
49. Macaulay, 55.

from religious organization. Again, law was most effective operationally when it dealt with overt action rather than with largely emotional values; this seems a reason why law had less to do with the family or the church than with the market.[50] Whatever the factors at work, the differential relations of law to other social institutions calls for attention it has not yet sufficiently received from legal historians.

I have sketched briefly some issues involving the law with the family, the church, and the school. Of course, even within its limits this treatment falls far short of covering the field. It does not include the press, or philanthropic organizations, or finance. Especially my catalogue so far omits any but slight references to three massive institutions—science and technology, the market, and the twentieth-century big business corporation. These I propose to deal with more broadly in two later chapters. Meanwhile, what is set out here perhaps suffices to suggest how much of legal history is bound up in the relations of law to social institutions apart from the law itself.

Integrating ideas. A second dimension of social experience in which law was much implicated was the formulation and application of concepts to integrate values into some ordered patterns of social living. To some extent the law's dealings with social institutions generally involved such integrations. Thus the doctrine of separation of church and state sought to bring these institutions into reasoned alignment and apportionment of roles. When the Supreme Court ruled that the state might not assert a monopoly of education, but must leave parents the option of sending children to qualified private schools, it marked out an important element of what was properly public and what was properly private in the state's relations to the family and to education. The central doctrine of substantive due process of law, that public power must be used only for a public and not for a private advantage, was important to separating roles of the market and the government in resource allocation.

50. Cf. Howe, 11–12, 18–19, 59–60, 154, 155; Levy (2), passim, but especially Chap. XIII.

But people used legal processes also to bring to definition and to use ideas that did not fit neatly into institutional roles. The next chapter examines the character of the powers of legal agencies that made them useful instruments for articulating social values. Here it suffices to note that as a result the formal output of law—in statutes, court decisions, and administrative rules and determinations—constituted probably the single largest body of evidence of wants and needs, ends and means, broadly held or prevailing in the society.

A cluster of middle-class attitudes and values stood out in the country's public policy over nearly two hundred years. This is not to say that these values had meaning for everyone; they left out great segments of the population and met with dissent and dispute of no mean proportions. But they held together as a working philosophy that prevailed through large areas of our uses of law. They included (1) regard for rational, peaceful order under the constitutional ideal, (2) favor for a diversity of outlets for active will, (3) belief in people's capacity to erect ideal values on an increasing material base as the foundation of justice, and (4) assertion of the quality of the individual life as the ultimate criterion of the good society.

(1) Though the society was marked by a good deal of roughness and violence in specific sectors (notably in race relations and in management-labor dealings), its working norms included high regard for peaceful order. It was symbolic that at the edge of settlement there was always early pressure to create the standard instruments of good order, the sheriff and the courts. The people were ready to write into law condemnations of the familiar offenses against person and property that represented individual or group deviance from social norms; and the law of treason and riot dealt with organized or group subversion of order. Within government itself the federal system sought order by offsetting federal and state power. Significantly, prevailing values did not identify order with a static condition of society. The framers wrote into constitutions regular procedures for their amendment, and the open-ended character of constitutional

grants of legislative power invited legislatures to grapple with new problems and adapt to new conditions. Desirable stability was seen as involving opportunity for orderly change.[51]

(2) Public policy promoted and protected diversity of outlets for the active, creative will of individuals. What most impressed Crèvecoeur in the 1780's and Tocqueville in the 1830's was the bustle of economic activity in the United States. Men bought land to exploit it for capital gains. The keynote was production for market, and everywhere the people were busy with contract dealings ("schemes" Crèvecoeur called them). This was the common reality expressed in the common-law doctrines favoring the active will—the presumption of the legality of duly made contracts, the burden of proof laid on one complaining of hurt from another's action, to show that the action should be deemed antisocial.[52]

Implicit in this favor for diverse expression of creative will was a deep-seated confidence in the feasibility and the morality of bargaining out almost any issue that might arise among individuals. The attitude was given classic expression in Benjamin Franklin's autobiography, where that master negotiator argued for the practical virtue of pressing points with deference to the other party's interests as well as his self-esteem. Plainly Franklin's advice assumed that the parties were at basis in a give-and-take relationship and not in a situation where one could prevail only at the complete subordination or defeat of the other. In a society where some individuals owned slaves, and where labor had to contend with violent opposition to its efforts to organize for bargaining, there was a good measure of unreality in Franklin's premise. But within a broad, middle-class frame of reference the bargaining mentality and morality prevailed and set the norms for many outside the middle class. The prime evidence for this is that, the slavery issue apart, public policy in the country

51. See Holmes, J., in Missouri v. Holland, 252 U.S. 416, 433 (1920); cf. Corwin (1), 184, 197; Hofstadter and Wallace, 3, 7, 12, 18–19, 24–28; Hurst (1), 24, 70–73, (3), 25–26, 95–101, 170–171; Wharton, 2:2186–2212.

52. Crèvecoeur, 52–56, 75–78; Hurst (2), 12, 18–20; Tocqueville, 2:99, 136–137, 157.

was not shaped within the terms of class warfare; the hardest battling that went on proceeded from the outrage of farmers and workers who felt that opponents were violating the bargaining ethic. This meant that legal order in the United States was less severely tested than it would have been in a different temper of dealing. The outcome largely vindicated the faith Hamilton expressed in *The Report on Manufactures* (1791) that promotion of wider exchanges in the market meant there need be no fundamental antagonism between the industrial and the agrarian interests. This faith was exemplified over one hundred years later in Samuel Gompers' business unionism, which eschewed the rhetoric of class war in favor of dollars-and-cents bargaining.[53]

(3) Closely tied to the belief that a bargaining society was possible was belief that in this country, the natural endowment and the substantially wide-open opportunities for economic development gave the people unexampled opportunity to erect ideal values on a material base. Again the text can be taken from Franklin and Hamilton. Franklin set himself an ordered list of virtues for cultivation and explicitly placed the economic virtues such as industry and frugality ahead of justice. He argued that individuals could achieve justice more practically from a foundation of material security. Hamilton argued that the law should promote factory-based production because this would bring both a fruitful division of labor and prodigious increase of output, which would permit developing more fully men's creative possibilities.[54] A long-lasting nineteenth-century expression of this philosophy was in public lands policy; generous disposition of the lands to increase private fee-simple ownership was trusted to produce the sturdy character of yeomen farmers as the best base for a democratic society.[55] In the twentieth century the same viewpoint was presented in the Employment Act of 1946, charging the federal

53. Dulles, 154–155; Franklin, 1:327–328, 338; Alexander Hamilton, 4:70, 78, 83, 95–99; Perlman, 168–169, 196–198.
54. Franklin, 1:327–328; Alexander Hamilton, 4:87–94.
55. Hurst (4), 24–34.

government to use its resource-allocating powers to assure broad employment opportunities that would bulwark a self-respecting population. So, too, when mid-twentieth-century foreign policy turned to offer economic aid first to war-ravaged Europe, and then to developing countries, the approach rested in effect on Franklin's priorities; economically despairing people could not be expected to maintain or move toward regimes of democratic justice, so the first effort must be to raise the material base of their societies.[56]

To draw from this premise that ideal values could be erected only on a sound material base the conclusion that a steadily rising, market-measured material standard of living was a self-evident public good was not necessary. It was, however, the conclusion that public policy tended to draw from the late eighteenth up to about the mid-twentieth century. This attitude put a premium upon rapid exploitation of natural and human resources for the speedier expansion of market transactions. This was a broad consensus through the nineteenth century that came under increasing question only when the first voices were raised on behalf of conservation values. Not until the mid-twentieth century did the country begin a substantial reassessment of the long-standing faith in the absolute value of a rising gross national product, measured by the calculus of market dealing.[57]

(4) The politically dominant opinion of the late eighteenth- and the nineteenth-century United States put high value on social arrangements that allowed large play for individuality. Individuals could realize themselves only in a healthy social context, but fulfillment of individual life and not conformance to social norms was the ultimate test of the good society. A principal theme in United States legal history, hence, was the enlargement of the definition of the legal person, by extension of the suffrage, by the married women's property acts, by the abolition of slavery, and

56. Bailey, Chaps. 1, 2; Myrdal (2), Chap. IX.
57. Frederick R. Anderson, 5–14; Hacker and Zahler (2), 54, 56; Hays, 1–4, 262–266; Hurst (4), 24, 26, 29, 31, 32–33, 42, 113–114, 172–175; Morison and Commager, 2:398–400, 609–612.

by the Fourteenth Amendment's guarantee of civil rights.[58] Another large theme relevant to values put on individuality was the effort to draw legally enforceable distinctions between what is of "public" and what only of "private" concern, so that government might not override the unique or intimate experiences of life by enforcing social roles wherever it pleased a legislative majority to do so. This is an area of policy marked by difficult compromises and adjustments, which legal historians so far have only scantly dealt with. Consider, for example, the matter of objective criteria of legal liability. It was a substantial protection of individuality that the law of crimes insisted that normally there must be proof of an overt act to establish criminal liability; a mere state of mind or feeling did not suffice to prove a crime. Where civil liability was in issue, law gave great reach to demands that individuals fulfill social roles, regardless of personal defects or peculiarities pleaded in extenuation of harm done; normally, at his peril, the individual must act within the bounds of reasonable and prudent behavior for one in his situation.[59]

Apart from the inherent difficulties of adjusting individuality and social roles, there were great ambiguities in practice concerning the society's support of individuality. First, the nineteenth-century preoccupation with gross economic development led to a tendency to equate individuality with the energetic individual will exercised in the market—essentially a producer orientation—to the relative neglect of both political and consumer personal values. Nineteenth-century policy was not in the end antagonistic to political civil liberties—witness the abolition of slavery and the adoption of the Fourteenth and Fifteenth Amendments—but on the whole it left them unattended, most damagingly so when in 1877 the North turned its back on further effort to bring the freed blacks into fair sharing in the society.[60] Nineteenth-century policy was relatively insensitive to values of

58. Friedman (3), 185–186, 434, 576, 579–580; Myrdal (1), 1:8, 12, 14; Pound (3), 4:193–194; Radin (1), 523–524.
59. Hurst (2), 18–22.
60. Frazier, 148–151; Hurst (2), 30–32; Rose and Rose, 137–140.

individual life that were not expressed through entrepreneurial will. Factory discipline brought new threats to the self-respect and security of workers, but labor lacked political power to bring law into play to redress the imbalance of power and found no effective allies to help press new claims. Larger, more impersonal markets brought new threats to consumer safety and fair dealing. But, again, effective political power lay with those who made claims on behalf of entrepreneurial will; the security of the individual as consumer or worker was not so much rejected as ignored in a prevailing temper that identified favored individuality with the position of the managing producer. Not until well into the twentieth century did legislation to protect labor and consumers begin a substantial reassessment of claims for individual security and realization in other than market terms.[61]

The headlong growth of the country was a second factor that created serious ambiguity in practice regarding protection of individuality. Great internal migration, with settlement of successive western frontiers, and great waves of immigration, beginning with the Irish in the early nineteenth century, brought here peoples of sharply different cultural background from those who had set the early patterns of social roles and values. Amid these turbulent changes were strong pressures to enforce conformity to social norms fixed by those who had dominated the country before the 1830's. An early area of tension was in religion. The First Amendment asserted the claims of the individual to privacy in respect to his religious belief and practice, and on the whole the law formally respected this value. But practice laid social and economic handicaps upon Catholics and Jews which law ignored.[62] On the other hand, a politically effective rural Protestant morality brought law into play over a broad range to regulate sex, gambling, and liquor in ways that later did not fit readily into mixed, urban populations and that fostered a good deal of

61. Edelman, 182–184; Fleming (2), 130, 135, 149, 151–152; Hacker and Zahler (2), 57–58, 447–448; Tannenbaum, 58–71, 75, 77–78; Wiebe, 48–50.
62. Ahlstrom, 7–8, 853–854, 927, 929, 973–974, 975, 1006–1007; Beer, 140–154; Herberg, 154–156, 248–258.

corruption in local government, climaxing in the sad experience of the 1920's with national Prohibition. Not until well into mid-twentieth century, with the passage of new civil rights legislation against religious and national-origin as well as racial prejudice, and with a new concern of the Supreme Court to define constitutional protections of individual privacy, did public policy show positive concern to strike a balance more in favor of the individual's realization of his own uniqueness and less on behalf of conventional social practice.[63]

But cross-currents continued to flow. The tensions attending the cold war brought new kinds of pressure for social and political conformity in the mid-twentieth century. Loyalty checks imperiled jobs, and charges of conspiracy and breaches of security classifications laid threats on political protest, reviving memories of the Alien and Sedition Acts of the 1790's. Controversy over the use of marijuana and dangerous drugs brought echoes of the battle over Prohibition. Despite the society's professions of continued high regard for individuality, the record made clear that demands for social conformity would continue to generate conflict over assertions of the political and the private claims of individuals to make their own distinctive contributions to the whole.[64]

Inertia: The Unplanned Course of Events. Both institutions and integrating policy ideas worked against the backdrop of influences that were not the product of calculation, but of accident, situation, or the accumulation of events. In almost any area of public policy, the historian needs to reckon with the operation of factors which people did not perceive or foresee, deliberate upon or choose, but which nonetheless profoundly affected the uses they made of law.

Facts of place and time loom large in the setting of public policy. The physical abundance of natural resources, such as the

63. Cf. Joseph Burstyn, Inc. v. Wilson, 343 U.S. 495 (1952); Griswold v. Connecticut, 381 U.S. 479 (1965); Stanley v. Georgia, 394 U.S. 557 (1969); Eisenstadt v. Baird, 405 U.S. 438 (1972).

64. Barth, 99–136; Gellhorn (1), Chap. VI; Grodzins, 232–237.

Lake States forest, encouraged people to believe that resources were inexhaustible, and so to take little or no heed for conservation.[65] Distance and variety of resources fostered distinctive sectional interests on the issue of the tariff, which pitted raw-materials producers against those in regions whose situation fostered commerce, finance, and industry.[66] The sweep of unoccupied land precluded successful adoption of feudal landholding.[67] The timing of events often was unplanned. Thus, the pattern of middle-class ideals noted earlier was self-conscious, but the fact that the country was settled at a time when its dominant settlers held a middle-class outlook was itself the product of a conjunction of factors—the art of navigation, the condition of commerce, politics, and religious controversy in England—which no one designed as the setting for the North Atlantic colonies.[68]

Population totals and distribution responded somewhat to deliberate policy; public lands and immigration policies favored increase and westward movement of people in the United States. But law worked only marginally on the total increase of population and on its distribution. Again, accidents of timing enter in. Pressures of hunger and political disturbance abroad produced large-scale emigration which, for want of capital to move onto the land, brought great increases in cities from the mid-nineteenth century on. In the twentieth century new kinds of population influences operated as blacks moved north and the automobile fostered urban sprawl. In either case the growth of cities was a phenomenon to which law contributed, but which, rather than being a chosen policy, thrust upon policy makers a host of unwanted problems in providing service and regulation.[69]

Factors of social caste and class were large and often ugly features of United States legal history. Law, of course, actively

65. Hurst (4), 107, 113, 119–122, 125, 461, 466.
66. Hurst (4), 476–477; Schattschneider, 93–94, 226–248, 250–254.
67. Bruchey, 62; Marshall Harris, 362–366.
68. Bruchey, 42, 44, 48, 50–53, 55–56, 59–64; Curti, 5, 35, 105, 120; Hurst (2), 35–36; Henry Nash Smith, 127–129, 135, 140.
69. McKenzie, 443; Morison and Commager, 2:364–366, 372–374, 383–384; Williams, 15–16, 464.

maintained slavery before 1862, and illegal use of legal power
was a key element in oppression of blacks thereafter. But slavery
and its aftermath wove into other factors outside the law—into
the structure of markets and education and class customs—to
create barriers to justice that were not only law-made.[70] For
whites, social class was a reality, affecting the respect or lack of
respect individuals got from law. The law did not formally recognize class lines, whether drawn on economic, ethnic, or religious
bases, unless the property qualifications put on the right to vote
are so considered. By the Jacksonian period the states had
launched a trend to drop the property qualification, and the
Fourteenth Amendment's equal protection clause after 1868 provided the base for outlawing any other formal legal creation of
social class lines.[71] Nonetheless, social class lines existed throughout the country's history as the product of differences in the distribution of wealth and income, in religion and in family practices, and in national origin. Law was implicated at a second or
further remove in the existence of many of these kinds of differ-
entiation, but on the whole law reacted to—however improperly
—rather than created the distinctions. Drastic redistribution of
wealth and income and unflinching enforcement of civil rights
legislation could deeply affect class alignments. But the lack of
politically effective demand for such changes ran too broad and
deep in the whole structure of the society to be attributed simply
to the legal order. The problem of assessment here is far from
simple. That law stood near a balancing point in responsibility
for phenomena of social class was reflected at mid-twentieth
century in the fact that the Supreme Court, while treating racial
classifications as suspect, was unwilling to treat indigency in the
same way. A majority of the Court continued to apply the ordinary presumption of constitutionality in behalf of statutes that
assigned significance to possession or want of economic means in

70. Myrdal (1), Chaps. 13, 14, 15, 17.
71. Hurst (1), 44, 238; cf. Harper v. Virginia State Board of Elections,
383 U.S. 663 (1966); Kramer v. Union Free School District, 395 U.S. 621
(1969).

determining legal rights. Evidently the majority view was that judgments on the social validity of given distributions of wealth and income were properly within a realm of considerable legislative direction.[72]

Nature, not law, created two sexes. But law bore heavily on women in many respects and lent its tacit support to social practices that discriminated in favor of men. Where law bettered the condition of women, the record was not always clear as to the force impelling change; there is some reason to believe that the married women's property acts were prompted as much by concern to help creditors attain the security of the wife's signature on her husband's note as to advance the woman's capacity to be a free trader for herself. This ambiguity points, as in the matter of social class lines, to the fact that women's subordinate position was the product of a conjunction of other-than-legal influences as well as of the law's doing. Again, Supreme Court doctrine in the late twentieth century puts law at a balancing point. A majority of the Court have been hesitant to treat sex as a suspect classification in measuring the validity of legislation and seem prepared to allow legislatures the same range of discretionary choice of policy in drawing lines on account of sex as in the case of ordinary economic regulatory statutes. The implication seems to be that the drawing of legal lines according to sex is so broadly implicated in a complex of community values and practices that constitutional law should not be asked to assume the full responsibility for the outcome. Obviously, however, this is fighting ground, and one cannot be sure that the balance might not yet tilt the other way.[73]

The law was capable of breeding its own inertia. Legal doctrine may originate as the resolution of particular value tensions, but then be drawn inaptly to serve other uses to which it is not

72. Dandridge v. Williams, 397 U.S. 471 (1970); Richardson v. Belcher, 404 U.S. 78 (1971); Weinberger v. Salfi, 95 Sup. Ct. 2457 (1975).

73. Reed v. Reed, 404 U.S. 71 (1971); Kahn v. Shevin, 416 U.S. 351 (1974); Geduldig v. Aiello, 417 U.S. 484 (1974); Schlesinger v. Ballard, 419 U.S. 498 (1975); Stanton v. Stanton, 421 U.S. 7 (1975).

truly relevant. Analogy is a useful analytical instrument, but also a two-edged one. Thus the law gave rights over wild animals to him who first reduced them to possession. This proposition, sensible enough within its original purpose, was misapplied by analogy in the nineteenth century to allot claims over oil and gas in ways that produced wasteful competition in extracting those resources among adjoining landowners.[74] Doctrine favoring freedom of contract among presumably equal bargainers in the market was carried over into late nineteenth-century substantive due process to rationalize decisions upsetting legislation designed to deal with grossly unequal positions in the market between employer and worker, or between seller and consumer.[75] Because law has been so massive an institution, a realistic legal history must take such doctrinal inertia more into account than it has.[76]

Responsibility for Justice and Injustice

The reach and diversity of law in United States society have been too great to be encompassed in a single essay; this account inevitably omits a good deal. But after we take note of core aspects of legal processes and their immediate products and of aspects of the social history of law displayed through institutions, ideas, and inertia, one subject still insistently demands inclusion. A stubborn tenacity about the constitutional ideal as part of the policy making of this society requires that legal history attend to questions of the justice or injustice of the social order to which legal order contributed.

Philosophers have explored the meaning of justice in varying terms, and their explorations constitute one aspect of legal history. The working concerns of policy makers and of those who have pressed or opposed the making of public policy in specific detail have also shaped certain main types of issues over the justice or injustice of using law. Philosophy is important to pro-

74. Hardwicke, 395–396.
75. Cushman, 737; Fine, 159–162; Pound (1), 454.
76. Hurst (3), 28–31, 62–75.

vide critiques of legal order. But the content of legal history has consisted mostly in the products of the actual operations of legal processes. Without denying an important place to philosophic critique, reality justifies legal historians in attending also to issues of justice as these gained definition in legal operations.

The ideas of procedural and substantive due process of law and the equal protection of equal laws pointed to three main kinds of issues of justice or injustice in social order.[77] All three related to the fact that life in society involved conforming to or departing from norms set by social institutions (including but not limited to those set by law), or by general ideas embodied in social custom or practice or given shape by shared private interest, or by the inertia always resident in social experience. These norms classified individuals or groups according to stated or implicit criteria, the end being to allocate different gains or costs of social experience among the defined categories. (1) Any classification setting a norm might be challenged as unjustly allocating gains or costs of social living because it intervened in people's lives without serving general interest or because the particular intervention was not a rational means to achieve a justifying general interest. (2) Some criteria for allocating gains or costs of social living raised sharply felt issues of justice or injustice because they were criteria of specially broad reach, with peculiarly penetrating effect on the content and quality of life. In this society the classifications that gave rise to peculiar concern allocated benefits and burdens according to criteria of age, sex, race, national origin, religious affiliation, or wealth. Recall that we deal not only with categories established by law, but also with those set primarily by institutions, ideas, or forces of social inertia deriving effect largely outside of legal processes. (3) One hazard of living in society was that, however legitimate a norm, those applying it might apply it mistakenly, irrationally, or abu-

77. Yick Wo v. Hopkins, 118 U.S. 356, 369 (1886); West Coast Hotel Co. v. Parrish, 300 U.S. 379, 391 (1937); Palko v. Connecticut, 302 U.S. 319, 325 (1937).

sively. Thus issues of justice and injustice arose regarding the
proper application of norms in particular instances.

Let me first take account of the place of the third type of issue
in the country's legal history. I put it first because, though proper
application of norms presented continuing difficulties and the
need for continual vigilance, the core principle was clear: a given
norm should be applied correctly, rationally, and fairly, lest the
meaning of the whole enterprise be stultified. The structuring of
legal processes to promote regular, rational, fair application of
general laws provided an important concern of legal history.
This was a prime object of some developments in the law of
procedure and evidence and in the law dealing with the functional independence and interrelationships of legislative, executive and administrative, and judicial officers. It was also a prime
object both of the general requirements of procedural due process
of law and of such particular constitutional guarantees as the
privilege against self-incrimination and the right to be free of
unlawful searches and seizures.[78] This aspect of legal history
deals to an unusual extent with impacts of law itself as a distinct
source of influence on the general society. The ideal of regular,
rational, fair application of legal norms was created largely from
the experience of establishing and operating the legal system
itself; the ideals of procedural due process and equal application
of norms were taught largely by lawmen to the laity or learned
by laymen from their immediate involvements with law. But law
did not confine these ideals entirely to its own processes. The
society put a high value on dispersion of power and division of
labor. Accordingly, the law was not quick to intervene in the
internal affairs of other-than-legal institutions, but it might intervene to require another social institution to administer its own
discipline correctly, rationally, and fairly according to its own
declared rules of procedure.[79]

78. Fellman, Chaps. 4, 8, 9; Griswold, 36–38; Patterson (1), 45–47, 406–
407; cf. Wigmore, 1:241–248.
79. Chafee, 993; Taft, Chap. I; Wellington, Chap. 4; Zollman, Chaps.
VII, VIII.

The ways in which highly focused special interest might prevail in law over other focused interests or over general interest were too various to lend themselves to ready generalization in terms of subject matter. One can generalize about matters of legal process and the ways in which legal process made it easier or harder to curb unfair or unreasonable measures of special interest. There is more history to be written of these aspects of law than has been written so far. Three lines of inquiry seem likely to be particularly fruitful.

(1) The more open-ended a lawmaking agency's jurisdiction —the wider the range of subject matter it was empowered to deal with, the wider its range of discretion in choosing responses to pressures for action—the greater the likelihood that its special-interest output would increase. This meant that the legislature tended to produce far more favors to special interests than did courts because legislatures did not regulate the kinds of petitions that could be brought or special favors asked of those who held legislative power; in comparison, access to judicial lawmaking moved through a more limited range of channels, narrowed by precedent and confined by the tradition that it was not the prime business of judges to make new public policy. Executive officers or administrative agencies could become targets of special-interest approaches as wider discretion was confided to them by delegating legislation. Experience showed that some structural or process curbs could be put upon the tendency of broad subject-matter jurisdiction to invite special-interest gains. If a field of policy developed toward generalization and standardization, pressures for special treatment could be reduced substantially because they could be made unnecessary; this was done when a combination of constitutional and statutory provisions substituted general incorporation laws for the thousands of special charters for business corporations that cluttered up statute books between the 1830's and the 1880's.[80]

80. Hurst (1), 24, 30, 70–74, 185–189, 407, 409, (3), 47, 52, 72, 320, (5), 134–137.

(2) Special interest prevailed over general interest, or prevailed at unfair cost to other special interest, largely because legal processes did not provide that all relevant interests had adequate representation. Adequate representation called for measures more positive than simply a procedural due-process right to be heard. In policy making by litigation—in the making of common law—there was the chronic danger that public policy of general import, or bearing heavily on other particular interests, would be made in response to too narrow a record and too limited a range of argument provided by the particular litigants to whom the precedent-making lawsuit was open. Opportunity for others to appear as friends of the court was a limited answer; their appearance depended on the court's permission, they must muster their own resources to appear, and they had no control of the record that would shape the terms of decision. The law was slow to develop hospitality to suits in which particular litigants might represent claims of whole classes of similar interests; and, again, it was left typically to the unassisted resources of particular suitors to find the means with which to bear the costs of a class action.[81] In policy making by legislation the norm was to open the legislative arena pretty much to all comers, but to measure them by the resources they could assemble, unaided, to make their case. As with private contract, the image of the bargaining process was not an unattractive solution to interest competition, especially compared with harsher alternatives; but, as with private contract, the formula promised to serve social interest only insofar as the parties did not stand in gross inequality of bargaining position. The presence of two legislative chambers could enlarge, but also could restrict opportunities for special-interest maneuver, especially when one chamber developed to have larger constituencies and longer terms and thus altered the mix of interest pressures impinging on it as compared with the other chamber. The chief executive's veto could offset more gen-

81. Arnold (1), 913–922, 944–947; Auerbach et al., 228–235; Fuller, 438–442; Llewellyn, 28–31, 227, 323.

eral concerns against special interest. The twentieth century brought efforts to regulate lobbies by publicity and by limiting lobbyists' spending; experience proved that it was difficult to enforce spending limits and that the greater hope lay in increasing publicity of interest-group activities.[82] Where statutes delegated rule-making power to administrators, presumably the specialized will and the expertise of the agency would provide adequate representation to the general interests the legislation was supposed to serve. But the specialization of the administrative agency proved to carry its own dangers of imbalance; the inevitable continuing relations between regulators and regulated gave the regulated particular opportunity to press their case, establish harmony with the public officers, and perhaps hold out to them possibilities of future private employment, all to result in sapping the energy the agency brought to fulfilling its mandate in the public interest.[83]

(3) We have considered situations in which legal agencies—legislative, executive, administrative, or judicial—confronted at first hand wants, needs, and pressures for or against action as these existed in the community apart from the legal apparatus. Judges confronted tensions between general and special interest at second remove by developing judicial review of the constitutionality of such initial responses as lawmaking agencies made to problems brought to them. Unless judicial review were to rob first-line lawmaking of functional significance, judges needed to draw doctrinal lines that would recognize that in enforcing constitutional limitations they were not to redo what the primary lawmakers had already done in finding relevant facts of community life and deciding what to do about those facts in the public interest. On some matters constitution makers lay down limiting rules—such as the prohibition of ex post facto laws—so specific in characterizing facts and values as to leave no room for

82. Joseph P. Chamberlain, 64–65; Gross, Chaps. 2, 3, 12, 13; Hurst (1), 53–56, 63–66, 236, 403.

83. Marver Bernstein, Chaps. 3, 5, 6; Hurst (3), 72; Kohlmaier, Chaps. 6, 21; Landis (3), 54–62, 87.

discretionary judgment in the primary policy makers.[84] But in most situations constitutions spoke in terms of standards and not rules—in such broadly framed criteria as requirements of due process and equal protection of law—under which primary lawmakers must exercise judgment in deciding, in the first instance, what facts of community life might fairly be deemed to have public-interest relevance, and what might reasonably be deemed proper public-policy response.[85] In these areas of constitutional standards, judges early developed the idea that primary lawmaking came into a reviewing court enjoying the benefit of a presumption of its constitutionality. This meant that a heavy burden of persuasion lay on the litigant who challenged the validity of a legislative product to show beyond reasonable doubt that it lacked foundation in fact or represented a value choice not supportable as serving public interest.[86] The presumption of constitutionality had a history of its own which deserves more detailed exploration. It took time to develop a full expression of the values for which the presumption stood; that the presumption applied to legislative fact-findings as well as to legistive value choices for long was not clearly recognized in legal doctrine.[87] Existence of the presumption was under varying challenge over many years. In the late nineteenth and early twentieth centuries an important line of decisions in effect rejected the presumption as applied to laws regulating market bargaining, declaring that freedom of contract was the norm of public policy and restraint the exception. By the late 1930's the Supreme Court squarely rejected this proposition, establishing that a strong presumption of constitutionality attached to all laws

84. See Hughes, C. J., in Home Building & Loan Association v. Blaisdell, 290 U.S. 398, 426 (1934).

85. Nebbia v. New York, 291 U.S. 502 (1934).

86. Powell v. Pennsylvania, 127 U.S. 678 (1888); Williamson v. Lee Optical of Oklahoma, 348 U.S. 483 (1955).

87. See Learned Hand, circ. j., in Borden's Farm Products Co., Inc. v. Ten Eyck, 11 Fed. Supp. 599, 600 (S.D.N.Y., 1935); cf. South Carolina State Highway Department v. Barnwell Brothers, Inc., 303 U.S. 177, 191–192 (1938).

regulating the market.[88] But the evolution of doctrine was not at an end. From about the mid-twentieth century the Court began to define other categories of preferred values (notably freedom of speech, press, and association) and of constitutionally suspect classifications (notably on criteria of race), and ruling that the proponent of a law limiting a preferred value or invoking a suspect classification must show compelling justification to uphold the challenged policy.[89] Application of the presumption of constitutionality had diverse implications for the bearing of judicial review on the tensions between general and special interest in a primary stage of making law. Though the burden of persuasion was heavy, an attacker had opportunity to rebut the presumption. This threat put some curb on lawmakers' yielding too readily to special-interest efforts, especially in the face of the equal protection standard embodied in the Fifth and Fourteenth Amendments. On the other hand, the presumption in effect strengthened the position of special-interest lobbies. All that need be shown to uphold a statute was that reasonable legislators could find the underlying facts and make a reasonable value judgment as to how to act on them; it was not hard to find plausible public-interest hypotheses to support a law that in fact responded to some particular interest. Moreover, after some wavering, the Court determined not to invalidate a statute, though it had been passed for an improper "motive"; in practical effect this meant that if a statute reasonably could be expected to produce one outcome of public interest and another of purely private interest, the Court would not undertake to judge which outcome predominated in the legislature's desires, but would sustain the statute on the basis of the public interest it could be deemed to serve.[90] Constitutional limitations did put cautionary pressure on law-

88. West Coast Hotel Co. v. Parrish, 300 U.S. 379, 400 (1937), overruling Adkins v. Children's Hospital, 261 U.S. 525 (1923).
89. Schneider v. State, 308 U.S. 147 (1939); Joseph Burstyn, Inc. v. Wilson, 343 U.S. 495 (1952); McLaughlin v. Florida, 379 U.S. 184 (1964).
90. Daniel v. Family Security Life Insurance Co., 336 U.S. 220 (1949); cf. United States v. Darby, 312 U.S. 100, 115, 116 (1941).

makers to resist narrowly focused efforts for private advantage. But the presumption of constitutionality meant that basic responsibility for dealing with the continual pull and haul between general and special interest rested with primary lawmakers and not with reviewing judges.

Apart from such challenges as might be raised to any classification by which law sought to apportion benefits or burdens, I earlier pointed out some criteria of classification that gave ground for peculiar concern because of their unusual reach and penetration into the quality of life. These were the criteria of age, sex, race, national origin, religious affiliation, and wealth. Social institutions other than law and patterns of social living derived from causes other than the action of law also applied these criteria. Hence a central problem in organizing the study of legal history is to mark out the varying terms and extent to which the law was specially implicated in differentiating gains and costs of life in society according to these measures.

Clearly these criteria enter into legal history as far as law directly assigned and enforced them as bases for fixing rights and duties, privileges or exemptions. Law made use of all of these criteria, and important phases of legal history emerged out of continuity or change in such legal usage. Law treated age as significant for a variety of purposes, as in decreeing compulsory schooling for the young, sanctioning parental control of children, exacting compulsory military service, imposing mandatory retirement at stipulated ages in public employment, or offering special tax benefits or provision of social insurance for the elderly. Law invoked sex as a basis for allocating gains and costs of social experience; subordination of wife to husband loomed large in nineteenth century law, for a time women were barred from the profession of law, the vote was limited to men. Slavery was law's strongest and most destructive use of race as a criterion for determining the content of life, but the Thirteenth Amendment did not end the invoking of racial criteria for determining legal rights, duties, and status; for decades law required segregation by race in public education and in public accommodations, while some parts of the criminal law—notably those concerning sex relations—turned on racial criteria. Law denied the vote to aliens, excluded them from some occupations, and barred them from holding title to land. Into the early nineteenth century the law of some states sustained establishments of religion; law regularly gave tax exemptions to churches, provided chaplains for the military and for prison populations, and made religious affiliation a test for exempting conscientious objectors from military service. Until about the mid-nineteenth century law often imposed property qualifications on the right to vote or hold office; early law imposed imprisonment for debt; law commonly limited access to legal process or legal services by requiring payment of fees; tax laws distinguished tax obligations according to types and extent of property ownership or income.[91]

Though criteria for allocating benefits and burdens might originate in social institutions or social practice outside the law, if the law stood ready to lend its aid to legitimize or enforce the criteria, this fact and the results of invoking it clearly were part of legal history. Social practice underlay many incidents of husbands' conventional subordination of wives within the family relation, but law in effect sanctioned these patterns as long as it denied divorce on grounds of incompatibility or mental cruelty.[92] Social practice brought into being private covenants against sale of land to blacks or Jews, but law in effect sanctioned these patterns as long as it stood ready to enforce the covenants. Similarly, social practice developed barriers to admission of blacks or Jews to resorts or restaurants, but law in effect sanctioned these patterns as long as the police would enforce laws of criminal trespass or disorderly conduct against those who insisted on entering the forbidden premises to demand service.[93]

91. Davidson, Ginsburg, and Kay, passim (sex discrimination); N. Edwards, 519–525 (schools); Heilbroner (2), 288, and Auerbach (2), 307 (wealth); Howe, Chaps. III, IV, VI (religion); Konvitz, Chaps. 5, 6, 7 (aliens).

92. Cf. Kanowitz, 14–15, 95–98.

93. Shelley v. Kraemer, 334 U.S. 1 (1948); Griffin v. Maryland, 378 U.S. 130 (1964); see United States v. Guest, 383 U.S. 745, 756 (1966).

Both where law directly mandated certain criteria for allocating benefits and burdens and where it simply offered its sanctions to support criteria originating outside the law, the record
was not unmarked by controversy, nor was it unchanging. No
area of policy was exempt from conflict; no area failed to show
some significant shifts of values. Thus, for example, compulsory
schooling did not become the norm of policy without bitter battles over legislating against child labor. The Fifteenth Amendment guaranteed blacks the vote, free of racial disqualification.
But long and weary battling stretched into the civil rights legislation and decisions of the 1960's to give some substance to the
constitutional assurance. Women got the vote only after some
seventy years of conflict. Aliens had to fight in court to obtain
the fair treatment which the equal protection clause of the
Fourteenth Amendment had told each state it must extend "to
any person within its jurisdiction." Conscientious objectors had to
sue to establish that exemption from military service should not
be read as limited to members of conventional religious denomi-
nations. Not until 1966 did the Supreme Court establish that the
Fourteenth Amendment meant that the right to vote might not
be conditioned on ownership of property.[94]

I have spoken so far of situations that are part of legal history
because the law was present, positively contributing to what
happened, either by taking initiatives to establish certain distributions of gain and cost in society or by lending its force to
legitimize and support distributions derived chiefly from other-
than-legal social forces. To define where the absence of law may
have contributed to what happened so as to make the situation
properly part of legal history is more difficult. Conceivably we
might declare law responsible for any ongoing patterns of social
organization, practice, custom, or interest, if law did not intervene where it might have affected what went on. But if we cast

94. Brandeis, 199–200, 208, 215–216 (child labor); Curti, 195, 386, 464,
625, 685 (vote for women); Rottschaefer, 553, 554 (aliens); South Carolina
v. Katzenbach, 393 U.S. 301 (1966) (vote for blacks); Harper v. Virginia
State Board of Elections, 383 U.S. 663 (1966) (poll tax).

a net so broad, we wipe out any analytically useful distinction of legal processes from other social processes, and all social history becomes legal history and legal history is all of social history. The law is too distinctive an apparatus, and too often exerts its own distinctive force, to make such obliteration of distinguishing marks sensible.[95]

It was part of legal history that in some areas of social relations law condoned, consciously accepted, or showed consistent neglect or indifference toward use of private violence to allocate benefits and burdens, privileges and deprivations. This was most marked in race and labor relations over many years. Here the absence of legal intervention belongs to legal history because the effective assertion of a legitimate monopoly of force was ordinarily a key element of the legal system. In standing by while private violence took over governance of an area of social life, law inherently contributed to defining the limits of reality in an essential element of legal order.[96]

The question of private violence apart, one criterion for demarcating the social history of law from the general history of society would be to treat a social concern as part of legal history only at the point at which the concern begins to be manifest in formal inputs to legal processes—in bills introduced in the legislature, suits begun in court, motions made to obtain administrative action. Before that point, there would be some reason in saying that given allocations of benefits and burdens are parts of the history of other-than-legal institutions but not of the law. In what sense, for example, was exclusion of women from voting a part of legal history in decades when both men and women took for granted social custom and practice limiting women's roles in society so that the idea of legal change did not enter the realm of substantial discussion, let alone legal action?[97]

95. Cf. Julius Stone (1), 743–758, 470, 479, 516–517.
96. Irving Bernstein, 152–153, 156, 170, 273–278, 285–286, 571; Dulles, 166–186, 277–278, 301, 304; Hofstadter and Wallace, 18–24; Hurst (3), 267–271, 274–280; Myrdal (1), Chap. 27.
97. Curti, 126, 166–168, 195–197; Hurst (3), 137–152.

But, for at least two reasons, we cannot let the matter rest. (1) The women's suffrage example shows that it is not the responsibility of the legal historian to do an original probe of all the other-than-legal causes of what happened; to put that burden on him would, again, be to destroy analytically useful distinctions and simply to put a label of legal research on all study of all social processes. But, just because law displays distinctive character and capacity among social institutions, legal history always needs to be concerned to understand the limits of effective legal action. To this end the legal historian does bear responsibility to borrow from the learning of other fields, to illuminate why law was not invoked in situations where other-than-legal processes explain what came about.[98] (2) Law is in itself often a cause of its absence from a situation because there are costs of using legal agencies. To get legislative action, for example, usually some people must expend a great deal of energy—in finding facts, in formulating proposals for action that can be put in the form of a legislative bill, in lobbying and bargaining out accommodations of interest to collect votes. These threshold costs often gave greater impact to criteria established largely by social forces outside the law, which determined positions of relative privilege and deprivation in the society. Youth or age, race, position as low-status foreigners or religious communicants, and above all inequalities of wealth and income put many individuals and groups at such disadvantage in meeting the threshold costs of invoking legal processes that for long periods their concerns found no expression at all in inputs to the working of those processes. The features of legal institutions that create such threshold costs are part of legal history, and here it merges with other dimensions of social history in explaining the absence of law in a given area of social relations over certain spans of time.[99]

The threshold costs of invoking legal processes have particular

98. Auerbach (1), 517–519; Hurst (4), 429, 466, 569, 601, 602; Patterson (1), 50–52.

99. Friedman (2), 798–806; Galanter, 121–122, 135–144; Hurst (3), 139–140; Truman, Chaps. XI, XV.

importance for estimating law's responsibility for allocations of gains and costs of social living according to such criteria as race or sex or wealth, where privilege or deprivation tends to be especially entrenched in a complex of social forces. Law was typically only a marginal force in determining the content of social life, but even so it could move affairs off dead center, toward improving the quality of life for increasing numbers of people. Since individuals and groups on occasion could use law for leverage against established privileges set by other-than-legal institutions, ideas, and inertia, it was the more important to learn from legal history all we could about factors that might enhance or reduce that leverage potential. Herein especially lay the answer to the question of how far the legal order itself was responsible for the absence of law from situations that presented grave issues of justice and injustice in allocation of gains and costs from life in society.

The varied factors relevant to appraising law's contributions to situations of privilege come to sharp focus where law relates to the positions of social classes in controlling the economy. Great inequalities in distribution of wealth marked most of the nation's history. From the 1870's on the content and quality of life were affected profoundly by high concentrations of ownership and practical control of the means of production in private decision makers moved by the search to maximize profit. Over a varying range from simplistic to sophisticated analysis, Marxist readings of these events took law to be shaped primarily by the drive for power of high capitalists, supported by the naiveté or ambitions of middle-class auxiliaries. The power of concentrated private ownership and control has bulked so large in the economy for the last century as to pose major problems for legal history. But the record shows more complex interplay of economic, political, and social processes than can be accounted for simply by the dominance of a capitalist elite. The law never legitimized the structuring of social power about a private elite; despite confusion of goals and inadequate enforcement, the general history of antitrust policy denied legitimacy to concentrated private power as the organizing principle of the economy, let alone of the whole society. True, in many ways law worked to assist trends toward more concentration of private ownership power, The federal system fostered markets broad enough to sustain big business; corporation law grew increasingly hospitable to providing means not only for large-scale mustering of assets but for focused inside control of business organizations; private pressures held tax policy within bounds that did not basically challenge accumulation and consolidation of great wealth by individuals, by families, and within tight circles linked by kinship and social and business affinity. Inertia in the course of public policy materially contributed to private concentration of economic power, especially as custom gave broad scope to the market to determine the impact of scientific and technological change. Other currents, however, moved with enough strength that to sum up the directions of public policy simply in terms of law's support of a capitalist elite is unrealistic. Expansion of the suffrage and concern for the independent vigor of the electorate helped keep political processes in competition with economic processes. Apart from antitrust policy, the persistent trend to enlarge legal regulation of the market on behalf of various constituencies—labor, investors, consumers, the commonwealth—showed that considerable dispersion of power still worked through legal processes. Tax programs often were regressive or at best proportional in over-all impact. Yet, the idea of progressive taxation showed a twentieth-century tenacity that made government's taxing and spending powers admonitions of caution to concentrated private interests. One could strike no neat balance among such factors. To untangle law's varied relations to creating and disciplining private-ownership privilege stands as a major challenge to the legal historian.[100]

100. Cf. Dahl and Lindblom, Chaps. 6, 7; Hofstadter, 188; McCraw, 159; Zeitlin, 1073.

CHAPTER II

The Powers of
Legal Agencies

The kinds of authority held by the major legal agencies, even more than their structure, determined the working character of law as an institution. There was more variety and change in the history of agency powers than of agency structure, warranting separate and more elaborate treatment than the first chapter gave to structural matters.

The nature of legislative power was central to United States legal history. Our inheritance from the Parliamentary Revolution put legislative power at the heart of representative government. Moreover, through the years of gathering tension with England the colonists found in the legislative branch—and particularly in the popularly elected lower house—the principal legal instrument to express their disagreements with imperial policy; governors and judges holding commissions at the pleasure of the crown were not dependable spokesmen for the local interest. Over the course of two hundred years following independence people made increasing demands on government for regulation and services that only the legislative branch could meet because of traditional and constitutional limits on executive and judicial power. Thus in important measure the historian best can establish the outlines of judicial and executive power by their relations to legislative authority.

Legislative Power: Declaring Standards and
Rules of Behavior

The authority of state legislatures. The norm set by the first state constitutions after the Revolution was simply to confer on designated chambers "the legislative power" of the state with no further description and virtually no limitations. Legislators and courts treated this open-ended grant as conferring the full law-making powers held in England by the Parliament and the crown together. Beyond that, the open-ended grant meant that the legislature was the agency empowered to entertain and bring to resolution any petition or grievance or any proposal for action about any subject it reasonably could deem to be of general concern. The legislature was the regular agent from which to seek response for both new or old problems of adjusting social relations by declaring standards or rules of behavior.[1] Of course, response did not always come, nor did it always solve the problem. Witness the lag between the 1890's and the 1950's in response to gathering concern about waste of natural resources. Or consider the lack of adequate legislation to deal with growing tensions in labor-management relations from the 1850's to the 1930's, which fostered a shameful history of violence in labor relations. Nonetheless, viewed in ten- to twenty-year perspectives, the legislative record showed the utility of the wide-open subject-matter jurisdiction of legislatures. For it was chiefly in the record of introduced bills, of committee hearings and reports, of amendments and reworkings and rejections and adoptions of proposals for statute law that we see the large movements of public policy in the states—in marking out the changing character of the market, of business organizations, of public utilities, of public health and sanitation, of communications and transport regulation.[2]

Constitution makers in the nineteenth century somewhat qualified the late eighteenth-century model of open-ended subject-matter authority. The qualifications did not change the basic working character of the legislature as the body to which, normally, concerned parties might bring any matter, however new, or whatever relations or interests were involved. Between the

1. Cf. Nebbia v. New York, 291 U.S. 502, 532 (1934); Bushnell v. Beloit, 10 Wis. 195, 225 (1860). See Walker, 12.
2. Horack, 41; cf. Lawrence H. Chamberlain, passim.

1830's and the 1880's constitution makers in most states developed a number of standard procedural limits on legislative process: for example, every bill must have a title that should describe
accurately the contents of the bill; every bill must be read three
times; on all bills of described character the yeas and nays must
be taken. Somewhat repenting the sweep of trust confided to
legislatures in the 1776–1780 state constitutions, people in the
next generation became distrustful of the integrity of legislative
processes. This distrust derived particularly from the pressure of
those who sought special franchises to engage in enterprises not
open at common law to everyone (putting a dam in a navigable
stream to generate waterpower; operating a bank in order to
profit by lending banknotes intended to be circulating currency).
Limitation appropriately began with imposing the requirement of
accurate titles on bills, in reaction to the deceptive title borne by
the Georgia statute that gave away state lands in the corrupt
Yazoo lands bargain between legislators and speculators.[3] Wielding their power of judicial review, for a time nineteenth-century
courts were ready to enforce these procedural limitations by refusing to recognize authority in statutes that could be shown to
have been passed in violation of the constitutional requirements.
Judicial review on these grounds was most unsettling to the
reliability of the statute books, especially because the internal
procedure of the legislature was in its nature subject to fictions
and manipulation of records. Thus a three-reading requirement—
apparently observed, according to the notations in official jour-
nals—was easily converted into what were in fact readings by
title only; the practice transformed the limitation from one to
promote knowledge of the substance of legislative proposals into
one that at most injected some deliberateness of timing into consideration of bills. By the twentieth century courts deferred to
legislative records or indulged in protective fictions to an extent
that substantially withdrew judicial enforcement from these pro-

3. Freund, 153, 154; Hurst (1), 242; Luce, 546.

cedural limitations, leaving them as admonitions to legislative conscience.[4] The point was emphasized when the United States Supreme Court ruled that there were not even judicially enforceable due-process requirements that notice and opportunity to be heard be given to affected individuals as prerequisite to the procedural validity of legislation affecting them.[5]

A second type of limitation that became standard in state constitutions between 1850 and 1880 was one on the subject matter of legislation: constitution makers forbade legislatures to enact special or local laws in specified areas of public policy. Thus legislatures no longer might enact special laws—ones dealing with the affairs of specified individuals—granting divorces, providing for adoption of children, authorizing named persons to act as a business corporation or to exercise a franchise to build a dam at a designated location on a navigable stream. Nor might legislatures any longer enact local laws—ones dealing with particular relations or arrangements within defined geographical areas—creating local courts, or other local units of government, or conferring on a particular local unit some specific authority (for example, to incur debt within stipulated limits for stipulated purposes).[6]

Like some of the procedural limits earlier put on legislatures, the bans on special and local legislation (and especially on special legislation) reflected growth of distrust of the integrity of legislative processes. From the 1820's on legislatures faced mounting demand to provide legitimated frames of organization for joint enterprises that ambitious men sought to press in expanding markets. This demand was at first mainly for franchises

4. Freund, 153–157; Read et al., 507–520; Sutherland, 1A:25, 32, 2:140, 143, 156–158; cf. Field v. Clark, 143 U.S. 649 (1896); United States v. Ballin, 144 U.S. 1 (1892).

5. Bi-Metallic Investment Co. v. State Board of Equalization, 239 U.S. 441 (1915); Norwegian Nitrogen Products Co. v. United States, 288 U.S. 294 (1933); cf. Townsend v. Yeomans, 301 U.S. 441 (1937).

6. E.g., Wis. Const., IV, 31 (1871); cf. Read et al., 543–547; Walker, 258.

to allow private action by some which common law forbade to all
or withheld from the generality: franchises conferring rights of
way and powers of eminent domain, usually exclusively, for
building toll roads, canals, or railroads; or franchises to operate
banks empowered to issue circulating notes. Most such venturers
found it convenient to operate as corporations and demanded
both special-action privileges and corporate status; the demand,
moreover, was not only for incorporation to do business, but also
to conduct philanthropic or public-welfare projects such as libraries, hospitals, and academies. Suspicion developed that those
who sought special-action franchises for business profit, particularly to conduct note-issuing banks, were ready to bribe legislators to get the authorization they wanted, especially if either
formally or in practical effect it would be a monopoly privilege.
Some impetus to limit special laws came from this distrust. For a
time, notably in the 1830's and 1840's, this distrust was applied
uncritically to grant of corporate charters as such, though on the
record the distrust was little warranted; despite their special
form, most business corporation charters carried no special-
action franchises apart from enjoyment of corporate status itself,
and one can scan hundreds of such statutory charters of the nineteenth century without finding evidence that they involved other
than standardized provisions valued simply for what became routine business utility.[7]

In the long run the spread of constitutional bans on special and
local laws came about mainly for reasons of efficiency in the
legislative process. The special corporate charters, along with
the special-action franchises for dams and river improvements
and railroads and banks, as well as the local laws chartering
particular counties, cities, towns, villages, and local courts, all
grew to overshadow in bulk the legislation of general application
and to crowd legislative dockets so as to impede proper handling
of general legislation. The demands back of special and local

7. Hurst (5), 16, 46, 113, 119, 131–138, 146.

laws did not go away—businessmen continued to want the corporate form for more and more enterprises, and there was continuing need to provide for local government—but legislatures needed to bring their energies to better focus on the general principles involved in meeting these demands.

Coupled with the new constitutional prohibitions on special and local laws went constitutional authorizations that legislators provide general laws for chartering local units of government and business corporations and even for organizing such truly special enterprises as banks, railroads, insurance companies, and other public utilities.[8] Where demand could be met by standards and rules spelled out in the statute books, as was true regarding the general run of business or philanthropic corporations, the legislature declared the full form of public policy and committed its routine administration to ministerial administrative officers, usually in the office of the state secretary of state. Where promoters sought special-action franchises, the impact on those dealing with the franchise holders (customers, suppliers, workers, investors) or on the general public usually called for more discretionary judgments than could be encapsulated in statutes; here, from about the 1880's on, but especially after the 1905–1915 decade, legislatures usually met the problems posed by the constitutional ban on special laws by delegating to specialized administrative agencies the implementation of general laws. To a workable degree, this outcome satisfied both constitutional policy and the practical pressures for special-action franchises or incorporation.[9]

Much less satisfactory was the outcome as to local laws. The legislatures responded to the new constitutional limitations by enacting general charter laws for types of local government units.

8. E.g., N.Y. Const., VIII, 1 (1846); Wis. Const., IV, 32 (1871); cf. Freund, 157.

9. Marver H. Bernstein, Chaps. 1, 2; Hurst (1), 420–422, (4), 604–605, (5), 56. Cf. State ex rel. Wisconsin Inspection Bureau v. Whitman, 196 Wis. 472, 220 N.W. 929 (1928).

But experience showed that local governments continued to encounter problems or local pressures too diverse and peculiar to their contexts to be resolved by statutory generalities. Despite the constitutional bans on their making local laws, legislatures continued to enact a significant amount of what in substance was legislation adapted solely to the affairs of particular localities, while failing to provide any administrative apparatus, comparable to that in the public-utility field, capable of dealing under statutory standards with the distinctive problems of the localities. The need to validate particular local demands remained, but legislatures had not met it directly. The result was to satisfy the demand under the cloak of legal fiction. Legislatures passed laws that in large terms were general ("Any city of the third class . . . ") but by further specifications (" . . . having a bonded indebtedness between $1,500,000 and $1,800,000) applied only to a given local government unit. After their first flush of enthusiasm for judicial enforcement of the new constitutional limitations had worn off, state courts in effect acknowledged the practical needs unsatisfied by general legislation in this field and usually refused to look back of the general language of statutes on local government to find that the legislation in substance violated the prohibitions on local laws.[10] The contrasting impact between the constitutional bans on special and on local laws indicated that real pressures for legal action would channel their own routes to some substantial satisfaction, if lawmakers failed to make effective response to them.

The net effect of formal constitutional change in the states was to leave to the legislative branch substantially all the freedom of choice and innovation with which the pioneer constitutions of 1776–1780 had endowed it. More substantial limitations on legislative options arose rather from the course of working relations with the other branches of government.

The courts had the first limiting impact. The Supreme Court

10. Hurst (1), 233–234; Read et al., 546, 567–569; Walker, 258–259.

early enlarged its scrutiny of state legislation measured against
the two key guarantees of the original federal Constitution. The
contract clause protected private commitments in the market
against retroactive state laws, and Chief Justice John Marshall
extended the protection over land titles and corporate charters.
Marshall, too, pointed the way to extension of the Court's role
under the commerce clause; after some doctrinal fumbling, by
the 1880's the Court had established its title under that clause
to refuse legal effect to state statutes deemed either unduly to
burden interstate dealings or to discriminate against them.[11] But
a much broader field for judicial review also developed.

Between about 1830 and 1860 state court judges began to
hammer out justifications for refusing legal effect to statutes they
deemed to infringe basic terms of the social compact. Their
formulas, which rang with the tones of natural law, served the
practical purpose of trying to preserve a broad arena for maneuver by private contract and property dealings within the market.[12]
It is questionable whether a simple appeal to natural law would
have sufficed to maintain the judges' legitimacy against rising
pressures for legislative intervention to redress imbalances of
power in the market, but the Fourteenth Amendment injected
a new factor. From the 1880's on federal and state judges
found in the due process and equal protection clauses warrant
for reviewing the validity of the substantive content of statute
law as well as the fairness of the procedures legislators provided to implement substantive policy. Proponents of the Fourteenth Amendment had envisaged that its terms would add
to the law courts would apply as cases came to them. But they
had expected that Congress—using the "power" given it by section 5 of the amendment, "to enforce, by appropriate legislation,

11. Fletcher v. Peck, 6 Cranch 87 (U.S. 1810), and Dartmouth College
v. Woodward, 4 Wheat. 518 (U.S. 1818) (contract clause); Welton v.
Missouri, 91 U.S. 275 (1876), and Wabash, St. Louis & Pacific Ry. v.
Illinois, 118 U.S. 557 (1886) (commerce clause).

12. Fine, 127–140; Hurst (1), 31.

the provisions of this article"—would supply the principal content of due process and equal protection standards as limits on state lawmakers. From the mid-1870's on into mid-twentieth century, however, Congress turned its attention elsewhere. In that interval the energy of businessmen-litigants and the ingenuity of their lawyers pressed upon the United States Supreme Court the expansive potentials of due process and equal protection for legitimating substantial judicial checks on state legislative power. The Court responded with a vigor of will unforeseen by the proponents of the Fourteenth Amendment.[13]

Between 1880 and 1930 the Supreme Court moved Fourteenth Amendment doctrine along three lines that enlarged judicial authority to restrict legislative policy making and one line that held down that authority; the over-all pattern represented a significant hierarchy of values. First, in domains where the Supreme Court was willing to recognize the force of the Fourteenth Amendment, it recognized that force as superseding the Tenth Amendment; legitimate national interests were at stake in measuring whether state legislation met standards of due process and equal protection, and national courts would enforce the newly declared national interests.[14] Second, these national interests concerned the substance of state public policy as well as the procedures for implementing that policy; the man in the street might be pardoned for thinking that "due process of law" simply spelled fair procedure, but the lawmen gave the constitutional formula much broader reach. As I have noted, this development was not wholly new. Judicial doctrine before 1868 had begun to invoke natural law or social compact ideas to warrant some judicial limitations on the substantive policy enacted by state legislatures. In the Dred Scott case the Supreme Court treated the Fifth Amendment's due process clause as imposing substantive limits on congressional policy making. Abolitionist pamphleteers had propagated the notion that there were substantive limits on what legislatures legitimately could enact. But if the Fourteenth

13. Cf. Flack, Chap. V; Kelly and Harbison, 458–463.
14. McCloskey, 103–105, 128–134, 151–160.

Amendment did not bring into being a wholly new concept, it provided the fresh doctrinal material that nerved the judges to grasp the full scope of review authority to which lawyers' arguments invited them.[15]

The third line along which the Supreme Court moved Fourteenth Amendment development was to interpret the amendment's guarantees of due process and equal protection for "persons" to embrace corporations. For a time in the early twentieth century some argued that the Fourteenth Amendment's coverage of corporations had not been within the true intent of most of the amendment's supporters, but had been concealed in its phrasing by a small conspiracy of lawyers and politicos solicitous for the interests of big business. This "conspiracy theory" has not stood up convincingly. The conspiracy must have been held to a select group; from the mid-1860's into the 1870's most lawyers representing business corporations grounded their resistance to state regulatory statutes on the privileges and immunities clause of the federal Constitution, apparently failing to see the possibilities in due-process language. The Supreme Court added its creativity at this point, but it seems more fairly assessed as creativity of will rather than as that of idea. Given the political origins of the Fourteenth Amendment in prime concern for the future share of the former slaves in the legal order—origins the Court often emphasized much later as it developed the doctrine that race was a suspect criterion for determining the reach of law—the Court plausibly might have read "persons" as intended to apply only to human beings. That the Court chose, instead, to read "persons" in the Fourteenth Amendment according to general legal usage, as embracing corporations, had warrant in the legal learning of centuries. But such a reading constituted a significant choice between alternative paths of Fourteenth Amendment doctrinal development.[16]

15. Howard Jay Graham, Chaps. 4, 5; Kelly and Harbison, 501–502, 508–518; McCloskey, 94–95, 116–118, 129–132.

16. Howard Jay Graham, Chaps. 1, 2; Hurst (1), 227–228; Kelly and Harbison, 462, 498; McCloskey, 132.

The one respect in which the Supreme Court held down its scope for action under the Fourteenth Amendment was by choosing the most restrictive of the options available under the legislative history of the amendment for determining when a state denied a person due process or equal protection of the laws. The combined weight of the centrist and the Radical Republican opinion in Congress behind the amendment would dictate that federal courts give relief to individuals—and particularly to the blacks—where they suffered discriminatory deprivation of civil rights because of the gross indifference or negligence of state lawmakers or state law enforcers. But from the 1880's into the mid-twentieth century, the Supreme Court interpreted the amendment's protection as extending only against affirmative action by state officers. The Court's value bias was clear and cruel: it would use the Fourteenth Amendment to enlarge judicial restraints on state legislation regulating the private market, but not on state policy that disregarded basic claims of personality.[17]

We must not exaggerate the limits judicial review put on state legislative power, even under the expanded Fourteenth Amendment. There is danger of exaggeration because decisions made between the years 1880 and 1930 created considerable political drama, as complaints rose when state and federal judges held unconstitutional various state laws designed to protect the health, safety, and earnings of workers, and especially of women and children, and to guard consumers against fraud and overreaching by superior bargaining power in the market. But the main currents of developing statute law in these fields moved ahead nonetheless. If one looks not just as the immediate impact of such court decisions, but at the course of public policy over the ensuing ten to fifteen years, it appears that the judges exercised a kind of delaying veto, and not a conclusive power to bar any major objective of legislative policy backed by substantial, sus-

17. Frantz, 1353; Hurst (1), 30; Kelly and Harbison, 491–492, 928, 945; McCloskey, 210–212.

tained pressure in the community. Mr. Justice Holmes spoke fact and not prophecy when he said, "Every opinion tends to become a law." This verdict does not negate the heavy costs to those who must wait until the delaying veto is overridden by community pressure, but realism calls for noting that time lay with the legislature rather than with the courts in establishing most generalized public policy. After the mid-1930's judges in effect recognized this fact by applying a strong presumption of constitutionality to economic regulatory legislation.[18]

State legislative power was limited at least as much—though through different operations—by the growth of organized lobbies as by judicial review. This was chiefly a twentieth-century development. The nineteenth-century legislatures were importuned by hundreds of individuals and small groups seeking particular relief or advantage. But these were episodic, ad hoc pressures. Beginning with the railroads in the last quarter of the nineteenth century, but mainly with the rise of trade associations, labor unions, farm organizations, and big business from the 1920's on, legislatures felt the impact of groups organized for continuity of representation of their special interests. These interests maintained salaried bureaucracies at group headquarters and found means to muster grass-roots pressure in broad-scale campaigns that brought home to each legislator where the votes and the campaign funds lay. The effect was more often negative than positive; such organized interests, of course, could gain through law (subsidies, franchises, taxes favorable to their enterprises), but much of the time their objects were to prevent other interests from getting competing gains or imposing regulations to burden their own freedom in the market. From the Progressive years of the early twentieth century, legislatures reacted somewhat to protect their own processes, requiring registration of lobbyists and some publicity of their operations, limiting the more outrageous tactics of pressure, putting some curbs on purchase of

18. Hurst (1), 31–32, 185; McCloskey, 138, 151–152; see Holmes, J., dissenting, in Lochner v. New York, 198 U.S. 45, 76 (1905).

legislative favor through campaign contributions. This kind of legislation was significant chiefly for reflecting the reality of the new-style lobbies and the unease they generated; into the last quarter of the twentieth century it had yet to prove effective in content or enforcement to curb the rising power of organized groups in legislative forums.[19]

An irony of the situation was that even the growth of self-restraint in the exercise of judicial review worked to give the lobbies leverage. I have already noted that from the 1930's on the United States Supreme Court led the way in applying a vigorous presumption in favor of the constitutionality of legislation regulating economic relations in the market; the courts would not hold economic regulatory legislation in violation of due process or equal protection of law unless the party attacking the legislation could establish that no reasonable basis could be deemed to exist for finding that the legislation might serve a public interest. It would be a rare measure for which skillful lobbyists could not provide a plausible public-interest explanation to satisfy the due-process standard, under this protective presumption.[20] A strong presumption of constitutionality was even more valuable to lobbyists when it was applied in the face of an equal-protection clause challenge to a statute, for otherwise distinctions among favored or disfavored groups offered readier points of attack on a statute than did questions of reasonableness of ends and means, which typically offered more room for reasonable debate. In either case, as long as a plausible explanation could be hypothesized, the courts refused to upset the statute because alongside a public-interest goal there might stand some private-interest goal; judges would not probe legislative "motive" by estimating which among the concurrent effects the statute might produce was the one the legislators really preferred. The strong presumption of constitutionality, buttressed by refusal to weigh legislative

19. Gross, Chaps. 2, 3; Truman, Chaps. XI, XII.
20. See, e.g., Daniel v. Family Security Life Insurance Co., 336 U.S. 220 (1949); Williamson v. Lee Optical of Oklahoma, 348 U.S. 483, 486, 487–488 (1955).

motive, represented sound separation-of-powers values.[21] Courts were small, relatively insulated bodies, often considerably removed by the age, experience, and knowledge of the judges from the varied interests brought to legislatures for adjustment; legislatures were more broadly drawn from the general community, subject by shorter tenure and the contingencies of elections to proper sensitivity to wants and troubles felt in the community; of the two forums, the legislative clearly should be primary in adjusting community-relations issues.[22] It is important, however, to recognize the full implications of this separation-of-powers position for the responsibility of legislators. The greater deference the courts paid to legislative dispositions, the more the legislators must bear alone the weight of organized interests.

General legislative authority in the states was more limited by twentieth-century developments in the executive and administrative arms than by what went on in the courts. The earliest state constitutions typically gave the governor no independent electoral base, no veto, and no patronage. But nineteenth-century state constitution makers provided for his election by the general voters and gave him a veto. In the twentieth century constitutional amendments increased his bargaining leverage vis-à-vis the legislature by conferring on him the authority to veto particular items of proposed expenditure.[23] Moreover, legislatures gave him substantial patronage as they implemented broader ranges of public policy by creating more and more new executive offices and administrative agencies, staffed at the top by the governor's appointees, though insulated in lower ranks by civil service. By mid-twentieth century, legislatures commonly brought the governor more intimately into programming public spending by charging him to prepare an executive budget. Budget preparation was not wholly a fiscal operation, but readily lapped over

21. Daniel v. Family Security Life Insurance Co., 336 U.S. 220 (1949); cf. Sonzinsky v. United States, 300 U.S. 506, 513 (1937); United States v. Darby, 312 U.S. 100, 115, 116 (1941).
22. Landis (2), 888; Thayer, 135–137, 150.
23. Dodd, 80, 229–237; Hurst (1), 235–236, 383, 402–404.

into issues of general legislation and the policy priorities it reflected. The sum of these developments was to increase the practical as well as the formal capacity of the state chief executive to
limit and channel the originally wide-open policy options of the
legislators.[24] Parallel to these developments, from about 1905 on
state legislatures themselves created a structure of legal order
that limited the range of legislative policy maneuver, as they delegated power to a variety of administrative agencies dealing
with public utilities, industrial accidents and factory safety,
public health and sanitation, insurance, regulation of the general
market, collective bargaining, and tax administration. In the nineteenth century and early twentieth centuries there was considerable unwillingness to legitimize such delegations openly in constitutional doctrine; early delegation was politely veiled under
formulas that insisted that the legislature was defining the law
and committing to administrators merely the responsibility to
find whether facts existed that would bring into play the rules set
out in the statute book. But from the 1920's on judges faced up
to the practical pressures in community life that were leading
legislators to entrust substantial policy-making discretion to administrative officers; court decisions now recognized that the
"legislative power" included authority to delegate lawmaking
responsibilities to new agencies.[25]

As the new executive offices and administrative agencies built
up their specialized experience, enjoyed continuity of their operations, and became immersed and (at least on a technical
level) skilled in handling the detailed flow of business within
their jurisdictions, they tended to gain substantial operating independence. Within their respective areas, they tended to pre-empt
the policy initiative, as far as anyone showed official initiative;
legislative investigation and follow-up typically proved slack and
episodic, so that the working content of public policy depended

24. Dodd, 231–233; Hurst (1), 235–236, 403
25. Hurst (1), 406–411; Kelly and Harbison, 645–651; Rottschaefer, 72–
80.

more and more in these delegated fields on what the delegates did on their own. Legislators attended usually only to the latest increment to an agency's budget and came to take for granted the funds traditionally provided for traditional programs. Thus, agencies enjoyed what amounted to budget tenure. Not surprisingly, in this context outside interest groups came to lobby at least as much with the administrators as with the legislators. After about two generations, the practical scope of legislative power in many a state was hedged in by the vested expectations, programs, and value patterns of executive offices and administrative agencies. The governing statutes usually granted the administrative agencies formal independence from supervision by the governor. Specialized continuity—and often a separate electoral base—conferred analogous practical independence on important executive offices. Thus, public policy making was substantially fragmented. The legislature continued to hold the general power that by historic inheritance made it in charge of public policy. Partly by constitutional change, but mainly by practice and default, the state legislature of late twentieth century was not in fact in charge. Too often for public good, no one was.[26]

The authority of Congress. Given the mingling of felt need and distrust with which the federal Constitutional Convention contrived the structure for a national government, the framers endowed the national legislature with substantial but only with enumerated powers. Their product thus stood in sharp contrast to the wide-open, unqualified grants of "legislative power" made by contemporary state constitutions. The contrast supplied argumentative basis for those who from time to time through the nineteenth and early twentieth centuries argued for a "strict" (that is, restrictive) construction of Congress's powers. But the effective pressures in the country's growth worked to enlarge congressional authority, primarily by practice, sanctioned ultimately by the Supreme Court, with the trend accented by two

26. Joseph P. Chamberlain, 192, 224–233; American Political Science Association, Chaps. 10, 11; Hurst (1), 404, 407–411, 424–425.

major constitutional amendments. The trend was not a repudia-
tion of federalism. Rather, it expressed the development of
broader perceptions of national interests. Though the Constitution enumerated Congress's powers, it conferred authority in
terms of general standards—regarding commerce, the money supply, public property, and the creation of means necessary and
proper for executing the enumerated powers. These standards
proved to have great expansive potential as people became more
aware of the economies of scale and the multiplying interlock of
cause and effect experienced in a continental economy and as the
growth of a more monetized market increased government's flexibility of maneuver by increasing its practical capacity to command resources by taxing and borrowing.[27] Formal constitutional
change added to and never materially subtracted from Congress's
substantive policy-making authority. Though its potential lay
dormant between the 1870's and the 1960's, section 5 of the
Fourteenth Amendment materially increased the possible range
of federal legislation "appropriate" to enforcing due process and
equal protection standards within the states.[28] Apparently narrower, but in its evolving impact almost as broad, was the Sixteenth Amendment. For as Congress broadened the range and
increased the weight of the income taxes it was now enpowered
to levy, federal tax law emerged as a body of economic regulation rivaling legislation passed under the commerce clause.[29]

As with state legislatures, so with Congress we cannot realistically define the bounds of legislative authority without consider-
ing interplay with the courts, with lobbies, and with the executive and administrative arms. In contrast to the confidently
restrictive line the Court took toward state economic regulatory
legislation between 1880 and 1930, with rare exceptions it applied a strong presumption of constitutionality in favor of federal

27. Cf. McCulloch v. Maryland, 4 Wheat. 316 (U.S. 1819); Wickard v.
Filburn, 317 U.S. 111 (1942).

28. South Carolina v. Katzenbach, 383 U.S. 301 (1966); Katzenbach v.
Morgan, 384 U.S. 641 (1966).

29. Blum and Kalven, 29–35; Paul, 97–99, 677–679, 685–694; Herbert
Stein, 83, 181–183, 187–190, 390–391, 410–421.

legislation. Prophetic were Marshall's hospitable readings of the commerce and fiscal powers of Congress in *Gibbons* v. *Ogden* and in *McCulloch* v. *Maryland*.[30] By violating the presumption of constitutionality in 1870 the Court held unconstitutional the retroactive legal tender aspect of United States notes (the greenbacks) which Congress had designed to circulate as currency. But in 1871 a new majority of the Court reversed that ruling, now in proper deference to Congress's appraisal of the facts and values at issue in the challenged legislation.[31] In 1895 the Court ruled that Congress lacked power to levy an income tax not apportioned among the states according to population. This was a serious blow to potential federal economic regulatory policy. But in the turn-of-century political climate it did not thwart any bold new policy directions that Congress was likely to take, and the Sixteenth Amendment removed the barrier in 1913.[32] In 1935 and 1936 the Court struck down a variety of federal statutes designed to cope with the disastrous downward spiral of the national economy; the decisions chose sharply restrictive constructions of constitutional grants of legislative power, especially under the commerce clause, and for the first time in some 145 years curbed Congress's discretion in delegating authority to administrators. But between 1937 and 1941 the Court reversed this restrictive course, returned to the strong presumption of constitutionality it had applied to federal economic legislation since Marshall's time, and upheld broad authority in Congress to regulate relationships not only immediately in interstate commerce, but also those which Congress might reasonably deem substantially to affect that commerce.[33]

30. McCulloch v. Maryland, 4 Wheat. 316 (U.S. 1819); Gibbons v. Ogden, 9 Wheat. 1 (U.S. 1824); cf. Missouri v. Holland, 252 U.S. 416 (1920).

31. Knox v. Lee, 12 Wall. 457 (U.S. 1871), overruling Hepburn v. Griswold, 8 Wall. 602 (U.S. 1870); cf. Juilliard v. Greenman, 110 U.S. 421 (1884); Hurst (7), 183–186.

32. Cf. Pollock v. Farmers' Loan & Trust Co., 157 U.S. 429 (1895); Lynch v. Hornby, 247 U.S. 339, 344 (1918).

33. McCloskey, 163–169, 174–179; Morison and Commager, 2:622–628.

The one policy area in which the Court limited Congress's legislative authority with long-lasting effect was that of race relations. By 1883, taking the most restrictive view of Congress's authority to implement the due process and equal protection standards of the Fourteenth Amendment, the Court had thoroughly defeated the apparently central intent of the majority coalition that pressed the amendment through to adoption in 1866–1868. Under the Court's reading, Congress might legislate only against affirmative use of state power to deny blacks civil rights or equal protection under the laws. Not until the middle 1960's did the Court begin to reverse this reading and return to the more extensive grant originally intended, under which Congress might legislate to make good sustained default or calculated indifference on the part of the states or state support of private action denying the substance of civil rights.[34]

Some contrasts in the influence of subject and timing are significant, as one compares the long-lasting practical impact of the Court's restrictive doctrine in the race area (from the climactic 1883 decisions to about 1966) with the Court's rapid reversal of restrictive decisions in 1870–1871 and in 1935–1937. Hamilton was correct in assessing the judiciary as the least powerful branch; for the judges to have lasting effect, their decisions either must be withdrawn from areas of broad controversy or must accord with deep and powerful currents of values in the society. Between the mid-1870's and the mid-1880's dominant sentiment in the North and West turned to urgent preoccupation with economic growth and wearily away from active concern with race relations in the South; prejudice against full sharing for blacks was a strong factor, too, in persuading the rest of the country to let Southern whites make their own dictated settlement with the blacks. Thus there was no power base from which anyone could mount a strong and ready reaction against the direction the Court took. In 1871 and in 1935–1937 the Court's restrictive line ran head on into immediately felt, urgent desires

34. Note 17, above. Cf. Civil Rights Cases, 109 U.S. 3 (1883); United States v. Guest, 383 U.S. 745 (1966).

of politically potent groups—the farmers and the growth-minded industrialists of the immediate post-Civil War years, distressed business and finance, labor, and farmers in the depression of the 1930's. The timing of Court action in relation to needs urgently felt by broad sectors of the public was such in 1871 and the 1930's as to bring the judges back to the presumption of constitutionality.[35]

No less than state legislatures, Congress experienced practical limitations on its capacity to make policy, arising out of the twentieth-century growth in the effectiveness of organized interest groups. Here, too, lobbies wielded power more effectively by veto than by sure ability to obtain positive benefits from government, though a sorry history of special-interest maneuvers over the tariff and the income tax testified to considerable ability of lobbyists to win particular gains for their clients. As compared with the states, a distinctive feature of the congressional scene was the fragmentation of jurisdiction among standing committees and the lively jealousy with which committees and key members entrenched by seniority guarded their prerogatives. Their strongly held positions made the congressional committees separate arenas for the play of contending interests, which in these narrower confines often could exert greater leverage on policy making than they might have enjoyed in a broader area of contest.[36]

The power formally and informally held by the President, as his office developed, set some material limits on the formal and the practical legislative power of Congress. A net balance was hard to strike, and the balance varied a good deal from time to time. The trend was to increase presidential capacity to affect Congress, but even after the increase, the most effective twentieth-century Presidents often found Congress intractable. This outcome was less because of the scope of congressional authority than because of the resistance of congressional structure to pro-

35. See notes 31, 33, above.
36. James MacGregor Burns, 19–23; Gross, 270–276, 278–280; Schattschneider, passim.

ducing programmed action; central factors were jurisdictional jealousies of committees, the leverage enjoyed by seniority-entrenched committee chairmen, and the high sense of their respective prerogatives in both houses, with relation to each other as well as to the chief executive.

The President held some advantages that were clearly legitimated by the Constitution or by statute. He was charged to inform the Congress of the state of the nation from time to time, and with the advent of mass media of communication this function allowed him to develop a forum for addressing general opinion such as no other body or officer could command. He held the veto; originally conceived as a means simply to protect the Constitution against legislative invasion, from Andrew Jackson's years this developed legitimacy as an instrument with which to express sheer policy differences with Congress and to bargain for legislative compromise. The Constitution and accepted practice gave the President primacy in the conduct of foreign affairs. In the twentieth century, inherent to legislation by which Congress delegated more and more important areas of public policy to executive offices and to independent administrative agencies, the President greatly increased the patronage at his command, as well as his capacity to affect the course of evolving policy through individuals he appointed. The federal budget grew along with growth of federal programs. In addition to its fiscal aspects, the management of the budget—through veto bargaining, but most of all through statutory provision of a Bureau of the Budget under presidential direction—spelled further increase in the President's ability to bargain on many fronts of policy other than fiscal, as he and his agents allocated priorities among requests for funds and for program authorizations for which executive offices or the congressional sponsors of particular measures sought to enlist presidential support.[37]

The office of President grew to wield power vis-à-vis the Con-

37. Lawrence H. Chamberlain, passim; Corwin (2), 264–281, 286–288; Koenig, Chaps. 6, 12, and pp. 135, 138–143; Neustadt, 43–45, 50, 150–151, 154–155, 169–170.

gress in other ways, the legitimacy of which stood more in question. Two twentieth-century developments, closely connected in origins and impacts, warrant particular note. Congress delegated increasing power to the executive, first in response to problems of war, then to those of peacetime depressions and recessions. In addition to enlarging the substantive powers of the President, Congress sanctioned the expansion of a White House secretariat, outside the cabinet. The two developments enabled Presidents greatly to increase the practical power derived from monopolizing information and knowledge of the grounds of policy. From the Eisenhower years on, the President enlarged claims of executive privilege against congressional requests to be informed of the existence of executive decisions, let alone of the grounds of those decisions. Congress compounded the growth in insulation of the White House from external view and criticism by a generally flabby assertion of its investigatory powers. In 1953 and 1974 the Supreme Court acknowledged that functional needs of the constitutional separation of powers warranted some assertion of executive privilege—qualified by subjection to some extent of judicial review—as against demands made to produce evidence in civil and criminal litigation. Whether or how far the Court would recognize executive privilege against the investigatory power of Congress remained an open question. But executive privilege was enough established in practice, and enough legitimated by judicial decisions, materially to bulwark the capacity of the White House to wield power with dangerous freedom based on the comparative secrecy of much of its operations.[38]

This twentieth-century development had the more significance because it reinforced another course along which presidential power had grown since Jefferson's purchase of Louisiana. The framers of the Constitution made clear their intent that the President should inherit none of the prerogative powers once asserted by the crown in England.[39] Nevertheless, strong-willed Presidents

38. Berger, Chaps. 3, 4, 5, 11; Corwin (2), 214, 281; Koenig, Chap. 7. See United States v. Nixon, 418 U.S. 683 (1974).
39. Hurst (1), 397–400, 470; cf. id., 382, 383.

built precedents for acting to fulfill what they saw as high national interest when neither the Constitution nor the statutes plainly validated executive action and when they judged that events pressed too urgently to take time to ask that Congress grant authority. Theodore Roosevelt gave the position its lasting shorthand expression when he said that the President was chief steward of the nation, and as a faithful steward he must be willing to take the responsibility of acting for his master's best interests in emergency, though he ran beyond his instructions. Such was the legitimation claimed by Jefferson in the Louisiana Purchase, by Lincoln when South Carolina fired on Fort Sumter, by Theodore Roosevelt when he intervened in the coal strike of 1902, by Franklin Roosevelt when he gave over-age destroyers to England in return for Caribbean naval bases, and by Harry Truman when he seized the steel mills during the Korean War. In 1952 the Supreme Court, invalidating the steel mills seizure, flatly rejected the thesis that the President enjoyed some constitutional authority to make general policy as an incident of his office, even under claim of national security. In 1972 the Court reaffirmed that position, this time denying any inherent presidential authority to use wiretaps on claims of protecting national security. The two decisions appeared to do all that the Court could to reaffirm the framers' determination that the President have no policy-making prerogative. However, the record of strong presidential initiatives taken under the claim of stewardship gives ground for questioning how far future Presidents will obey the Court, if events press them hard.[40]

As on the state scene, on the federal the multiplication and entrenchment of executive offices and independent administrative agencies tended to limit the practical scope of congressional policy making. This outcome was not required or even provided

40. Youngstown Sheet & Tube Co. v. Sawyer, 343 U.S. 579 (1952); United States v. United States District Court for the Eastern District of Michigan, 407 U.S. 297 (1972). But cf. Corwin (2), 152–157; Hurst (1), 397–400.

by law; Congress delegated these powers in the first instance, and in law could take them back, modify them, or issue fresh mandates for action at any time. In practice, policy making was increasingly fragmented, as executive offices and administrative bodies built up their own constituencies, consolidated their ties with friendly congressmen and senators entrenched in committees which in turn enjoyed large autonomy, and traded on the insulation they derived from the specialization or sheer bulk of detail of their work. As far as Congress was concerned, the dominant working mode was to scrutinize closely the newest increment of activity in an agency field, with scant, episodic, and tardy concern for large patterns of executive or administrative policy making as these emerged out of the whole of agency activity over five-, ten-, or twenty-year terms. The longer Congress left a policy area without close, continuing surveillance, the greater grew the weight of inertia, want of expertise, and bureaucratic and third-party vested interest against major legislative intervention. That this result was mainly the product of congressional default did not lessen the difficulty of overcoming it.[41]

Legislative Power: Resource Allocation

In the states. Scarcity of economic resources means that important issues in social relations turn on the institutions that allocate those resources. The principal resource-allocating institutions in the United States were the market, government, the family, and nonmarket philanthropic and religious associations. Among these, the principal competitors for influence were the market and the government.

Within government, the legislature holds primary authority to allocate resources by law, normally through the power to tax and to spend tax-derived funds. Legislative primacy in this field was the clear-cut inheritance our constitution makers drew from the

41. Fenno (1), 286–290, 307–313, 317–320, 333–340, 566–568, 577; Galloway, 84–88; Redman, 175–182; Truman, 416–426, 437.

seventeenth-century English clash between crown and Parliament; this inheritance was so taken for granted that there never has been controversy over it in the states or in the national government. Government has allocated resources in the United States by other means, than taxing and spending: by borrowing (the feasibility of which rested on the taxing and spending powers), by using government property (notably public lands and control of franchises for special use of common resources), and by controlling the system of money.[42] This chapter emphasizes taxing and spending because these were the most-used channels of resource allocation by law. But some note must be taken of the other resource-allocating techniques, for their own importance, and because in some times and in some places their use predominated in public policy.

State constitutions did not specifically grant resource-allocating authority any more than any other kind; this authority simply was embraced in the broad grant of "legislative power." For the first generation of national life the only constitutional limitations on state power in this domain were in the federal Constitution. Evidence of the early, strong bias of public policy toward fostering the market is that these federal constitutional limitations were designed largely to protect market autonomy, vis-à-vis government. Such was the purpose of the clause that forbade any state to pass any law that would impair the obligation of contracts; state laws must not interfere retroactively with the collection of debts incurred in the market to shift income and capital from creditors to debtors.[43] Of broader reach than the contract clause was the limitation on states to deal with the money supply. The Constitution forbade the states to coin money, implicitly forbade them to try to define the value of the coinage, and declared that no state should emit bills of credit (that is, issue paper currency), or make any object except gold and silver coin a

42. Bator, Chaps. 2, 3; Hurst (7), 74–91; Mosher and Poland, Chaps. 2, 3, 7.
43. Wright, 3–18.

tender in payment of debts. Taken in conjunction with broad
money-supply authority given to the Congress, the Constitution
thus determined that ultimate control of the money supply was a
matter of national policy.[44]

The later development of commercial banking revealed a gap
in the constitutional policy not foreseen by the framers. From the
1820's state legislatures granted an increasing number of special
charters empowering banks to issue circulating notes. In 1837 in
calculated dicta the Supreme Court validated such note issues as
not offending the ban on state bills of credit, which it treated as
forbidding only issues based directly on the faith of the state.
Under this protection private state bank notes provided the bulk
of circulating media of exchange, lending ill-governed stimulus
to a growing economy through the 1850's. For a few years after
Congress in 1862–1863 provided for chartering note-issuing national banks, state bank notes held their own against the new
competing currency. But Congress drove state bank notes from
the market by a prohibitory federal tax, which in 1869 the Supreme Court sustained as a valid exercise of federal tax power.
Shortly, however, state-chartered banks learned that they could
profit satisfactorily without note issues, by loans that took the
form of deposits against which borrowers drew checks. State-
chartered banks thus continued to make a large contribution to
the national money supply through deposit-check money.
Though state constitutions added no limits on this money stock,
state legislation tardily and unevenly imposed some regulation of
bank lending. But this regulation was, at best, designed to guard
the solvency of individual banks rather than to adjust the general
supply of money to the changing currents of the economy.[45]
When significant money-supply controls again entered the picture, they were federal. As the Federal Reserve System learned
techniques of money-market management—especially from the
1950's on—the impact of its policies fell on state as well as on

44. Hurst (7), 9–18.
45. Id., 11–12, 16–18, 138–146, 153–172, 179–181, 189–195.

federal banks, whether or not they were members of the system. After Congress set up a Federal Deposit Insurance Corporation (FDIC) in 1934–1935, competition for depositors tended to bring into the deposit insurance plan substantially all banks in the country, including state-chartered banks. In consequence, FDIC decisions to grant or withhold desired insurance inherently worked as a check on chartering new state banks, and FDIC bank-examination procedures worked as another check on lending policies of individual state-chartered banks. Federal impact on the ebb and flow of the total money supply depended, however, on Treasury and Federal Reserve System policies.[46]

State taxing power also was limited significantly by the Supreme Court's development of commerce clause doctrine. By its terms the commerce clause was a grant of power to Congress, rather than to the Court. Congress showed little initiative in creating federal statutory protections of interstate dealings against state taxes, however, so the Court provided most of the federal-system protection of national and sectional markets. The Court justified its intervention most readily in striking down state taxes (or regulations) that in terms or by substantial effect discriminated against interstate commerce; this kind of state action clearly had been a prime target of the framers in writing the commerce clause. Somewhat bolder judicial creativity was involved as the Court elaborated another head of doctrine, curbing state tax (or regulatory) laws which in the Court's judgment unduly burdened interstate commerce, even though not by discriminatory treatment. Of similar functional meaning was a line of Court-made due-process doctrine, striking down state taxes (or regulations) affecting transactions that were shaped or had effect outside the state's boundaries, without material connection to the state's internal affairs. The Court's impress against discriminatory state tax policy was definite and sharp. More wavering—now more restrictive, now more tolerant—was Court policy under the doctrines of undue (direct) burden or extraterritorial effect. The balance tended to be struck, though, in favor of limit-

46. Id., 200–211, 218–227.

ing state tax (and regulatory) authority in the interests of national or sectional markets. Particularly revealing of this bias of policy were indications that the Court would not always apply the ordinary presumption of constitutionality in favor of state statutes charged with infringing commerce clause values; out-of-staters lacked voting leverage on a state legislature and hence might be seen as deserving more solicitous protection from federal judges.[47]

From about mid-nineteenth century two state constitutional limits on the fiscal powers of state legislatures emerged. First came the imposition of flat constitutional limits on the legislature's authority to borrow money, apart from the federal Constitution's ban on borrowing by emission of bills of credit. The success of the Erie Canal stimulated Ohio and Mississippi Valley states into inflated expectations of advancing their economies by comparable ventures. They financed their undertakings with bond issues, which brought the states into default and near insolvency as the new canals failed to pay off. Policy makers drew the lesson that borrowing tended to extravagant extension of the states' demands on resources because it did not carry the immediate, sharp impact of taxes; borrowing, hence, must be curbed rigidly. The 1848 Wisconsin constitution contained a limitation that became common among the states: that except to repel invasion, suppress insurrection, or defend the state in war, the state should never contract public debt exceeding in the aggregate $100,000.[48]

Disenchanted with ambitious internal improvements, and for some fifty years subjected to no other imperative demands for large public investment, state legislatures conformed to the debt limits until about the 1920's. Then pressures rapidly mounted on state legislatures for two new kinds of social capital investment—for hard-surface roads to subsidize mass use of the automobile and for extension of educational opportunities, especially at the

47. Welton v. Missouri, 91 U.S. 275 (1876); Robbins v. Shelby County Taxing District, 120 U.S. 489 (1887); Allgeyer v. Louisiana, 165 U.S. 578 (1897); Bibb v. Navajo Freight Lines, Inc., 359 U.S. 520, 528–529 (1959).
48. E.g., Wis. Const., VIII, 6 (1848); Brown, 46–47.

secondary-school and university levels. Some of these new demands, as for roads, were met by ad hoc constitutional amendments, carving out specific exceptions to the debt limitations. But the rigidity of the mid-nineteenth-century constitutional debt limitations and the cumbersome processes of constitutional amendment did not always permit ready response to these fresh demands. In some states ingenious lawmakers circumvented the limitations by erecting nonprofit corporations to build and lease to the state physical facilities to meet new service demands with money borrowed on security of rents or fees to be paid by the state or by users of the facilities. State courts cooperated by refusing to see that in reality the state was assuring these nonprofit corporations—or in case of breakdown would have to assure them—the funds with which to pay interest and amortize principal. In Wisconsin, by 1969, despite the $100,000 debt limit, there was outstanding some $500 millions of debt contracted by corporations set up to build university dormitories, state office buildings, and like facilities. The situation had generated undesirable fictions that cast disrepute on constitutional legal order and clouded proper legislative and public scrutiny of state finance. In the second half of the twentieth century states slowly began to correct the problem at its root, by getting rid of the nineteenth-century fiscal strait jackets. Thus in 1969, Wisconsin amended its constitution to sanction state borrowing for tangible social capital investment (in land, waters, highways, buildings, equipment, or facilities for public purposes) within a limit adjusted to the course of the state's general economy (with total public debt not to exceed a percentage of the aggregate value of all taxable property in the state). The lesson was tortuously learned: it was unwise to confine legislative discretion to deal with changing circumstances within bounds rigidly defined in terms of experience of a particular time.[49]

49. E.g., Wis. Const., VIII, 7 (1969); Loomis v. Callahan, 196 Wis. 518, 220 N.W. 816 (1928); State ex rel. La Follette v. Reuter, 33 Wis. (2d) 384, 147 N.W. (2d) 304 (1967). See Wis. Legis. Ref. Lib., Bull. No. 152.

One other constitutional limit on state spending was wholly court-made. In the later nineteenth century state courts asserted their authority to enjoin any expenditure of public funds that the judges found could not reasonably be deemed to be for a statewide public purpose. Auxiliary to this judicial role was the recognition, concurrently, that a state taxpayer had standing in court to challenge the legality of spending of state funds. For several decades the courts exercised a broad surveillance under the public-purpose doctrine, consistent with the leeway they were allowing themselves in reviewing the constitutionality of state legislation under criteria of due process and equal protection. But after the 1930's judges tended to limit the impact of the public-purpose doctrine in line with their general enforcement of a strong presumption of constitutionality in favor of economic regulatory legislation. This turn of policy was analogous to the contemporary relaxation of state debt limitations by judge-made fictions and by constitutional amendment. By late twentieth century constitution makers and state judges had restored to the state legislatures substantially all the fiscal policy freedom with which the 1776–1780 constitutions had endowed them.[50]

Increased executive and administrative power in the states put formal and informal limits on legislative fiscal freedom. Contrary to the first state constitutions, nineteenth-century constitution makers gave the governor a general veto on fiscal as well as on other legislation. In the twentieth century state constitutional amendments made it general policy to give the governor authority to veto appropriation bills in whole or in part. This power of the item veto materially increased not only the governor's formal power but also his bargaining power with the legislature, compared with the all-or-nothing options to which the general veto restricted him. By late twentieth century the item veto has become a firmly entrenched part of state fiscal policy, in controversy only insofar as a governor might in practice try to stretch

50. McAllister, 139–148, 244–248; Mills, 40, 282.

it to allow him to strike substantive policy items from a bill because the bill appropriated money. More broadly limiting than the item veto was the legislatures' tendency in handling fiscal policy to focus only on the last or newest increment of action of executive offices or administrative agencies. As executive office and agency budgets grew bigger and represented the accretion of bulky and specialized detail as well as of internal and external vested interests in familiar lines of action, the legislatures tended to take for granted the established items of budget and to examine only the latest additions. From about mid-twentieth century state legislatures began to authorize and charge the governor by statute to fashion a comprehensive budget as a frame of reference for the legislature. To some extent this innovation promised more rational over-all resource allocation, but it did not eliminate the limited incremental approach taken to most items.[51]

In Congress. The federal Constitution endowed Congress with broad potential authority to allocate resources. Despite temporary setbacks, this authority expanded over the years. Most obvious was the grant of power to tax to pay the debts and to provide for the defense and the general welfare of the United States. James Madison early argued that Congress could tax only to raise money to support action taken under its other powers. Hamilton countered that in terms the tax power was a distinct authority conferred on Congress, properly invoked whenever Congress reasonably decided that a given tax or spending policy in itself would promote national interest. In later years the Hamiltonian view won out in congressional practice. Finally, in 1936 and 1937 the Supreme Court committed itself to the Hamiltonian reading. Meanwhile, Congress's taxing power had been much enlarged by the Sixteenth Amendment, and again congressional practice enlarged on the constitutional language. From modest beginnings, the federal individual and corporation income taxes evolved into broad-ranging and intricate structures so pervasive in economic

51. Wis. Const., V, 10 (1930) (item veto); Wis. Stat., 1973, secs. 16.43–16.47 (executive budget); Joseph P. Chamberlain, 224–233.

life that these taxes had major economic regulatory effect, apart from their growth in importance to federal revenues.[52]

These formal expansions of federal tax authority took on greater meaning because of two doctrines of self-restraint adopted by the Supreme Court. First, the Court built a line of precedent refusing to probe behind the revenue justification apparent on the face of federal tax laws to discover a regulatory purpose that arguably might be of dubious validity. The Court adopted the formula that it would not examine legislative "motive"; a more realistic summary would be that if a statute might be expected to produce both a revenue result and a nonrevenue result, the statute would be allowed to stand on the revenue base, at least as long as the nonrevenue result was not one (such as racial discrimination) forbidden as a goal of any government action. Thus the Court gave Congress a free hand to use its tax power for regulatory purposes.[53] Second, in 1923 the Court ruled that, for want of sufficient focused interest in fact, a federal taxpayer lacked standing to challenge the constitutional validity of federal expenditures. The ruling is a puzzle in Supreme Court history. It substantially closed the door on judicial review of federal resource allocation through the spending power at a time when a majority of the Court was zealous in invoking due-process doctrine to protect private market values against state economic regulation.[54] In 1968 the Court drew a poorly defined qualification of the 1923 decision when it recognized that a federal taxpayer could protest the spending of federal funds in aid of church schools; the First Amendment ban on an establishment of religion was, said

52. See United States v. Butler, 297 U.S. 1, 64–67 (1936); Steward Machine Co. v. Davis, 301 U.S. 548 (1937); cf. Douglas v. Willcutts, 296 U.S. 1, 9 (1935); Commissioner of Internal Revenue v. Glenshaw Glass Co., 348 U.S. 426, 429–430 (1955).

53. Veazie Bank v. Fenno, 8 Wheat. 533 (U.S. 1869); McCray v. United States, 195 U.S. 27 (1904); Sonzinsky v. United States, 300 U.S. 506 (1937). Cf. Bailey v. Drexel Furniture Co., 259 U.S. 20 (1922) and United States v. Darby, 312 U.S. 100 (1941).

54. Frothingham v. Mellon, 262 U.S. 447 (1923).

the Court, so specific a limit on the spending power as to warrant enforcement by a taxpayer suitor. But in 1974 the Court pulled back from extending this specific-limit rationale when it denied standing to a taxpayer who wished to compel the Treasury to disclose publicly in detail expenditures of the Central Intelligence Agency, despite secrecy provisions in the act creating the agency. The Constitution commands that a regular statement and account be published from time to time of expenditures of all public money. This direction seems as specific a limit on the spending power as any derived from the no-establishment clause of the First Amendment. That the Court would not treat it so indicated renewed determination to keep judicial review out of federal fiscal policy. The outcome fits the historic primacy of the legislative control of the public purse.[55] Perhaps, too, these twentieth-century decisions convey a judgment that Congress's expanded use of its taxing and spending powers has made fiscal policy so innovative, varied, and pervasive an influence that it should be appraised only through the pull and haul of political processes and not within bounds set by records made and precedents invoked in lawsuits.

Congress held other resource-allocating powers as broad and as free of outside check as its taxing and spending authority. The Constitution authorized it to borrow money on the credit of the United States, and in contrast to the fiscal history of the states no federal constitutional amendment imposed any limit on federal debt. Congress has power to dispose of and make all needful rules and regulations respecting the territory or other property of the United States. For the first seventy-five years of national life Congress's most effective command of resources was through its control of the public domain, embracing substantially all the land in the nation west of the Appalachians. The Court recognized no limits on congressional discretion, as Congress disposed of public lands to promote a family-farm economy in the Mississippi Valley and to underwrite development of a national railroad net-

55. Flast v. Cohen, 392 U.S. 83 (1968); United States v. Richardson, 418 U.S. 166 (1974).

work.[56] Resources also can be allocated by shifts in purchasing power that attend inflation or deflation of the money supply. The Constitution committed to Congress a monopoly of direct government of coin and currency; to this grant, congressional practice, ratified in key respects by judicial decision, added assertion of authority to put ultimate control of credit (deposit-check money) in national agencies under statutory delegation.[57]

The President enjoyed no formal grant of a special role concerning the resource-allocating powers of Congress. He had the general veto power, and in this as in other policy areas Presidents learned to use the threat of general veto to bargain with Congress. In contrast to the state scene, however, no federal constitutional amendment ever gave the President the greater bargaining leverage of the item veto.[58] There was a possible analogue to the item veto in presidential impoundment of appropriated funds. Beginning with Jefferson, Presidents occasionally took the responsibility of deciding not to spend money Congress had appropriated. The record of such presidential actions was not clear either in weight or in justification. Through the nineteenth century impoundment of funds was occasional and sporadic; the incidents became a bit more frequent from the 1930's on. Until Richard Nixon's administration, however, impoundment was of limited character, typically involving relatively small amounts of money and on limited grounds of avoiding waste in light of peculiar circumstances or marked changes of circumstances after Congress had acted. The meaning of presidential action was clouded, moreover, because Congress often was fuzzy in the terms of appropriation acts, leaving uncertain whether it meant to command or simply to permit spending. In a few general acts Congress vaguely authorized the executive to withhold spending in order to retain funds against contingencies or for limited efficiency reasons. Thus it was unclear how far presidential impound-

56. Hurst (4), 13, 20, 56. See United States v. Gratiot, 14 Pet. 526, 538 (U.S. 1840); Gibson v. Chouteau, 13 Wall. 92, 99 (U.S. 1871).
57. Hurst (7), 8–18, 200–227.
58. Koenig, 23, 139, 153–154.

ings were authorized by Congress. President Nixon raised the matter to the level of a separation-of-powers issue for the first time. He did so partly by the scale of his impoundments; by early 1973 he had refused to commit or to use some $12–$15 billion of appropriated funds. He made clear that he was not only making limited adjustments warranted by marginal efficiencies, but that in important instances he was impounding funds because he disagreed with the substantive policies of the appropriation acts involved. The point became most clear when he refused to make commitments of some $6 billion of funds provided under a bill that was passed over his veto; in this context impoundment constituted the assertion of a second veto, and one not within the regular procedure by which Congress might override it. Arguably, the President's conduct here was a sufficient breach of the separation of powers to be a ground for impeachment; the point was not pressed within the House Judiciary Committee as it framed articles of impeachment, perhaps because members felt that Congress itself was too much involved, by default and by lack of clarity in past appropriations procedures, to allow it now to make such drastic complaint against the President. But the 1973–1974 controversies of the Nixon administration caused sufficient concern with impoundment to produce a 1974 bill, which President Nixon signed, requiring that in future the President must have Congress's approval or acceptance for impoundments.[59]

The greatest practical separation-of-powers limitations on Congress's allocation of resources were the same as the principal limitations on the fiscal powers of state legislatures—the failure of the legislative branch to keep abreast of the growth of the executive branch and the independent administrative agencies. As in the states, in the federal government the working rule was that Congress tended to focus only on the newest increment in executive or administrative spending and the programs financed

59. 88 Stat. 333 (1974); Louis Fisher, Chaps. 7, 8; Harvard Law Review, 1505.

by such spending. From about the 1920's, executive and administrative handling of federal fiscal and monetary policy tended to become somewhat more centralized and more rationalized through creation of a powerful budget office in the executive, through a Council of Economic Advisers to the President (created under the Employment Act of 1946, with a modest congressional offset in the Joint Committee on the Economic Report of the President), and through the consolidation of monetary policy direction partly in the Treasury and partly in the Open Market Committee of the Federal Reserve System (under the Banking Act of 1935). These developments still fell short of achieving full coordination of fiscal and monetary policy, but they moved executive and administrative offices much further toward that end than Congress could go while it left power and responsibility fragmented among mutually jealous committee baronies. As late as 1974 Congress took hesitant steps by statute to create its own apparatus for comprehensive budgeting to match executive capacity.[60]

The analysis so far has focused on legislative resource-allocating authority as this stood defined by constitutions, statutes, and more or less accepted practice of legislatures and executive and administrative officers. Another useful aspect from which to appraise the purse power is to sketch the development of the principal goals legitimated by government practice as properly pursued by using resource-allocating authority. Three sanctioned goals emerged—the support of government operations, the promotion of general economic productivity, and the redistribution of purchasing power (and, implicitly, to some degree the redistribution of wealth). Through most of the nineteenth century the main use of federal and state taxing-spending power was to finance the staple operations of government—paying salaries of officials and staff, providing legislative chambers and court-

60. 88 Stat. 298 (1974); Hurst (7), 82, 209, 211, 220, 235, 237, 241, 247; Kimmel, 5, 283–288; Smithies, Chap. IV, and pp. 81, 92, 138–147, 163–165, 175–178, 183–192.

houses, and meeting expenses of prosecuting ordinary crimes. The relative place of this use of resource-allocating powers declined as government took on broader ranges of programs. By mid-twentieth century provision for the nonmilitary overhead costs of government operations probably accounted for no more than 10 to 12 percent of the total economic resources channeled by official action. This is not to deny social importance to this auxiliary role of the purse power; to meet the overhead cost of legal agencies meant to sustain operations—legislation, administrative rule making and adjudication, judicial enforcement of law, and resolution of conflicts—that helped to sustain social institutions outside the legal apparatus and gave the community significant leverage on new problems. But it is desirable to keep the auxiliary goal of the purse power in due perspective in order to appreciate the importance of other objectives sought through the resource-allocating powers of government. Also, recognizing that law made quite limited demands on the general economy to pay such overhead costs of legal processes pointed up the fact that at least in the twentieth century this was not a realm in which retrenchment could achieve substantial economy in government. It was not in the focused regulatory efforts of law, but in its more diffuse service and social planning roles that law made large-scale demands on economic resources in the twentieth century. Hence only by changes in service and social planning programs could there be major reductions of law's claims on resources.[61]

In his *Report on Manufactures*, Hamilton prophesied the development of the second great objective in use of resource-allocating authority. This was to promote substantial, steady increase in over-all economic productivity. Though the goal stayed the same from the early nineteenth into the later twentieth centuries, a massive change in techniques of pursuing it began about the 1920's. From 1776 into the 1870's the economy was marked by an abundance of fixed capital (arable land, minerals,

61. Bator, 21–23, 26–28, 33–34; Fabricant, 11–12, 42–46, 51, 56, 63, 73–74, 77–79, 82.

timber, waterpower) and a frustrating scarcity of fluid capital (money—representing capacity to buy time while awaiting the fruition of delayed returns from capital commitments). As symbolized by the Whiskey Rebellion in 1794, a cash-scarce society placed sharp political, let alone economic, limitations on how far government could allocate resources by taxation. By the 1870's, however, the country began to experience marked increases in material productivity based on rapid, cumulating changes in the technology of physical production and of social organization. These changes were reflected in growth of the money supply, especially in the volume of credit translated into deposit-check money. A more monetized economy was one on which government could make heavier tax demands, which it could affect in relatively flexible ways by developing varieties of official management of the money supply, and in which it thus had a much greater practical capacity to intervene to affect the general course of economic activity. Monetary-policy controversies occupied much of national politics from the 1870's to 1913—over the role of the greenbacks, of silver, of the gold standard, and of central banking. These disputes reflected groping efforts to realize new economic management roles for government in light of the possibilities opened up by the transition from a cash-scarce economy to one capable of generously providing fluid resources.[62]

Use of resource-allocating authority to increase over-all productivity translated into three more particular goals, the expression of which reflected the transition from a physical-asset to a money-based economy. (1) Congress—and, subordinately, the states with means delegated by Congress—acted to overcome the country's early gross imbalance among the factors of production. Through the nineteenth century Congress pursued this task chiefly by disposing of the public lands. It encouraged movement of labor onto the land by setting low prices and by offering land in exchange for the work of bringing it into cultivation. It encouraged movement of cash capital to support growth of com-

62. Alexander Hamilton, 4:70, 78, 83, 87, 89, 95–99; Hurst (7), 74–91.

mercial agriculture by public land subsidies to build roads, canals, and railroads. In the twentieth century this kind of policy was continued mostly by spending dollars instead of acres, as government directly or indirectly subsidized training in needed skills to correct deficiencies in the supply of teachers, doctors, and skilled craftsmen.[63] (2) Congress and the states acted to encourage or provide long-term capital commitments. To this end public policy sought to enlarge markets that would support such capital commitments by shouldering some material part of the risks of investment. In the nineteenth century the federal government pursued this effort, as it underwrote new railroad construction with public land grants that could provide security for bondholders and made land available to settlers on terms that provided an equity against which private lenders would be willing to advance money on mortgage. Of related impact was the erection of tariff walls to reduce risks of domestic industrial investment. The technique continued in the twentieth century in such forms as the Export-Import Bank's underwriting of private firms' sales of goods abroad. Functionally similar was the provision of great amounts of federal money to take on the high risks of translating esoteric science into workable technology in nuclear energy and space travel, providing a base on which private investment might build if the public gamble paid off. The private market would not supply some important long-term capital commitments quite apart from risk because gains and costs were too diffuse to be captured within market transactions. Provision of roads and schools constituted the bulk of this kind of social capital investment. Here the states always played the largest, continuous part, but from about the 1930's federal spending grew significantly.[64] (3) From the controversy over retirement or retention of the greenbacks (1875–1884), through the silver battle (1880–1900), the panic of 1907, the creation of the Federal

63. Goodrich, Chaps. 5, 8; Heller, 74–75; Hurst (4), 24, 34–40, 107–112, 230, 471.

64. Bator, 26–28, 32–35; Dupree, 290–292, 373–375; Goodrich, 183–204, 289–294; Mosher and Poland, 102–111, 116–127; 49 Stat. 4 (1935) and 59 id., 526 (1945) (Export-Import Bank).

Reserve System in 1913, and the departure from the gold standard in 1933–1934, events moved in halting fashion toward increasingly ambitious efforts at national government resource allocation by managing the money supply; the object was to promote healthy growth in productivity by affecting the timing of the general flow of economic transactions. This kind of effort was paralleled by and tended toward merger with use of the taxing and spending powers to the same end, as in the New Deal's revived spending program in 1938, the commitment to business-cycle management in the Employment Act of 1946, and the overt use of a tax cut to stimulate the private economy in 1963–1964.[65]

The third and latest goal of government resource allocation to gain legitimacy by legislative practice was that of redistribution of income among private persons; redistribution of capital among private persons by law went on only within the narrow confines of eminent domain procedures, almost wholly limited to benefiting public utilities. The one precedent as old as government in the United States for redistributing income by law among private persons was taxation used to pay interest on government bonds. When government used the borrowed principal to buy wood and steel to make a warship, it removed control of economic assets from the market into the sphere of public disposition of resources. But in spending tax-derived money to pay bond interest, government was using its power to transfer purchasing power from the taxpayer to the bondholder, leaving that purchasing power ultimately within market disposition. Relatively few such transfer payments occurred in public policy until the 1930's, but between 1930 and the 1960's the economic resources thus shifted by federal taxing and spending policy among private individuals in the market increased some fifteen times, compared with about a tenfold increase in government spending that took economic goods out of the market for government use.[66] Government-ordained

65. Heller, 32–37, 59–62, 74–76; Hurst (7), 74–85, 99, 216–218; Herbert Stein, 88–89, 116–123, 148–151, 412–420, 428–440.
66. Bator, 12–16, 130–131.

transfer payments of the late twentieth century have had two related, yet somewhat different, objectives. One aim of social security payments, unemployment insurance payments, and payments to farmers to hold land out of production is to help manage downswings of the business cycle by maintaining private purchasing power. Another aim of these programs, and the primary aim of welfare payments to dependent individuals and of educational subsidies to war veterans, is to enhance individual life opportunities. In 1937 and 1942 the Supreme Court found the federal social security legislation and revised farmer-aid legislation within the protection of the presumption of constitutionality.[67] By the 1970's public opinion had firmly ratified—indeed practically mandated—transfer-payment programs designed to help even out the business cycle. But as late as the 1970's the legitimacy of taxing and spending to enhance individual life quality continue to include areas of spirited controversy; there is little dispute over aid to veterans, but much over the terms of public welfare payments. Even in the disputed field, however, conflict seems to be over the extent and conditions of such transfer payments, not over the legitimacy of government use of its resource-allocating authority to some extent to increase the life options of individuals of small means. We must not overestimate agreement on values in this realm, however. As late as the 1970's public policy has not pressed income redistribution to a point of major confrontation between haves and have-nots; the over-all impact of taxation probably is more proportional than progressive, and possibly is regressive, bearing hardest on those of less income.[68]

Legislative Power: Investigation

In the states and in Congress, legislative power has allowed inquiry into affairs both inside and outside of government that

67. Steward Machine Co. v. Davis, 301 U.S. 548 (1937); Helvering v. Davis, 301 U.S. 619 (1937); Wickard v. Filburn, 317 U.S. 111 (1942).
68. Blum and Kalven, 5; Lampman, 24–26, 199, 204, 207, 217. Cf. Dandridge v. Williams, 397 U.S. 471, 484–485 (1970); Richardson v. Belcher, 404 U.S. 78, 81 (1974); Weinberger v. Salfi, 422 U.S. 749. 768–774 (1975).

legislators determined to be of public concern. Auxiliary to this right to ask questions is considerable authority to compel answers, under subpoena enforceable by legislative or judicial process. I do not put this item third in appraising types of legislative authority because it was a latecomer. Power to ask questions was as much a part of our legislative inheritance from the rise of Parliament, and particularly the House of Commons, as were the powers to tax and spend and to enact general standards and rules of behavior. I put this item in third place because, though as old in origins and in practice as the other two, it was the last to develop in broad use, and as late as the 1970's it is treated by policy makers as subordinate in importance and prestige to the resource-allocating and general lawmaking authority. Especially in the twentieth-century context, this subordination of the investigatory power has been as damaging a defect of process as any in the history of this legal order.

Successive stages of legislative practice in Congress primarily defined the legitimate uses of the legislature's power of investigation. The earliest goal of investigation concerned the purse power. Legislators wanted to know for what the executive wanted funds, and then whether the executive had spent the money for the proposed uses and how efficiently it had been used to pursue the programs it was to support. Since the supply of public funds had been the lever by which the House of Commons raised its authority over the crown, this use of the investigatory power could hardly be challenged as lacking historic legitimacy. Congress invoked this base of authority as early as 1792 when it inquired into the causes of General Arthur St. Clair's defeat by the Indians.[69] Through the years, both in the national and in the state governments, inquiry into executive budget requests and executive performance within the means provided by the legislative branch regularly formed the largest category of use of the investigative power, and, indeed, in the twentieth century has been the largest single category of all legislative business. Compared with the relatively limited amount of executive and administra-

69. Landis (1), 170.

tive operations that came under review in court cases, questions pressed in budget hearings provided the bulk of review of executive and administrative action.[70] When in 1927 the Supreme Court validated scrutiny of executive performance as a proper objective of legislative inquiry, it simply accepted an authority which 135 years of congressional usage had put beyond serious challenge.[71]

Legislative investigation could serve broader concerns than scrutiny of the executive branch. For general lawmaking the legislature needs to know what is going on in the society or within any particular frame of people's relations that may be of public interest. Legislators bring with them considerable knowledge of the community, the more so because an elected body draws its members from diverse parts of the whole community; accordingly, the Supreme Court has ruled that there is no judicially enforceable requirement of due process of law that a legislature conduct a special investigation before passing a law.[72] Congress showed that it did not feel the need of investigation in aid of general lawmaking as much as it did for scrutiny of the executive as it performed in the St. Clair investigation, for not until 1827 did Congress first use its power of inquiry for the broader purpose. From the late nineteenth century on Congress increasingly brought into play its power to conduct inquiries through its standing committees or through select committees specially designated to determine whether facts existed warranting general legislation. Once again, when in 1927 the Supreme Court declared that investigation in aid of general lawmaking was a legitimate use of the power of inquiry, it only ratified usage so long established as to be beyond reasonable challenge.[73]

A third objective of legislative inquiry developed in practice only with the rise of mass media of communication in the twentieth century: its use to inform or even to generate public opin-

70. Fenno (1), Chaps. 6, 7, 11.
71. McGrain v. Daugherty, 273 U.S. 135 (1927)4.
72. Townsend v. Yeomans, 301 U.S. 441 (1937); Maryland v. Wirtz, 392 U.S. 183, 190, n. 13 (1968).
73. Hurst (1), 79–81; Landis (1), 177–178.

ion. Before the day of the big-circulation newspaper, the radio, and television there was usually little likelihood that information or sensation produced by legislative inquiry would reach beyond the capital city. The new media quickly created new audiences of unprecedented numbers and range, which presented both creative opportunities and new dangers. In this high division-of-labor society interests grew more varied and more diverse, and chains of cause and effect in social relations became increasingly intricate and hard for anyone save the specialist to understand. The society also was more and more gathered into the impersonality of urban living, its members tempted by a rising material standard of living into withdrawing from public concerns into private-consumption pleasures. Thus powerful tendencies worked toward political apathy and despair; individuals felt cut off from understanding the social currents that tossed their lives, lost confidence that they could significantly affect what happened to them, had difficulty in perceiving where common interests lay. This setting created a constructive role for legislative inquiry directed at informing public opinion, and even at arousing public worry, anger, or urgent demand. But the availability of the new mass audience was tempting to ruthless political ambition. Armed with committee subpoena powers, a headline-hunting legislator now could find a new avenue to personal power, perhaps build himself into a leading contender for a presidential nomination, at whatever expense to individuals or groups pilloried by his shrewd manipulation of damaging testimony. The hazards of abuse became plain in mid-twentieth century as both House and Senate investigations—notably those of the House Un-American Activities Committee and of Senator Joseph McCarthy—exploited the country's cold war fears. Thus by the 1970's a balance of gains and costs is difficult to strike in estimating the use of legislative investigation for this new goal of informing and creating public opinion. Probably the verdict ultimately will be one familiar in appraising legal processes—that the danger of abuse is not enough in itself to warrant abandoning powers that can serve constructive and highly important public interests. In the late twentieth-century United States there is enough danger that political apathy and despair will subvert the working minimum of public involvement necessary to representative government to provide warrant for this new use of legislative investigatory power.[74]

Judicial review never imposed much restriction on legislative investigation. Relatively few cases came to court challenging legislative inquiry. In large part the legislature was asking questions of individuals on government payrolls, whose employment precluded them from contesting the authority of the body that paid the bills. When the witness was not a government official, he found that courts were wary about venturing into this area of controversy; judges made quite plain their opinion that legislative investigation was so integral to the legislative process that deference to the separation of powers dictated caution in telling legislators how to go about their business. Especially marked was the absence of judicially declared limits on the permissible subject matter of legislative investigation. In 1880 the Supreme Court ruled that a private witness need not answer questions about matters so particular to claims of the United States as creditor of an insolvent bank as to be proper subject matter of a lawsuit, or matters so particular in impact on persons as to be fairly deemed only of private concern.[75] Later decisions cast grave doubt on the continuing vitality of this lone precedent, and properly so; Congress might have been presumed to have concern whether further legislation was needed to protect the government as creditor, and Congress would seem warranted in inquiring into particular transactions that might demonstrate the need of legislation. No further cases developed constitutional separation-of-powers or privacy limits in this field; as of the 1970's there appeared to be no judicially enforceable limitations on the subject matter of legislative inquiry.[76]

74. Griswold, 63–66; Taylor, 83–88, 168–173; cf. Watkins v. United States, 354 U.S. 178 (1957); Barenblatt v. United States, 360 U.S. 109 (1959).

75. Kilbourn v. Thompson, 103 U.S. 168 (1880).

76. See McGrain v. Daugherty, 273 U.S. 135, 173–175 (1927); Sinclair v.

Courts did provide some procedural protections to witnesses called by legislative committees. Judges plainly would enforce only two constitutional limitations against legislative inquiries: they upheld a witness's right to claim the privilege against self-incrimination before a legislative committee and to object to production of evidence in violation of the Fourth Amendment guarantee against unreasonable search and seizure.[77] However, particularly in the 1950's when investigatory power was abused to attack politically unpopular causes or individuals or to promote the power hunger of particular legislators, courts responded with protections to witnesses derived from limits set by Congress or one of its houses on the operations of its committees. Thus, decisions upheld witnesses in refusing to answer questions that judges found to be beyond the scope of inquiry authorized by the parent house, or questions found irrelevant or immaterial as measured against the authorized subject matter of inquiry, or questions put by a subcommittee that lacked authority conferred by the parent committee. This development seemed an adroit compromise between deference to legislative prerogative and concern for fair treatment of individuals; it did not bring judges into a constitutional confrontation with legislative power, but rather invoked the supervisory authority of the legislature as basis for checking the conduct of its own agents.[78] Of related import was the assertion of authority in the courts to protect their own processes against invasion. Thus, a court would not enjoin legislative inquiry; but if by their inquiry legislators generated publicity that precluded a fair trial, the court could order dismissal of an indictment to protect the integrity of its own operations.[79]

Claims of executive privilege to withhold testimony or docu-

United States, 279 U.S. 263, 291–292 (1929); cf., however, Watkins v. United States, 354 U.S. 178 (1957).

77. See Watkins v. United States, 354 U.S. 178, 188 (1957); cf. Gibson v. Florida Legislative Investigation Committee, 372 U.S. 539 (1963).

78. Watkins v. United States, 354 U.S. 178 (1957); Barenblatt v. United States, 360 U.S. 109 (1959); Russell v. United States, 369 U.S. 749 (1962); Gojack v. United States, 384 U.S. 702 (1966).

79. United States v. Delaney, 199 Fed. (2d) 107 (1st Cir., 1962).

ments from legislative inquiry involve the potentiality of both executive and judicial power to limit legislative investigation. As of the 1970's the courts have not had occasion to decide a conflict between legislative investigation and claims of executive privilege. In 1953 and in 1974 the Supreme Court recognized that on some grounds the executive might withhold evidence in either civil or criminal litigation to protect military, national security, or diplomatic secrets, or more generally to protect such confidentiality among high officials and their advisers as might be functionally necessary to exercising constitutionally granted executive power. The Supreme Court asserted that the judicial branch had authority to review the facts and arguments advanced on behalf of such privilege; the courts should pay substantial deference to executive judgment, especially if the claim rested on assertion of military, diplomatic, or national security secrets, but some measure of judicial review apparently could be asserted in all instances.[80] Whether this doctrinal frame would embrace a clash between legislative and executive remains an open question. The Supreme Court has taken jurisdiction over such matters as the relative powers of Congress and the President over the tenure of federal officeholders,[81] and thus likely would take jurisdiction in a clash between legislative inquiry and executive privilege. But the historic primacy of the legislative branch in structuring executive offices and the programs the executive was empowered to pursue enhanced the likelihood that the deference paid to claims of executive privilege against efforts of private litigants or public prosecutors would not obtain against Congress, but rather that the presumption would favor the claims of legislative inquiry.

The most significant limitations on legislative investigation grew out of executive and administrative structure and practice, not lawsuits. The idea of executive privilege derived its operative

80. United States v. Reynolds, 345 U.S. 1 (1953); United States v. Nixon, 418 U.S. 683 (1974); cf. Berger, Chap. 7.

81. Myers v. United States, 272 U.S. 52 (1926); Humphrey's Executor v. United States, 295 U.S. 602 (1935).

content from the practical pull and haul between the legislative and executive branches. Sporadic and relatively limited claims of privilege were made from time to time through the nineteenth and early twentieth centuries. The bulk of executive assertions of privilege came from the 1950's on, originally inspired by President Dwight D. Eisenhower's desire to protect his subordinates from the harassment of Senator Joseph McCarthy. Measured by the number of assertions, the privilege developed to sizable proportions quite late in United States history. Generally, the executive had the advantage and prevailed; on the other hand, he usually made at least some response to congressional requests for information so that through most of the years claims of executive privilege were not a major factor in the working relations between the branches.[82]

Of more weight than executive privilege were structural advantages of the executive that made it increasingly difficult for the legislature to use its investigatory authority to keep close, effective surveillance over the money it provided and the programs it authorized. As both state and national governments expanded their service and regulatory functions, the apparatus to implement these functions also expanded. Executive and administrative offices gained in specialized knowledge of their fields of operation, brought to their assistance experts' learning in those fields, were immersed in a daunting volume of rules, adjudications, field procedure policies, and files upon files of documents. Confronting these developments were all-purpose legislators—relative amateurs confronting specialists—baffled or frustrated by the time and money costs of probing sufficiently into executive or administrative mysteries to control policy.[83]

Apart from these difficulties of understanding there was a problem of will. Specialization of function enabled an executive office or administrative agency to bring will to a focus in a degree

82. Berger, Chaps. 6, 8.
83. James MacGregor Burns, 7, 99–100, 103, 106, 111, 114–116; Fenno, 410–411; Gross, 104–105.

hard to match on the legislative side, where many issues competed for legislators' time, attention, energy, and courage. This difference between focused and divided will showed itself in two characteristics of legislative behavior, vis-à-vis the executive and administrative arms. One was the legislature's tendency to grapple with a problem and to treat its resolution as a final disposition, leaving the policy area without broad scrutiny for years thereafter. Symbolic was Congress's treatment of regulation of securities trading; having created a wholly new field of federal intervention in the economy in 1933–1934, Congress waited until 1962 to provide a full-dress inquiry into the working of the stock exchanges within the new framework.[84] Such inertia with reference to the broad delegations of power so characteristic of both state and national law in the twentieth century was matched by the persistent tendency of legislators, if they gave any continuing supervisory attention to their delegates, to attend only to the marginal increments to public policy. When the legislature looked at the activity or plans of an executive or administrative agency, typically it gave its attention only to the latest request for an addition to authority or for new money; rare indeed were instances of legislative scrutiny of the full scope and depth of what an agency had done with its statutory authority and its funds over a substantial span of time.[85]

Organized demands on government steadily mounted. A working society required more and more services and regulations which no other institutions showed themselves able to provide. Thus the twentieth-century development of executive and administrative influence and apparatus is likely to be sustained. In contrast to the simpler eighteenth- to nineteenth-century situation, basic reassessment of legislative priorities is needed. Resource allocation and definition of standards and rules of be-

84. Cary (1), 71–76, 92–94; cf. Lowi, 152.

85. James MacGregor Burns, 103, 106; Otto A. Davis et al., 66, 85, 87; Fenno (1), 410–411; Joseph P. Harris, 35, 41, 43, 54–56, 62, 65–67, 69, 75, 77–78, 79, 83–86, 101–103, 105–106; Wildavsky, 15–16; cf. Lowi, 73, 86, 90, 101, 111, 144, 155.

havior undoubtedly will continue to be important legislative contributions. But the functional logic of the rise of executive and administrative roles dictate that the legislature should regard its investigatory authority as the most important of its powers and should make more effective use of its powers of inquiry its primary concern. John Stuart Mill saw in the 1870's that "in legislation . . . the only task to which a representative assembly can possibly be competent, is not that of doing the work, but of causing it to be done."[86] His appraisal is even more applicable to the realities of the separation of powers in the 1970's. Unfortunately, by the 1970's the operative values and the working practice of state legislatures and the Congress have not caught up with these realities. Legislators fail to invest sufficient staff resources to arm their investigatory functions, and they fail to innovate in styles and techniques of investigation. Back of both of these deficiencies are deficiencies of perception and of will—failure to see the direction in which the shift of power into the executive and administrative arms should move the emphasis of legislative effort, failure hence to make the investigatory function the prime instrument both of legislative ambition and of legislative service. Default in this area means that the legislative branch tends to fall farther and farther behind in capacity properly to direct and to pass judgment on what executive and administrative officers do. Moreover, in its general affairs apart from the working of legal processes, the society is increasingly difficult to understand; relationships interlock in more intricate chains of cause and effect, and interests are multiplying in diversity and intensity. Wise public policy making thus calls for more effort to heighten awareness of interests and gains and costs at stake in social behavior. As Louis D. Brandeis had foreseen, government has no more important function than that of education—of the people and of lawmakers.[87]

86. Mill, 1:237.
87. On Brandeis: Mason, 521, 585, 602; Urofsky, 155–158, 160. See Hurst (3), 137–152; Woodrow Wilson, 303; cf. Doob, 207–220; Knight, 27–28, 32–35, 125–127, 163; Truman, 218–223, 503, 505–506, 518.

Legislators are using their investigatory power somewhat more effectively to respond to this general need for increasing knowledge of society than they are in coming to terms with growth of executive-administrative power. But in the larger field, too, investigatory effort tends to be discontinuous, inadequately funded and staffed, and not motivated by sufficient perception of its importance. The sum of the matter is that the legislative branch is confronting the principal challenge to its social utility in matching its use of its investigatory authority to the imperatives laid on it by events and that by the late 1970's it has signally failed to meet the challenge. The future of legislative power lies more in this area of action than in any other.

Judicial Power: Making and Applying Law

State constitutions conferred on courts authority defined typically without qualification as "judicial power." Article III of the federal Constitution vested "judicial power" in the Supreme Court and in such inferior courts as Congress might create, adding that this power should extend to "cases" and "controversies." In practice the central idea of judicial power proved substantially the same in both state and national governments, and for present purposes we can consider the two court systems together. The staple job of judges was to hear and decide disputed issues of law and fact between litigants who had focused, adversary interests in the claims for which they sought resolution. Through the nation's history, practice indicated the centrality of the case-or-controversy concept as shaping and defining judicial authority. The concept was reflected in the consistent emphasis on translating the matter in dispute into a formal record of procedural steps and of evidence taken and in the sheer bulk of procedural issues that figured in shaping records in litigation much more than in legislative or executive or administrative process. The idea that the proper business of courts and the scope of their authority was simply to decide real and particularized disputes under existing law took further shape in a number of doctrines of judicial self-restraint. One who would present a claim for judicial determination must show standing in court; standing was an ill-defined requirement, but its core was an insistence that a litigant must show that he had at stake a focused material interest (whether of benefit or detriment) that his opponent's claim would affect. A court had power to dismiss a suit on a finding that it was collusive—that is, that the contenders were sham contenders and in truth sought the same outcome. A court might refuse to decide a case for reasons of ill timing—that the issue was raised prematurely because events as yet presented no concrete threat of gain or loss to the suitor; or that the issue was moot because intervening events had changed the situation so as to deprive the intended issue of meaning.[88]

The impact of this case-deciding function on people's lives is hard to define with precision, if only because for most of the country through the nineteenth and into the early twentieth centuries no reliable series of data exist on the whole flow of business through the courts, and particularly through trial courts, whose proceedings only rarely were evidenced in any published reports. The evidence available suggests that probably most of the time a very small percentage of all disputes that might have been litigated were litigated. Probably the lawsuits that were begun in the nineteenth century involved plaintiffs who represented a wider range of economic interests and of wealth than in the twentieth, when plaintiffs seem to come in greater degree from the ranks of business creditors, property owners, and established institutions.[89] In any event, probably consistently through all the years, only a small percentage of legal proceedings begun in court came to determination on the merits by the court. Though forms differed, a similar pattern follows in civil and

88. Auerbach et al., 200–235; Hurst (1), 180–188; Mermin, 174–187, 192–197; Patterson (1), 564–570.
89. Galanter, 97–114; Hurst (1), 171–179; Laurent, Chaps. 2, 3; Mermin, 75–76.

criminal suits; most civil suits either were not pressed to any resolution or were settled by the parties' out-of-court bargain; most criminal proceedings were resolved by out-of-court plea bargains struck between the prosecutor and the accused, simply ratified by the judge. This record did not mean that the courts lacked significant impact, but that their impact needs realistic definition. Their dispute-resolution function created pressure on the contending parties on both the civil and criminal sides of the docket to adjust their relations by their own immediate bargaining. The judges made themselves felt more by their readiness and their availability in the background than by the direct impact of their activity in deciding cases.[90] This estimate of judicial function is clouded with disturbing practical and moral ambiguities. To a great extent judicial process created pressure for out-of-court settlements not because courts were available, but because they were not, because the out-of-pocket costs of suing or defending were beyond the means of one or the other party. To a great extent pressure for out-of-court settlement existed not because the courts were ready, but because they were so unready; crowded dockets spelled delays that claimants or defendants of modest means could not afford. By the second half of the twentieth century state trial court operations in metropolitan areas were near breakdown from crowded civil and criminal dockets, a condition that had been building since the last quarter of the nineteenth century. A somewhat more limited jurisdictional base helped to keep federal courts from falling into so acute a crisis of the case-deciding function, but from the late nineteenth century on in the urban areas the federal courts, too, were in chronic trouble.[91]

There were structural causes for these difficulties. Despite the prominence of courts among the symbols of legal order in the United States, Congress and state legislatures generally left the judicial branch in a condition of budget starvation because, until the creation of official judicial councils and offices of court

90. Hurst (1), 171–175; Jacob, 149–167; Mermin, 75–76.
91. Barrett, 85; Maurice Rosenberg, 29.

administration about the mid-twentieth century, the judicial branch had no legitimated lobby before the legislature. It was typical, too, of the narrow pragmatism of our legal processes that policy makers only tardily recognized the institutional implications of the importance of out-of-court settlements by giving attention to matters of pretrial practice, conciliation, and mediation or arbitration; even by the 1970's there is little well-formulated, openly scrutinized policy on plea bargaining between the prosecutor and the accused.[92]

Despite such structural factors, aspects of the substantive authority of courts, relative to the uses the legislature made of its authority, contributed profoundly to unsatisfactory social yield from the courts' case-deciding function. Legislative default concerning substantive public policy was largely responsible for overcrowded court dockets. Judge-made (common) law grew out of one-to-one confrontations of parties, which invited resolution by assignment of fault rather than by adjustment of the total situations in which the parties found themselves. Fault issues were inherently costly of litigating time, but legislative inertia—in areas of personal injury, consumers' rights, and nuisance law particularly—allowed these costly issues to dominate resolution-of-conflict situations. Apart from crowding the dockets, the alternatives posed by public-policy emphasis on fault too often gave the judicial process doubtful social utility. Common law too readily put solutions in terms by which a claimant either gained total recognition of his claim or no recognition at all, when a more workable as well as a more just appraisal of the parties' situation called for doctrine and procedures for spreading and sharing gains and costs in social relations, as statute and administrative law did through promoting the device of insurance in industrial accident cases.[93] A still more profound limitation on courts' effectiveness derived from the limits of their authority. Lacking

92. Barrett, 87, 94, 108–110, 113, 115–116, 121–123; Hurst (1), 93–96, 98–107; Jacob, 139–144, 156–157.
93. Maurice Rosenberg, 38–41, 52, 54.

the power of the purse, the power to initiate and sustain their own policy investigations, or the power to create new forms of official and private organization, courts could do relatively little to produce policy to prevent social ills. Preventive legislation and preventive administrative action could help to relieve courts of burdensome dockets; thus the federal land survey tended to reduce boundary disputes, public health regulations and requirements of disclosure in market transactions tended to reduce seller-consumer disputes, statutory and administrative protection of collective bargaining tended to keep out of court criminal or civil cases arising from employer-worker relations. Insofar as legislation lagged in structuring situations to avoid or reduce clashes of interest, the defaults of the legislature mingled with the built-in limitations of judicial power to increase court loads without increasing courts' ability to make useful social contributions.[94]

Though both doctrinal and practical limitations confined courts to the work of disposing of particular lawsuits, judges in fact created a substantial amount of generalized public policy out of ordinary litigation. In our constitutional tradition courts worked under an ideal of equal administration of equal law. This ideal meant that normally judges should decide disputes not by considerations unique or personal to litigants, but by categorical values and under uniform procedures and rules of evidence. If constitutions or statutes failed to provide standards or rules, obedience to the constitutional ideal called on judges to fashion the generalizations themselves. The doctrine of stare decisis reinforced this claim to the legitimacy of some judicial policy making by holding the judge duty bound to search for existing judicial precedent to govern the case before him. Judicial practice supported other devices that helped judges to advance policy in directions of their choosing—by calculated dicta, by alternative grounds of decision, by entertaining test cases be-

94. Cardozo, 68–71, 81, 113–114; Hurst (3), 182–215, 293, 326–330. See Holmes, J., in Southern Pacific Co. v. Jensen, 244 U.S. 205, 221 (1917).

tween good-faith adversaries. From the early nineteenth century the presses turned out a growing volume of reported opinions of courts, mostly of appellate courts, to facilitate the accretion of judge-made law. John Marshall gave authoritative form to the process of judicial lawmaking by establishing the practice that a several-member court normally would speak through one of its members, delivering "the opinion of the court."[95]

The courts contributed to the substantive content of the law in three principal forms: in law shaped wholly by judges (the common law); in application of rules (such as the ban on ex post facto laws) or development of standards (such as due process of law or the meaning of the commerce clause) derived from state constitutions and the federal Constitution; and in interpreting and applying statutes and administrative legislation. As I noted earlier, these three types of judicial lawmaking had distinctive chronologies. Common-law growth was prominent between about 1810 and 1890, and then steadily declined so that from about the 1920's it was a relatively minor part of new public policy. Judicial interpretation of statutes and administrative rules rose steadily in importance with the ascending curve of statute and administrative law after the formative decade, 1905–1915. Judicial review of the constitutionality of legislation flourished confidently and sometimes arrogantly in checking statutory regulation of the market between about 1880 and the mid-1930's, and then declined drastically as the Supreme Court led in applying a stronger presumption of constitutionality in favor of economic regulatory legislation; from about 1950 on, judicial review developed strong new curbs on statutes, administrative action, and even judicial decisions that adversely affected nonmarket interests, especially interests in open political processes (free press, free speech, free association, equal voting rights), in deference to individual dignity (against discrimination on account of race, religion, sex), and in freedom of in-

95. Auerbach et al., 43–64; Cardozo, Chaps. II, III, and pp. 149, 164; Patterson (1), 300–320, 469.

dividual emotional experience (through the arts, in sexual relations).[96]

Both strengths and limitations of judicial power were reflected in the relative subject matter of common law and statute law in the nineteenth and twentieth centuries. A pattern emerged in the relations of these two main heads of law, shaped within the bounds set by constitutional doctrine:

Subject Matter of Law

Common Law	Statute Law
Contract	Government organization
Tort	Schools
Property	Roads
Mortgages and other security	Taxation
Domestic relations	Public health
Basic crimes against person	Corporate organization
and property	Public utilities
	Antitrust law
	Securities regulation
	Collective bargaining
	Insurance regulation

The common-law side of the listing includes areas of public policy involving one-to-one relations or confrontations, or one-to-society relations. Aside from the criminal law, these were fields of activity in which individuals brought will and assets to bear on highly focused projects. The particular interests of immediately concerned actors supplied motivation and means to invoke legal processes to shape supportive, protective, or regulatory public policy which the moving parties thought to be useful to their relationships. The staple law of crimes presented a somewhat different situation. The offender represented a specific focus of will, emotion, and interest. But from early in the

96. See Chap. I, notes 23–29.

nineteenth century public policy substituted the public prosecutor, and later an increasingly professional police, in place of
the victim as the source of initiative for using legal process.
Until the late nineteenth century, however, the community sense
was that criminal sanctions should be invoked only for the classic
offenses against person and property, and these seemed to offer
a simple enough catalogue to be developed through court proceedings alone. The listing of statute law consists largely of
subject matter entailing diffuse gains and costs; everyone—or so
many everyones as to constitute big, amorphous groups—is
affected in some measure by the character of government organization, of public education, public roads, public care against
contaminated food and water. A breach of contract involves
primarily two contracting parties; personal injury (tort) involves an actor and a victim; trespass involves a landowner and
an identifiable invader. These situations were readily brought
within the frame of lawsuits. But a smoky factory might pollute
the air of a whole city; a poor road might cripple whole markets
along its extent; inadequate schooling could deprive the general
economy of skilled labor and the polity of a literate body of
voters. These problems were too broad in reach to be defined
handily, let alone resolved, by any litigation.[97]

The contrasts presented by the pattern express key differences
in the authority and structure of the legislative and judicial
branches. Judicial power traditionally meant authority simply to
resolve sharply defined conflicts of interests within relatively
simple, commonly agreed patterns of community values; the
subject matter on the left-hand side of the listing could be
handled by simple legal authority through the first three-quarters
of the nineteenth century. The subject matter on the right-hand,
the legislative, side of the listing, called for authority to tax and
spend and create new forms of public and private organization;

97. John Maurice Clark (2), 139–141, 226–235; Freund, 20–33, 69–71,
96–99, 185, 248–251; Kapp, 8–9, 11, 14, 16, 18–20, 230–231; Posner, 320–
332.

it also largely represents response to major changes of community circumstances, calling for the kind of open-ended authority to deal with change and novelty that was implicit in grants of unqualified legislative power. Implicit in much of the subject matter on the right-hand side is the need for specialized knowledge, will, and resources such as only legislative power could provide in the form of an expanding variety of executive offices and administrative agencies. The executive and administrative arms grew fast in the twentieth century with resources only the legislative branch could supply, responding to three main types of pressures to which general-purpose courts were not adequate —to needs in some areas for expert knowledge and technique (as in regulation of drugs), in others for the creation of expertness theretofore lacking and to be built out of specialized resources (as in the regulation of public utilities, collective bargaining, and corporate security issues), and in others for the provision of sufficient specialized apparatus to handle the huge detail inherent in implementing certain kinds of public policy (as in creation of a social security system).[98]

The twin-column pattern is handy to summarize important aspects and consequences of the differences in authority between courts on the one hand and the legislature and its delegates on the other. We must treat it only as a handy device for that purpose, however, and not be misled by its apparent rigidity. In the twentieth century there was a tendency for policy fields to shift from the left-hand (common law) side of the pairing to the right-hand (legislative and executive-administrative) side. This society throughout put high social value on fostering, servicing, and protecting the market as an institution. Contract law was a prime legal instrument to those ends. Until the late nineteenth century a single body of contract law doctrine, fashioned by judges, served to meet most of the felt needs for a public policy concerning private agreements. For a long time one set of working concepts—offer, acceptance, consideration, measures of per-

98. Hurst (1), 23–26, 70–74, 185–187.

formance or breach—seemed to serve equally well whether an agreement was about trade in wheat, horses, land, or personal services. Beginning with a rudimentary statute law of public utilities in the late nineteenth century, and flowering into a broad range of new areas of statute and administrative law from about 1905 on, public policy specialized its responses to social concern with private agreements. By mid-twentieth century the old general doctrines of offer, acceptance, consideration, and the like served only peripheral or wholly new types of transactions. The bulk of private transactions now fit within specialized bodies of doctrine, defined and administered more and more by specialized executive or administrative offices, concerning management-labor relations, insured and insurance company, electric power consumer and electric power utility, stockholder and corporation, or stock trader and stock exchange. Some of the oldest staple market situations now had their specialized statutory standardization—sales of goods under the Uniform Commercial Code, leases presumptively under statute-fixed standard forms.[99] Similar transformations in the same or in less but still substantial degree showed in relational problems earlier handled by the law of property (nuisance issues translated into zoning and pollution-control regulations), or tort (personal injury cases in industry brought under workmen's compensation, auto accident injuries increasingly brought within some frame of statute-required insurance).[100]

A somewhat analogous shift appeared in judicial interpretation of statutes. Nineteenth-century judges elaborated a catalogue of abstract canons of construction: remedial statutes should be liberally construed; penal statutes should be strictly construed; statutes in derogation of common law should be strictly construed; and many more. Indeed, so many canons grew that there was one for any purpose. Their proliferation indicated that their

99. Friedman (1), Chap. IV; Friedman and Macaulay, 812–818.
100. Babcock, 3–16; Kapp, 51–56; Keeton and O'Connell, 339–344; Murphy (1), 184–185, 237.

function was less to guide and confine judicial discretion under statutes than to legitimize interpretations the judges chose for reasons which the canons did not expose or explain; in their diversity the canons were a charter for judicial escape from the policy leadership that courts formally conceded to legislators.[101] But after 1900 legislation and executive and administrative action under statutory delegation pre-empted the making of public policy so sharply as to reduce the opportunities for value choice enjoyed by nineteenth-century judges. Courts reflected this change by a marked shift toward a less abstract, more particularistic, data-based approach to interpreting statutes. The generalized canons of construction more and more faded from judicial opinions, to be replaced by concern to elicit the policy indicators found in the specific course of legislation in a given subject-matter area; if a court resolved doubt in favor of increasing rather than limiting the coverage of a workmen's compensation act the judges were now less likely to explain their decision on the ground that the statute was remedial than because the legislature had pointed the way with successive amendments always enlarging and never restricting the definition of the benefited class. Of similar import was the courts' increasing readiness to use material outside the statute book to guide or rationalize interpretation. Where such material was available in the nineteenth century, judges made relatively little use of it; indeed, there was some indication that judges might adopt the English doctrine that barred almost all material outside the statute book as incompetent evidence to show legislative intent. But from about the 1920's on judges increasingly turned in aid of interpretation of the statutory text to legislative committee reports, legislative hearings, executive messages, comparison of successive drafts or amendments in the course of consideration of a bill, and to continued, consistent, practical construction of a statute by officials charged to administer it. By mid-twentieth

101. Llewellyn, 521–535; cf. Jackson, J., in Securities and Exchange Commission v. C. M. Joiner Leasing Corporation, 320 U.S. 344, 350 (1943).

century courts were using extrinsic evidence so much and so selectively as to evoke criticism that the technique was unfair because not all litigants could get access to or afford the cost of searching out such materials; that the technique could provide cover under which, by picking and choosing among diverse sources, judges could insert their own policy bias under the guise of deferring to legislative intent.[102] The criticism injected a healthy note of skepticism. But as of the 1970's it has not mounted to the point of substantially curtailing judges' use of legislative history materials. For the heart of the matter is that the twentieth century has witnessed an apparently permanent shift toward dominance of legislative and executive-administrative over judicial policy making; it was functional to this change that judicial development of the policy content of statute law should proceed within lines marked by the particular course of legislative history.

Executive and Administrative Authority

Executive and administrative authority is considered last because it best fits the course of United States legal history to do so. One deeply felt legacy from the tensions with England was a profound distrust of executive and administrative power, matched with determination to rely primarily on the legislative branch to shape public policy. This attitude showed itself in the first state constitutions, which in general left the fashioning of executive apparatus to the legislature and in important instances created only a weak office of governor as chief executive. Under some state constitutions the legislature at first selected the governor; at the outset he was given no veto; and since the legislature set up executive offices, no patronage was inherent in his office. This

102. Wright v. Vinton Branch of the Mountain Trust Bank, 300 U.S. 440, 463, n. 8 (1937); Hurst (1), 186–188; cf. Jackson, J., concurring, in United States v. Public Utilities Commission of California, 345 U.S. 295, 319–320 (1953); Dickerson, Chap. 10.

pattern of policy on the whole continued through the nineteenth century, though, as I noted earlier, later constitution makers gave the governor veto power and in the twentieth century enlarged his bargaining capacity vis-à-vis the legislature by adding the power of item veto over appropriation bills.[103] By 1789 there was disposition to create a potentially strong executive in the new federal government. The federal Constitution gave the President a separate electoral base—originally in the electoral college—a substantially longer tenure than was enjoyed by the chief executive in the states, a veto power, authority to report from time to time on the state of the nation and to take some initiative thereby in policy programming, authority to appoint federal officers, and special leading roles as commander in chief and treaty maker. But at Philadelphia, as in the earlier framing of state constitutions, a lively fear remained of executive usurpation of power against the legislatures and against the people. Thus the framers contented themselves with a relatively sketchy outline of the presidential position—especially compared with the detail given to the Congress—and made plain in their discussions that they intended to confer on the President no inheritance from the prerogative powers of the English crown. Formal constitutional doctrine changed little from the original pattern. The Twelfth Amendment assured that electors would vote separately for President and for Vice President. The Twenty-second Amendment stipulated that no individual might hold the office of President for more than two terms, implicitly setting a barrier against political dynasty while also reducing the bargaining power of a second-term President.[104]

In this constitutional context, the working character of executive and administrative power at the outset stood little defined, either in the states or in the national government, and for further definition waited on development by interaction with the

103. Hurst (1), 382–383, 403; Kallenbach, 15, 25–29; Zimmerman, 108–109.

104. Hurst (1), 383–384, 397.

other branches. Thus what executive and administrative authority have been in United States legal history for the most part is to be found by examining what legislative and judicial authority have been in relation to the executive and administrative officers. The earlier parts of this chapter have sketched key aspects of these relationships and thus already have outlined essential elements of the history of executive and administrative authority. It remains here only to align what has been said with a few other factors to bring out the large relief of the subject.

The great rise in executive and administrative roles and power came quite late in the country's legal history. This was a twentieth-century development. From the late eighteenth through the nineteenth centuries most state governments and the national government operated with a minimum executive establishment and with almost no counterparts of the later independent administrative agencies. The governor's office in the states continued as weak in practice as it often was in original endowment.[105] Strong-willed Presidents began to create precedents extending the chief executive's role. Thus Jackson's veto of the rechartering of the Second Bank of the United States opened up use of the veto power as a means of expressing policy differences with Congress, instead of limiting it—as the framers intended— to use against bills the President deemed unconstitutional. And Abraham Lincoln's responses, in proclaiming a naval blockade and calling for volunteers after the firing on Fort Sumter, added to Jefferson's Louisiana Purchase as precedents for presidential "stewardship" power. But such uses of the presidency were limited to unusual situations; they did not foreshadow pervasive, powerful, day-in-day-out presidential shaping of public policy over a broad range of concerns.[106]

A turning point in the states was the decade before World War I. Then state legislatures responded to pressures to expand legal

105. Dodd, 231–234; Hurst (1), 402–404, 419–420; White, 1405–1408; Zimmerman, 120.

106. Corwin (2), 29, 310–316; Hurst (1), 398–399.

regulation of the market by delegating broad powers to a growing catalogue of newly invented administrative commissions, notably in regulation of public utilities, insurance, banking, public health, and conditions of health and safety in industrial employment. From the 1920's on governors had more leverage on affairs through the item veto, increased patronage, and the executive budget.[107] Expansion of executive and administrative powers began in the federal government a bit earlier, as Theodore Roosevelt pushed through creation of a Department of Commerce and Labor and a Bureau of Corporations in 1903 and in 1906 the grant of substantial rate-regulation powers to the Interstate Commerce Commission. Woodrow Wilson gave further impetus to the trend when he pressed successfully to obtain the Federal Reserve Act in 1913 and the Federal Trade Commission and the Clayton (antitrust) Acts in 1914. The federal bureaucracy expanded immensely out of the problems of mobilizing for World War I, as it did again from 1940 on under the urgencies of World War II. Franklin Roosevelt's buoyant pragmatism fostered a new array of federal regulatory and service agencies from 1933 to 1941, including the Federal Deposit Insurance Corporation, the Federal Housing Administration, the National Labor Relations Board, and the Securities and Exchange Commission. From limited nineteenth-century beginnings, Presidents learned to use the executive budget as an instrument to shape programs and mark the bounds of agency jurisdictions. And under the impetus of two world wars and the popular demand for more positive response from national government to declines in the business cycle, Presidents from Franklin Roosevelt on tended to build larger roles as policy programmers, vis-à-vis Congress.[108] A powerful, distinct current of policy stemmed

107. Fine, 353–362; Kallenbach, 15, 25–29; Morison and Commager, 2:357–366; Nesbit, 428–430; Raney, 399–403, 409–415; Wooddy, 1292–1296, 1304.

108. Lawrence H. Chamberlain, passim; Hacker and Zahler (2), 50–58, 129–139, 199–205, 404–424; Heller, Chap. I; Morison and Commager, 2:391, 394–397, 431–438, 471–475, 591–612; Herbert Stein, Chaps. 5, 7, 15, 16, 17.

from early twentieth-century Progressive faith in rational and objective expertise as the answer to problems both complex and sharpened by demands of special interests. Out of this faith came the confident creation of independent administrative agencies to regulate such key areas of the economy as public utilities, banking, and insurance. It took just about one generation, starting in 1933, to build up an array of presidential, departmental, and independent agency power of such unprecedented sweep as to put in question Congress's capacity significantly to determine national public policy. If the trend of events was somewhat less dramatic in the states, it moved in a similar direction; the typical state legislature found its practical options and room for maneuver more and more reduced as it confronted the specialized skills and experience and the vested interests centered in the state executive-administrative establishment.

That executive and administrative power developed so relatively late and at so hard a pace has unsettled separation-of-powers values in the late twentieth century. Especially the lateness and speed of executive-administrative growth help to explain, though they do not justify, the extent to which the legislative branch gave ground by default; will was mustered more readily among the smaller numbers and more specialized concerns of executive and administrative officers than in the legislature, whose greater numbers and greater range of exposure to diverse interests fostered inertia more often than drive.[109]

To consider relative will to action points to a second major feature of executive and administrative authority as these took their twentieth-century course. Significant differences appeared in the roles of the chief executive and of executive departments and independent administrative agencies. A good deal of what happened was common to both the national and the state governments, but was more marked on the national scene.

Beginning with Theodore Roosevelt, Presidents built up their

109. Kenneth C. Davis, Chap. II; Lowi, Chap. 5.

role as leaders in programming legislation. Jefferson, Jackson, James K. Polk, and Lincoln had set notable precedents for this role. But twentieth-century Presidents enlarged the range of their involvement in legislation beyond that of their predecessors—in no small part because the twentieth-century social context brought more diverse and broad pressures for public policy of national scope. However, the spotlighted drama of presidential action tended to exaggerate the relative contributions of presidential policy leadership. Twentieth-century federal legislation typically originated through a sifting process (that might last from a few years to a decade or more), in which the content of policy developed through a succession of introduced bills, legislative hearings, committee deliberations, bills voted by one house and amended to death in the other, bills pressed by one set of lobbies and opposed by other alliances, along with the shaping of supporting or opposing or qualifying opinions in diverse "publics" affected by the proposed policy. Usually there was little or no presidential input in this essential formative process. The presidential contributions typically occurred in the last stages, such as the negotiation of final items needed to strike a voting bargain in Congress or the exercise of final pressure through presidential prestige, patronage, and appeals to the country. Typical was Wilson's last-stage intervention to obtain the Federal Reserve Act. Wilson's action was critical both in exerting pressure for congressional votes and in fixing some key terms of the achieved compromise (notably, that the Federal Reserve Board should be wholly a public body, named wholly through official process). But Wilson could be effective only because he had an existing legislative situation to work upon. He came into a situation where proposals already had been defined and tested by prior inquiry and interest-group interplay with legislators because the congressional process had been at work for some five years on issues of national regulation of the money supply. Moreover, he could not dictate a program; like other Presidents, he found that, though Congress might rarely generate a driving will for final action, it could effectively brake action, and that its committees and key members must be conciliated. The twentieth-century President developed his capacity to be a dynamic factor in legislative lawmaking. But it was, for all that, a limited capacity, effective usually only within potentials for action shaped by years of congressional consideration of a policy field. It was effective usually by last-stage intervention rather than by sustained contributions to the long business of bringing issues to awareness, defining competing values and alternative modes of implementing them, mustering support, and striking bargains to get support.[110]

From World War I on Congress delegated large areas of policy discretion to the President. Beginning with Franklin Roosevelt's administration, Congress also began to provide an enlarged secretariat for the office of the President, allowing the chief executive to name confidential advisers not subject to Senate confirmation, reporting directly to him, and available for assignments that could cut across the jurisdictional lines of executive departments and independent administrative agencies. The tortuous course of policy on the war in Southeast Asia, from John F. Kennedy through Nixon, showed that the combination of these two factors, together with the public deference built for the office by tradition since Washington, allowed the President to use delegated discretion in ways and to ends that could long be effectively insulated from outsiders' knowledge or criticism. The impeachment counts reported by the House Judiciary Committee against President Nixon in the summer of 1974 were special to his administration, but they pointed to a dangerous insulation of the executive office of the President that had been developing since the 1930's. This insulated use of delegated power—along with the practical precedents for presidential emergency power claimed as the duty as well as the prerogative of a chief steward of national interest—represented a much more

110. James MacGregor Burns, 40, 121, 164–172; Lawrence H. Chamberlain, 11–19, 450–464; Gross, 99, 100–103, 426–430; Link, Chaps. VII, XIII.

severe disturbance to the separation of powers than was presidential influence on the course of legislation. In the 1970's, after some forty years of this course of events, it was evident that the future vitality of the Congress would depend largely on Congress's capacity to delegate with more care and caution and to use its great investigative authority to hold its chief delegate under effective scrutiny.[111]

The extended reach of federal and state service and regulatory programs that began about 1900 brought great growth in executive departments and independent administrative agencies. Positive values were served by this multiplication and dispersion of executive and administrative apparatus, which met real needs for using the established expertise of fields of knowledge outside legal processes, as well as for building needed experience through the specialized activities of government offices and coping with the huge volume of detailed business that was inherent in many of the new program areas. But there were also two types of heavy costs in providing these positive values. First, growth of executive offices and independent administrative agencies fostered fragmentation of policy making. The wider the array of its delegates, the more the legislature tended to scrutinize only the last increment of agency funds or programs. The dispersion of policy responsibility among agencies promoted development of vested interests of congressional committees in their own jealously guarded subject-matter areas; a standing committee and an agency under its jurisdiction were inclined to become a closed corporation vis-à-vis the Congress itself, particularly agencies and the related subcommittees of the House Appropriations Committee. Policy fragmentation also was manifest in the time and energy agencies and legislative committees spent in fighting with each other for jurisdiction or program leadership.[112] Second, disper-

111. Kallenbach, 243–251; Neustadt, 43–51, 146–154; Reedy, 10–12, 30, 70–72, 78–85; Schlesinger, Chaps. 1, 2, 11.

112. Fenno (2), 316–324, 333–336, 344–348; Gross, 101–105, 155–161, 450; Redman, 40–52, 61–66, 175–182.

sion of programs accentuated problems of fair representation of interests in determining the practical content of public policy. By sweeping delegations of policy discretion, both Congress and state legislatures deflected from themselves onto their delegates much of the pressure that special interests otherwise would turn onto the legislators. To some extent by their special focus of will and their specialization of knowledge departmental offices or administrative agencies were peculiarly qualified to stand up to interest partisans and to make more realistic appraisal of their claims than could legislative generalists. But countervailing factors often proved to overbalance such gains. In a given agency there were fewer responsible actors to spread the burden of special pressures; the agency's specialization meant that its heads had fewer opportunities to play pressure in one program area against pressure in another; agency officials had no general voter constituency out of which to build political capital to offset the economic prestige and arguments that a regulated group could bring to bear. In all such respects a legislative body was better structured to strike balances among special interests and between special and diffuse interests than was an isolated departmental office or administrative agency. Back of the constitutional doctrine that said a legislature might not delegate powers save within carefully defined standards to guide and confine its delegate lay practical political wisdom: the legislature should not expose a separate agency to more heat of interest combat than it fairly could be expected to bear. By the 1970's a considerable public disenchantment with delegated powers attested that legislators for some two generations had tended to violate this practical principle.[113] Closely related was a type of conflict of interest peculiar to the growth of executive-administrative authority. The bulk of the work done by twentieth-century executive and administrative agencies did not in the first instance draw on knowl-

113. Marver H. Bernstein, 76, 79–81, 87–90, 92–95, 154–163, 184–187, 254, 261–271; Landis (3), 50–52, 54–55, 59–61, 68–70, 75, 78; Truman, 395–398, 417–421, 454–457.

edge or occupational patterns already established outside the law. Utility rate regulation, regulation of insurance or of securities markets, income tax administration—and most other areas of delegated policy—constituted new types of activity that had to develop their own skill and knowledge out of the government service or regulatory experience itself. The closest analogues in occupation or knowledge were among those regulated—in the ranks of the public utilities, insurance companies, specialized tax lawyers, and industry lobbyists. Such expertness as was to be found was likely to be among those employed by the regulated groups. As far as government staffed key posts with individuals drawn from outside the regulated groups, these officials learned on-the-job competence that qualified them as future recruits for private employment by those regulated; the possibility of such employment after leaving government service could exert subtle influence on the zeal with which policy-level agency officers pursued their official duty.[114]

Policy fragmentation and conflicts of interest within the ranks of public officials could have the more effect because courts matched the expansion of executive-administrative authority with a growing disposition to restrict judicial review of the use of delegated powers. In interpreting statutes, judges gave strong weight to continued, consistent, practical construction of such legislation by those charged with its administration.[115] Judges would sustain particular findings of fact and particular exercise of judgment by administrators as long as the record showed that the official action was supported by evidence. Such judicial self-restraint could be justified as appropriate recognition of the problems to which delegated legislation had responded—the need for specialized knowledge and experience and focused will to achieve desired goals of public interest. But, as legislative

114. Douglas, 49–52, 62–63; George A. Graham, 213–217, 244; Kohlmaier, 73–74.
115. See Cardozo, J., in Norwegian Nitrogen Products Co. v. United States, 288 U.S. 294, 315 (1933).

delegation grew more generous, judicial self-restraint in practice left executive and administrative officers substantially exempt from effective scrutiny through the courts. This outcome was the more assured because so often the interests most aggrieved by administrative error or default were too diffuse to muster resources to pay the costs of litigation, or perhaps to establish standing in court to complain. In the second half of the twentieth century legislation—notably the federal Administrative Procedure Act and the National Environmental Protection Act—legitimated the courts in broadening the definitions of those with standing to seek review of administrative action or inaction. But practical barriers of cost as well as barriers of legal doctrine continued to block broad-scale judicial review of the exercise of delegated powers.[116]

The logic of events led back to the legislature. Executive and administrative authority had grown mainly by the legislature's delegation of powers, with apparatus created by statute, moved and sustained by funds provided by legislators. Too many positive uses were served by expansion of departments and independent administrative agencies to make realistic the expectation that the legal order would work with any drastic cutback in executive and administrative jobs. But in this society there continued to be political vitality in the constitutional ideal that all powerholders be held effectively responsible to others than themselves. Unchecked expansion of executive-administrative authority was not consistent with constitutionalism. The constitutional ideal called on legislators to reappraise the delegated powers they had allowed to accumulate; without an unrealistic effort drastically to reduce executive and administrative roles, it should be possible to reduce the extent of discretion the legislature had committed or would in future commit to its delegates. Beyond this step, a healthy separation of powers called on the legislative branch to revitalize the power it could wield through its control of the public purse and to reorder its own priorities to put sustained,

116. Kenneth C. Davis, 152, 155, 158–161.

efficient use of its sweeping investigatory authority as its first order of business. The 1970's brought more urgent meaning to the judgment Woodrow Wilson had passed in 1885: "It is the proper duty of a representative body to look diligently into every affair of government and to talk much about what it sees. It is meant to be the eyes and the voice, and to embody the wisdom and will of its constituents. Unless Congress have and use every means of acquainting itself with the acts and the disposition of the administrative agents of the government, the country must be helpless to learn how it is being served; and unless Congress both scrutinize these things and sift them by every form of discussion, the country must remain in embarrassing, crippling ignorance of the very affairs which it is most important that it should understand and direct. The informing function of Congress should be preferred even to its legislative function."[117]

117. Woodrow Wilson, 303.

PART TWO

LAW AND CHALLENGES OF THE NATURAL AND THE SOCIAL ENVIRONMENTS

CHAPTER III

Science, Technology, and Public Policy

No part of the legal history of the United States is more important than the relation between substantive public policy and the acquisition and application of scientific and technical knowledge. The state of knowledge critically affects the character of any society, but it proved to be unusually significant in the United States, and hence unusually significant for uses of law. In the twentieth century the state of knowledge was largely dependent on "research and development"—a good pair of terms to represent two dominant trends: (1) the dynamic, changeful condition of knowledge, and (2) the insistent drive to put knowledge to working use. Both characteristics profoundly affected and were affected by roles of law.

Knowledge grew at three principal levels. First, basic science dealt with cause and effect—or at least with relationships—among phenomena traced as far back along a line of analysis as the searcher's skill permitted. The objective was to understand the terms of existence, without limiting the search to such learning as could be turned to particular use; indeed, as it accumulated, knowledge at this level tended to find expression in ideas more and more abstracted from concrete experience. Second, applied science dealt with perceptions of cause and effect ordered into formulas that individuals could put to specific use to satisfy their wants or needs. This was knowledge pursued for the sake of what people could do with it, by rationally planned and measured search and within rationally constructed patterns of principle. At a third level knowledge existed as skill acquired on the job, in

157

grasping cause-effect patterns or in manipulating relations of facts—products of trial and error and of practice and custom in striving for immediate, concrete satisfactions. This was the knowledge of the skilled carpenter or metal worker, as the second level was the knowledge of the laboratory scientist. These distinctions are relevant to the history of public policy, for policy differently affected, and was differently affected by the three levels of knowledge. A salient example: the nearer one moves to the basic-science end of this spectrum the less likely he is to encounter broad or diverse legal regulation of knowledge-seeking enterprises; largely because of its abstraction from immediate experience, until the mid-twentieth century, basic science moved substantially free of public-policy restraints, which on the other hand tended to grow in proportion as knowledge foreshadowed concrete application.

The example points to another basic distinction. Adding to knowledge was a different activity, of different impact, from applying knowledge in sustained ways. "Research" and "development" interacted, but they also elicited different responses in public policy. Law usually dealt with the close-at-hand order of social relations, and, thus, more with the application than with the fresh acquisition of knowledge. Public policy showed more concern with Thomas Edison's development of electric light systems than with his laboratory work with electric energy; the laboratory work brought into play the narrow specialty of patent law, but development of generating plants and transmission lines gave impetus to the growth of a complex law of public utilities, with immediate consequences for the everyday lives of millions.

At least as pervasive a public-policy response to the challenges in applying knowledge was the law's growing concern with education. Jefferson had urged public schools as means to increase the society's economic productivity as well as to promote a healthy political balance of power. But he could not foresee the pressures the growth of technology would exert to assure that people would have the literacy and related skills to let them serve and be served by an increasing division of labor. The growth of publicly supported education in the twentieth century, with the myriad problems that attended it—affecting the impact of class and racial lines, the separation of church and state, and the maintenance of order, for example—must be counted among the public-policy products derived rather from the "development" than from the "research" side of scientific and technical advance.

This chapter deals mainly with public policy related to the physical and biological sciences, to applied science, and to empirical (on-the-job) knowledge bearing on physical production of tangible goods and services. It notes some value problems connected with basic and applied science concerning individual and social psychology. It does not deal with problems of using applied or empirical knowledge about how individuals organize activities for cooperation or combat, and thus does not deal primarily with government, nor with the organization and operation of markets or business corporations. This limitation is adopted more for practical than for theoretical reasons. Individuals put varying kinds of knowledge to work to effect social arrangements as they adapted knowledge about the physical and biological terms of existence to their wants or desires. In both areas the state of knowledge at all its levels was critical to what happened. Thus one cannot distinguish the physical and biological realms as areas dominated by basic or applied science, in contrast to rule-of-thumb governance of most social arangements. There was plenty of rule of thumb in dealing with the physical and biological setting; on the other hand, from the framing of the federal Constitution into the twentieth-century development of the administrative process, leaders of opinion and action used what they took to be the best-ordered knowledge available of the arts (if not the science) of government.

Analysis is not advanced by merging the stories of public policy involving the science and technology of physical, biological, and (to some extent) psychological phenomena with policy bearing on structure and process in human relations. The two

areas involve different sources of initiative and energy, different
people with different working processes and goals. Moreover,
though common social effects sometimes came from developments
in both areas, physical and biological knowledge and its application produced public-policy responses separate from those concerning the organization or play of human relations. The Office
of Science and Technology in the White House, for example, was
a distinctive segment of federal government apparatus at mid-
twentieth century, apart from the Council of Economic Advisers,
also in the White House. The problems of the Food and Drug
Administration as it coped with a swelling number of chemical
additives in foods were different from those of the Federal Trade
Commission as it acted against false advertising. So our concern
here is with public policy related to science and technology
dealing mainly with the physical and biological terms of existence; to Chapter IV are left some problems of social organization and adjustments.

Institutional Supports for Acquiring and Applying Knowledge

The long-term trend of public policy in the United States was
to promote additions to the stock of scientific and technical
knowledge. A prime element of this policy was to use law to
legitimize, protect, and provide sustaining facilities for the search
—to give the steadiness of an institution to scientific and technological effort.

Favor for private ingenuity. Through most of the nineteenth
century the principal uses of law were to sanction and protect
private ingenuity wherever it operated, in advancing technical
command of nature, with a minimum of formal organization. In
this country, government erected no legal barriers to the movement either of individuals or of technical knowledge. The English
apprentice, Samuel Slater, had to bring here in his memory the
secrets of textile machinery which English law tried to keep at

home.[1] But he could come to the United States because up to 1917-1921 its policy generally was to welcome the skills of immigrants; conversely, United States policy left our citizens free to go abroad to seek out new technical knowledge.[2] Within the country the creation of the federal system meant that individuals could move from state to state free of legal hindrance, taking their technical skills wherever the legally free labor market offered scope for them.[3] A free press encouraged production of handbooks that collected and spread a wide variety of craftsmen's lore, as in building design and construction, road building, and machine-tool construction.[4]

Curbs on acquisition of technical knowledge were imposed by the law of patents and trade secrets, not to preserve industrial situations from disturbing change, but rather to encourage private investment in innovative products and techniques. The federal Constitution declared an activist bias when it empowered Congress to create a patent system "to promote the progress of science and useful arts." A trade secret in the manufacture of goods was protected largely to encourage the investment of time and money necessary to foster production under the superior technology, as well as to allow the possessor of the secret safely to employ workmen in putting it to use.[5] Of course, particular holders of patents or claimants of trade secrets might abuse these protective doctrines to stifle technical change to their own profit. But law set limits so that the ultimate bias of policy favored technical in-

1. Boorstin (1), 27; Burlingame (2), 158–162; Morison (3), 31.
2. Ferguson, 19, 20, 23–24; Handlin (2), 5, 205–206, 286–293; Morison and Commager, 2:185–188.
3. Crandall v. Nevada, 6 Wall. 34 (U.S. 1868); Edwards v. California, 314 U.S. 160 (1941).
4. Boorstin (1), 151; Ferguson, 14–16; Kirkland (1), 1:102; Larkin, 83, 84, 154, 156, 168; Nye, 190, 194, 196, 240, 262, 272.
5. U.S. Const., I, 8 (8) (patents). On protection of trade secrets as promoting investment: Tabor v. Hoffman, 118 N.Y. 30, 23 N.E. 12 (1889); Du Pont de Nemours Powder Co. v. Masland, 244 U.S. 100, 102 (1917); B. F. Goodrich Co. v. Wohlgemuth, 192 N.E. (2d) 99, 105 (Ct. App. Ohio, 1963); N.Y. Times, March 22, 1963, 11:4. Cf. Seidel and Panitch, 32–33.

novation. One who sought freedom of action could overset the claim of patent or trade secret by showing that a given device or process belonged to an already existing stock of scientific or technical knowledge, or that another came by the secret by fair, independent work, and legal redress lay against a patentee who sought added leverage in the market by tying sales of the patented product to sales of goods that lay outside patent protection.[6]

Individuals or groups might try to bring private force against disturbing changes fostered by a free market for the development of technical skills. For example, in scattered episodes unorganized workers used violence against machinery that threatened traditional jobs. But the optimistic temper of the United States was alien to this response, and it never became a central concern for public policy; the ordinary law against riot was sufficient to meet episodic challenges; confidence prevailed that advances in technical capacity were a self-evident good.[7] Knowledge generally passed freely among shops and mills; it was taken to be a sign of a free republic that all classes might participate in the discovery and application of technical skill, while through the nineteenth century economic growth so outstripped the labor supply that machines seemed less fearsome to workers.[8] The rise of trade

6. Chadwick v. Covell, 151 Mass. 190, 23 N.E. 1068 (1890) (trade secret fairly acquired); O'Reilly v. Morse, 56 U.S. 62, 112–114 (1853) (patent sustained on telegraph, but not on broadest claims for use of electricity and magnetism to send messages); Great Atlantic & Pacific Tea Co. v. Supermarket Equipment Corporation, 340 U.S. 147 (1930) (no patent for subject matter obvious to one with ordinary skill in the art); Motion Picture Patents Co. v. Universal Film Manufacturing Co., 243 U.S. 502 (1917) (tying arrangement invalid).

7. That Luddite-style violence against technical innovations was present, but episodic, see Meier, 88. Commonwealth v. Paul, 145 Pa. Super. 548, 21 Atl. (2d) 421 (1941) treated as riot what was probably a forcible attempt to prevent technological change. Luddite-type disturbances are markedly absent from the examples of major violence in the United States, collected by Hofstadter and Wallace. Cf. id., 13, 18–19, on strike violence.

8. On free exchange among shops, see Ferguson, 24. Such exchanges were a sign of healthy freedom to an extent that Europeans were puzzled by the

unions might have provoked an organized Luddite reply to the machine, but the bitterness and strife that attended the efforts to create union strength centered on wages and conditions of labor in the factory. Through the nineteenth and early twentieth centuries workers did not for the most part use unions to try to block technological change, but rather to get a better share of the gains and to mitigate the dangers and rigors of machine-governed production.[9] Only in the twentieth century did substantial trade-union effort go into checking technological changes that threatened jobs. The threat of increasingly automated production processes especially brought this concern to the fore about mid-twentieth century, as with the typographical unions and those that organized stevedores, meat packing, and steel workers. Even though such responses did not mount to a wholesale counterattack on technological change, government began to direct more positive attention to social tensions attending drastic shifts in workplace techniques.

By the 1870's, broad, diverse currents of practical experience in producing goods and services for the market had built a great stock of technical capacity in the United States. This asset was made up of the competence of countless individuals and firms, not bounded within narrow lines of highly skilled crafts or guilds, nor within jealous monopolies of knowledge held by particular firms. Technology born of production practice thus took on the sustained life and momentum of an institution. Indeed, practice-bred technology became an institution of major social impact substantially before basic or applied science became organized forces in the country's growth; craftsmen, mechanics, and pragmatic inventors preceded scientists as principal movers through

---

good will shown here to the introduction of machinery. Meier, 81, 89, 90. Cf. Barber, 210, 215. The nineteenth-century labor shortage made machines less fearsome to labor. Burlingame (4), 37. Acceptance of technological as well as scientific advance continued to be treated as a self-evident good well into the twentieth century. Etzioni and Nunn, 195, 196.

9. Dulles, 73–94, 99–100, 107–109, 119–122, 137–140, 155; Hacker (1), 269–279; Ware, 26–100, 201–212, 229, 240.

the nineteenth century. Like the market, practice-based technology was an institution the law had not made,[10] but the law contributed a favoring, supporting context for its growth. Public policy gave this assistance mainly by legitimizing and protecting the freedom of workers to move about, of business firms to organize, and of technical information to flow generously among workers and entrepreneurs. In this domain law played its least active role in fostering technological development, but what it offered was, nonetheless, of high importance. To see this, one needs only to contrast the fluid state of technology in the nineteenth-century United States with the cramping limits set earlier in England by guilds, crafts, and early industrialists and later by mercantilist state policy.[11]

Empirical technology as a by-product of internal improvements. Next—in weight of influence, though not in chronology—was a more positive contribution of public policy to the growth of practice-bred technology. In effect, though not by design, state and federal government promotion of internal improvements in the nineteenth century provided on-the-job engineering schools to spur technical innovation as well as to train individuals in applying the results. The building of the Erie Canal provided a training school for practical engineers, as did other state canal projects inspired by it, along with public projects to build roads and to construct water supply systems and public encouragement of like private enterprises. Similar impetus to on-the-job advance and training in engineering and mechanical skills came from the money subsidies, franchises, and public land grants with which

10. Boorstin (1), 33–34, 106, 148–152; Bruchey, 162–163; Cochran (1), 143, 147; Conant, 7, 24; Dupree, 46, 48; Morison (3), 22, 26–33, 37–38, 90–91, 95, 109, 110.

11. Hill, 28–35; Letwin, 23–32; Polanyi, 35, 38, 40, 63–65; Thorelli, 14, 23–26. One must not exaggerate the novelty of the Industrial Revolution; eighteenth-century manufacturing built on productive potentials that had been growing over a long past. Lampard, 17, 20, 21, 22. But technological change about 1760–1830 was unprecedented if not absolutely new. Id., 4, 5; see Whitehead, 97, 98.

state governments and then the United States promoted the private building of railroads.[12] First on a modest scale between 1790 and 1815 and then massively out of demands of the Civil War, government military contracts and operations provided a new scale of opportunities for broadly applying techniques already developed and to some extent fostering new ones in producing goods and services for the market and for public-purpose use, from mass production of standardized clothing (soldiers' uniforms) to provision of large-scale sanitation facilities. The Civil War perhaps retarded industrial growth already surging in the 1840's and 1850's, but government's wartime purchases, in the North at least, sustained currents of technological development.[13] The federal government's military supplies contracts grew enormously as influences on the development of technology in the twentieth century, from World War I production of planes and ships to World War II and later cold war promotion of electronics gear and nuclear energy facilities. These twentieth-century events, however, involved much more use of basic and applied science and of science-based techniques of production. Thus they represent different, more sophisticated functional relations of government spending to the roles of technology in the society than did the growth of job-based skills as by-products of nineteenth-century internal improvements.[14]

The twentieth-century situation points up another contrast to that of the nineteenth. At least from World War II and its aftermath, science-based technology and government investments in it took on distinctive force as moving factors in shaping the eco-

12. Burlingame (2), 241–242, 252–256; Ferguson, 10; Goodrich, 10, 23, 28, 33, 35, 60, 81, 106, 108, 280, 285; Kirkland (1), 1:101–102, 119–122, 296–298; Morison (3), 20–29, 44–45, 60–67, 71; Scheiber, 47, 64, 76, 122–123, 164–165.

13. Boorstin (2), 98, 100, 188, 314, 315; Burlingame (1), 127, 506, and (3), 172–181; Victor S. Clark, 41, 43–45; Cochran (3), 148, 154; Woodbury, 49–54, 57–58.

14. Cochran (2,), 33, 44, 46–47, 110, 127, 132, 133–139, 160; Cochran and Miller, 225, 298, 301–302; Hacker and Zahler (2), 510, 511, 517–519; Jones and Angly, Chaps. 22, 23, 26.

nomic and social character of the society. Thus, twentieth-century public policy had to take account of technological development as in itself a significant element in such modest economic and social planning as government undertook. For example, the geographical distribution of government contracts and the impact of government-financed technological advance among industries and among firms within a given industry emerged as active concerns of Congress and the federal executive for the bearing these factors had on distribution of power and influence in the society.[15] Such issues were involved in the nineteenth-century government's relation to technological change, but advances in technical knowledge, as such, were not then seen as distinct matters for public-policy decisions. Of course, nineteenth-century policy makers saw large economic planning stakes in internal improvements; the fate of whole regions and not merely of localities or of particular states turned on the building of canals and railroads. But the development of engineering and mechanical capabilities was a taken-for-granted by-product of such enterprises, and as such never became a focused topic of public policy. At this stage the lines of influence ran simply from government to the growth of technical skill, and little or no heed was given to the influence that technical developments might have in posing choices for general public policy.

Legal favor for private associated effort to promote growth of scientific and technical knowledge. From an early time public policy encouraged development of rationally ordered knowledge of physical and biological phenomena, in the forms both of basic and of applied science. Policy took two lines—direct government provision for scientific research, and delegation of research to private direction under government encouragement. Such official promotion of science overlapped in time the two styles of public policy this chapter already has examined, but lagged considerably behind them in extent and impact. Indeed, public policy designed

15. Hacker and Zahler (2), 508, 512, 519, 573–574, 576; Newman and Miller, Chaps. 7, 8, 9; Price (1), 170–184.

to foster growth of ordered physical and biological knowledge did not become a substantial factor until the late nineteenth century and took on prime influence only after 1940.

Through the nineteenth century government promoted basic and applied science mainly by legitimizing and encouraging scientific pursuits by private persons and organizations. This approach was consistent with a broader tendency to delegate to private hands the accomplishment of purposes of public interest. Save for occasional tariff-derived surpluses, through most of the nineteenth century government found it impracticable to command sizable resources by taxation in a chronically cash-scarce economy. The country inherited no practice of sophisticated public administration in the relatively simple circumstances that prevailed until after the Civil War. Congress and the state legislatures typically were amateur bodies. From the break with England we derived a sharp distrust of executive power, which hindered development of apparatus capable of directing affirmative programs of any complexity. In this context a premium was placed on mustering from volunteer private sources talent, energy, and resources to meet all sorts of public needs, including the advancement of knowledge.[16]

From the late eighteenth century public policy favored freedom and diversity of private association for purposes deemed to promote the general interest. States adopted general incorporation acts for philanthropic undertakings—libraries, academies, religious groups, charities, literary societies—long before they provided general incorporation laws for business enterprises. Early favor for granting special charters of incorporation went to business undertakings seen as furnishing facilities of general utility—in banking, insurance, provision of turnpikes.[17] It fit easily into these patterns that common law in this country presumed the legality of unincorporated associations for philanthropic purposes and

16. Hurst (2), 11, 15, 39, 53, 63–65, 87; (4), 92–93, 215–216, 384–385, 459–461; (5), 4, 7, 15, 17–18, 22–24, 35, 43.
17. Id. (5), 17, 37, 40, 51, 134.

that legislatures were ready to charter private associations for the advancement of knowledge.[18] The American Philosophical Society existed in unincorporated form and with varying vitality from Benjamin Franklin's proposal of its organization in 1743 until the Commonwealth of Pennsylvania granted it a charter in 1780. Also in 1780 the Massachusetts legislature granted a charter to the American Academy of Arts and Sciences. The stated purposes of both organizations combined the promotion of basic and applied science in a fashion fitting the intellectual ambition of their founders and the pragmatic temper of the country. Thus, the Pennsylvania charter declared itself grounded in the confidence that "the cultivation of useful knowledge, and the advancement of the liberal arts and sciences in any country, have the most direct tendency towards the improvement of agriculture, the enlargement of trade, the ease and comfort of life, the ornament of society, and the increase and happiness of mankind."[19] The early nineteenth century saw the creation of new educational institutions focused wholly on research and training in the sciences, with particular attention to acquiring and using ordered knowledge for improved technology. Such, for example, was the Franklin Institute founded in Philadelphia in 1824 for "the promotion of the mechanical arts." The Institute's activities show how such a specialized, private association could provide facilities for dealing with public-interest problems at a time when the country had little developed official apparatus. The Institute established a *Journal* that provided a forum for advancing technology on lines of general utility; thus its *Journal* early gave much space to the matter of boiler explosions on the new steamboats, and in its pages a leading machine-tool builder, William Sellers, launched a campaign for standardizing screw-thread design. Again, while

18. Id. (5), 14, 21, 31, 33, 118. Cf. Friedman (3), 296–297. Compare the caution shown in defining the crime of conspiracy as limited to associations for unlawful ends or operating by unlawful means. Hurst (2), 19, 87; Levy, 188–190, 203, 205; Sayre, 404–406, 413, 416, 420.

19. General Court of the Province of Massachusetts Bay, 1779, Chap. 46; Pa. Stat., 1780, Chap. DCCCXCIV.

Congress floundered about over the losses from steamboat boiler explosions, in 1830 the Institute empowered a committee of its members to investigate the causes of explosions; Congress provided some supporting funds, in the first grant by the federal government for technological research; six years of experiments carried out by the Institute resulted in a factual report and recommendations (1836, 1837) that provided indispensable impetus for moving Congress to enact a first—if inadequate—federal steamboat boiler regulatory statute in 1838.[20]

From mid-nineteenth century on the business corporation took center stage as the most influential type of private association sanctioned by a more and more hospitable public policy. Industrial and commercial technology grew, though mainly as byproducts of business profit seeking. Andrew Carnegie assembled talented lieutenants who promoted on-the-job learning to improve steel making, and he was alert and bold in investing in proved technological gains. But he did not make his mark by investing in research.[21] Not until the turn of the century did the big business corporation emerge as a source of planned commitment of resources to scientific and technical research. In 1900 the General Electric Company created within itself a laboratory to do basic research in physical science. By 1920 key chemical companies (Du Pont, Standard Oil, Kodak, U.S. Rubber) had set up laboratories. In 1925 the American Telephone and Telegraph Company consolidated various small units into the Bell Telephone Laboratories. By 1930 there were twelve hundred industrial laboratories in the United States, and by 1950 some twenty-two hundred. We must not exaggerate the significance of this trend. Most work done in these laboratories understandably focused on narrow, relatively immediate, commercially realizable gains. If they pursued more basic research other business corporation laboratories confined themselves to narrow channels fixed by their companies' estab-

20. Burke, 107; Curti, 297, 325; Dupree, 50, 88; Morison (3), 121; Sinclair, 66, 72–73.
21. Hacker (2), 348–350, 356; Wall, 473, 499, 502, 504–505.

lished lines of business.[22] From World War II on the research role of business corporations changed from one simply incident to private profit seeking to one primarily oriented by massive government contracts toward primary objectives set by government.[23] Despite these qualifications, the rise of big business did add its own distinctive strand to the advance of science and technology. At first the law made only passive supporting contribution to this development; General Electric could pioneer with its laboratory within the broad acceptance that law gave to freedom of private associated effort. Federal taxation brought a more positive element into the picture. From the first mild corporation income tax of 1909, the pressures of the depression in the 1930's and then of World War II and its cold war aftermath brought increasingly heavy levies. These gave more and more relevance in business decision making to what the tax laws allowed as deductions for corporate spending on research and development. By the same token, the allowed deductions put a more affirmative stamp of public-policy approval on such effort; a 1969 estimate put the revenue effect of expanding corporate research and development expenditures at $500 million.[24]

The early twentieth century saw a major new development in private allocation of resources for research in basic and applied science. By the absence of sustained or substantial income or inheritance taxes, nineteenth-century public policy fostered the accumulation of great private fortunes out of the unprecedented rise of big business. A few holders of such wealth felt moved to devote it to the advancement of knowledge for the betterment of life. In 1907, New York's legislature incorporated the Russell Sage Foundation to administer a great gift from Sage's widow for "the improvement of social and living conditions in the United States of America," by means including research, publication, and education. John D. Rockefeller's effort to obtain a national charter

22. Morison (3), 126–128, 140–141; Price (1), 37.
23. Cf. Price (1), 37, 68, 70, 73, 79, 86, 91–92.
24. Aaron, 43; cf. Ratner, 294–295 and Appendix, Table 3.

for a research endowment failed in 1910, partly from general opposition to the wealth and power symbolized by the name Rockefeller, partly from objections that the proposed charter was too vague and appeared to create an institution of permanent life that might command huge tax-free resources. Opposition was less in 1911, but a second charter bill failed when it became caught in the time pressures for Congress's adjournment. At that point in 1911, Rockefeller obtained a charter from the state of New York, creating the Rockefeller Foundation. Also in 1911, Andrew Carnegie established the Carnegie Corporation of New York under a New York charter, granting broad authority for an institution that might support basic and applied scientific research. Except for the flurry of controversy in 1910, these pioneer foundations and many that followed gained acceptance in public policy with little difficulty. They set new precedents in the scale of their assets. Otherwise they fit readily into the long-standing favor of our public policy for delegating to private associated effort the pursuit of objects of public interest.[25] True, the distrust of great wealth that had produced rejection of a national charter for the Rockefeller Foundation in 1910 surfaced again in 1915 in hearings of Congress's Commission on Industrial Relations. The majority of the commission saw a sinister threat in an industrial relations study sponsored by the new Rockefeller Foundation; two dissenting members of the commission—Professor John R. Commons, University of Wisconsin economist, and Florence Harriman, New York social worker—would not accept the majority's dark reading and urged that there be no legislative action against foundations without a complete investigation of all of them. Interest in the matter quickly dropped away, and the foundations went their way substantially undisturbed until new issues arose from the 1950's on.[26] Meanwhile, since the later

25. Glenn et al., 1:4–12; Nevins, 2:645–648; Wall, 882–883, 1046; Weaver, 34–38. On the general hospitality of United States law to charitable trusts, see Scott, 4:2783, 2786, 2789, 2895.

26. Nevins, 2:671; Weaver, 170–171.

nineteenth century, another private institutional trend paralleled the impetus the foundations gave to scientific growth. Led by Johns Hopkins, universities moved beyond older, narrower boundaries of study to develop scientific graduate departments, all also under the broad favor public policy showed to private philanthropic initiative.[27]

The new issues regarding foundations were first ideological and, later, fiscal. Big government loomed ever larger in the society at a time when racial tensions and distrust bred of the cold war generated fears of domestic difference and desires for a safe conformity. The situation brought to the fore a separation-of-powers value heretofore scarcely perceived in the law's legitimization of private foundations. The foundations could provide support for inquiry and assessment of social policies separate from official doctrine and action. Foundation activity thus might help to implement the values of free and full examination of public policy symbolized by the First Amendment. But this was not a role accepted by all as a public benefit. In the early 1950's two House investigations probed allegations that foundation money was supporting subversive movements. From the Cox Committee investigation of 1952 came a report substantially vindicating the social utility of the foundations and acquitting them of charges of financing subversion. From the Reece Committee in 1953, in contrast, came slanted hearings and findings that earned for the committee broad condemnation. But, however appraised, the two episodes showed that privately endowed research in the second half of the twentieth century had taken, or had had thrust on it, a significance for the over-all distribution of power in social policy making that gave a new dimension to legal history in this field. And the 1960's brought another new policy concern. Congress became properly concerned that high levels of federal income taxation were encouraging individuals to evade taxes by throwing the cloak of philanthropic foundations around private profit seeking. Congressman Wright Patman mounted what was prac-

27. Curti, 514, 585; Curti and Carstensen, 1:545, 641, and 2:368–372; Dupree, 157.

tically a one-man investigation of such possible abuses of the foundation device. His effort produced desirable improvement in annual reporting by tax-exempt philanthropies, both under changed Treasury Department procedures and regulations and then under statute. The tighter regulation and the better accounting were not achieved without costs. The investigation did not differentiate fairly between responsible and sham foundations, and Congress wound up by imposing taxes on foundation income that contradicted the social value involved in preserving foundation funds for research not immediately dependent on official favor. The fiscal issue did not carry quite the threat of censorship of ideas carried by the investigations of the 1950's, but the threat was there, if somewhat submerged. Policy history was clearly still in motion in this emotionally charged area, moved by considerations that had not been material before the 1950's.[28]

Direct government support of scientific research and development. From early, small beginnings the states and the national government—mainly the latter—after mid-nineteenth century built up official institutional support for advancing basic and applied science and fostering development of scientific knowledge into sustained action programs. The first measures provided for single ventures. Hamilton's *Report on Manufactures* (1791) urged government bounties or subsidies to scientists and inventors to encourage industrialization.[29] Of more immediate effect, in 1803, Jefferson persuaded Congress to finance the Lewis and Clark expedition to lay a base of knowledge for settling and using the land west of the Mississippi. In 1807 he got still more generous funding from Congress to begin planning a coastal survey, which did not get under way until 1816.[30] In the summer of 1838 the United States put to sea a flotilla for a four-year, broad-purpose study of Pacific waters.[31] Also in the early nineteenth century

28. Weaver, 172–179 (Cox and Reece investigations), 179–186 (Patman investigation); cf. 83 Stat. 502 (1969).
29. Alexander Hamilton, 4:70, 78, 83, 87, 89, 95–99; Price (1), 6.
30. Dupree, 26–27, 30, 32; Malone, 173–180.
31. Dupree, 56–61; Struik, 196.

states supported particular scientific research ventures. The Massachusetts legislature showed the way in 1830–1831 by providing for a botanical and geological survey of the state's resources. In the next three decades other states created like natural resource surveys, which were important not only for the data they accumulated but also for the career opportunities they provided for scientists.[32] These undertakings built acceptance of the propriety of direct government action to advance knowledge. Indeed, before 1860 federal and state activities may have supplied more money and employment for science than did all private societies or colleges.[33] But such particularized activities inherently were subject to the chances of politics and lacked continuity. Policy took a more important direction as government began to institutionalize its relations to research and development.

Two measures looked toward generalized relations of the federal government to science. After years of delay and political and ideological bickering, in 1845, Congress chartered the Smithsonian Institution, as the instrument of James Smithson's bequest to the United States for "an Establishment for the increase and diffusion of knowledge among men." The charter reflected the compromises necessary to its passage by providing a frame within which the Institution's regents could use its resources for varied services to learning. In 1863, with scant consideration and almost casually, Congress chartered the National Academy of Sciences, a body entitled to select its own membership and charged when called upon by any department of the government to investigate and report "on any subject of science or art." Into the early twentieth century the Smithsonian grew to be a major research center, notably in meteorology, zoology, botany, and anthropology, though it tended to lose leadership with the rise of more specialized government research offices. The National Academy had less substantial impact. It recognized established scientific talent and thereby contributed to the prestige of basic research—

32. Dupree, 45, 46, 63, 92, 116; Hurst (4), 446–449, 452–453, 463, 507; Struik, 185, 187, 194.
33. Dupree, 130.

a useful counter to the dominant, narrow pragmatism of this society. But the government made only episodic calls on the National Academy, and on the whole it supplied no effective, comprehensive leadership in relating science and technology to public policy making.[34]

Through the nineteenth century and to about 1940 the federal government made its principal contributions to basic and applied science by multiplying and consolidating research undertaken incident to the missions of particular bureaus. When in 1802, Jefferson created an Army Corps of Engineers stationed at West Point, he laid the foundation for the first engineering school in the United States; Army engineers put to use such science as was available in surveying and developing the West and became a prime factor in providing internal improvements, to the extent of developing as the core of a powerful public-works lobby in Congress. In scientific terms, the growth of an established coastal survey organization dominated the years before the Civil War. Thereafter, in the 1880's, the United States Geological Survey became an agency of research influence, and about the turn of the century the Forest Service gained stature in its work for natural resource conservation. Other offices of the Department of Agriculture bulked large in governmental support of research; as late as 1938 the Bureau of Entomology and Plant Quarantine spent almost as much for research as did the Public Health Service. The specialized bureaus were not all-powerful. They some-

34. 9 Stat. 102 (1846) (Smithsonian Institution), 12 id., 806 (1863) (National Academy of Sciences). Cf. Dupree 76–79, 83–90, 283–284, 335 and Price (1), 17 (Smithsonian Institution); Baldwin, 577, Dupree, 135–141, 241–244, 294, and Weaver, 112–113 (National Academy of Sciences). Up to 1900 the forest policy report of 1896 was the one major issue of science-related policy on which the advice of the National Academy was asked. Baldwin, 577. The National Academy played a more active advisory role in public policy making after 1950. N.Y. Times, May 25, 1962, 15:1. Its advisory role had been broadened by creation of a National Research Council, by Wilson's executive order in 1918; the Council could recruit specialists who were not members of the Academy. Baldwin, 577, 578; McCamy, 60; Price (1), 41–42.

times met hostility, or more often indifference, from Congress. Some did not survive. Research sponsored by private foundations and by industry in the first third of the twentieth century tended to overshadow federal bureau efforts.[35] After 1940 the demands of World War II and the cold war competition with Russia gave a new scale to what was at basis, still, the same type of federal involvement. Action was now at the level of the Department of Defense and of new agencies, the Atomic Energy Commission (AEC) and the National Aeronautics and Space Administration (NASA), along with the expanded medical and biological research apparatus represented by the National Institutes of Health. But the emphasis was still on particular, mission-oriented support of research and development.[36] Projects sponsored by the Department of Defense, the AEC, and NASA were large scale and tied research and development closely into what policy leaders and general opinion estimated to be critical substantive programs for national security. These characteristics effectively denied the possibility of bringing the national government's roles regarding science and technology under one broad direction.[37]

On a much smaller, but yet not insubstantial scale, various states institutionalized research and development efforts so that by the mid-twentieth century they had become integral parts of state government. These efforts were mostly in the life sciences; the bulk of the money went to agriculture, to health-education-welfare agencies, and to natural resource development and public works. Typically, the principal emphasis was on applied research, usually in aid of particular state regulatory or service functions, usually related to crops or industries salient in the states' economies. Two-thirds to 80 percent of the state money put into research and development came from state legislatures; the rest came from the federal government. The state programs shared one

35. On the Corps of Engineers: Dupree, 29, 37; Goodrich, 39, 42, 65, 285; Kirkland (1), 1:121, 131; McCamy, 48. On the later bureaus: Dupree, 376–378, 380–381; Price (2), 60, 61, 64, 66.
36. Baldwin, 573; Price (2), 57–59, 67–73, 125–129.
37. National Academy of Sciences, 111–114; Price (2), 257.

dominant characteristic with federal efforts: typically there was no steady effort at top policy-making levels to create a comprehensive state scientific program. Thus, too little attention was given to rational ordering of priorities or to the achievement of significant balance in the over-all state efforts.[38]

As the federal government's research and development expenditures mounted, particularly after 1940, there were suggestions that Congress create a cabinet-level department of science to coordinate these diverse, massive investments. But the size of the new commitments and their involvement with the missions and ambitions of major departments and agencies worked against the political practicability of coordination of such scope.[39] The nearest Congress came to institutionalizing a coordinator of federal support of scientific and technical research was in creating the National Science Foundation (NSF) in 1950. Impetus originally came from scientists who had taken leading roles in the government's rapid expansion into the field in World War II. These proponents envisaged an agency analogous to a great independent foundation under close and exclusive direction of the scientific community, empowered to sponsor research, to assign priorities, and to determine the scale of federal investment in research and development among other departments and agencies. In part this ambitious blueprint failed of realization because President Harry S. Truman opposed it as encroaching on proper prerogatives of his office. In part the original blueprint failed to be translated into action because it represented a politically unrealistic estimate of the power resident in the Department of Defense and in other agencies whose traditions already gave them the bulk of appropriated funds, bulwarked by working ties at high levels in the executive branch and in the congressional committee structure.[40]

Congress did not empower the foundation to operate its own

38. Cleaveland, 20, 21, 41, 57, 66, 76, 89, 146, 147–148, 150, 152, 153; Murphy (2), 28, 147.
39. McCamy, 103–104; Price (2), 257, 258.
40. Baldwin, 563, 572, 584; Price (1), 55, 57, 61; Schaffter, 7, 9, 11.

laboratories; though its statutory authority was to "initiate and support basic scientific research," it was designed to be a granting and not an operating agency. Subject to this limitation, its statutory authority allowed it to concern itself with a wide range of subject matter, in "the mathematical, physical, medical, biological, engineering and other sciences." The foundation relied on panels selected from outside government, working with its own staff, to evaluate applications; Congress, fortunately, only rarely undertook to pass on specific research proposals. Thus, this much of the original sponsors' intent was made good—that the foundation provide a means through which responsible scientific judgment could be brought to bear with substantial independence in determining some important areas of federal research support. In 1966 a House subcommittee criticized the foundation for taking too passive a role in waiting for talented outsiders to suggest programs to it. But the NSF's approach seemed best calculated to fit and protect a relatively independent status for the agency. Other agencies—notably the Department of Defense, AEC, NASA, and the National Institutes of Health—far overshadowed NSF in the size of funds at their disposal, and substantial parts of the funds administered by these more specialized offices went into basic research. NSF never enjoyed the practical capacity that some of its proponents had desired for it to assign priorities or allocate funds among these big competitors. But after twenty years it had established a distinctive role as sponsor of basic research, less tied than any other federal agency to particular mission-oriented work.[41]

General legal agency dealings with science and technology. Top legislative, executive, and judicial agencies existed to deal with the full range of matters that became of public-policy concern, among which the impact of scientific and technical developments was only a part. Among the most common problems of government are tensions created as jack-of-all-trades agencies try to cope with special interests and specialized subject matter. But

41. 64 Stat. 149 (1950); Baldwin, 561–563, 572, 573, 579–580, 582, 584, 589; Price (1), 55, 57, 58, 59–60, 61, and (3), 108; Schaffter, 209, 222, 223.

these problems took on particular difficulty where legislators, executive officers, or judges confronted scientific or technical matters that were peculiarly hard for the amateur to appraise. Thus there is in this domain special reason to ask how far general agencies institutionalized their dealings with scientific and technical issues.[42] The over-all verdict must be that, up to the 1970's, government had in this respect more often fumbled than commanded the direction of events. Until mid-twentieth century there is little basis on which to distinguish state and federal agency roles; from about 1940 on, however, the most striking efforts to give general policy-making processes some special focus on science and technology center in the national government.

Least impressive in the record was the use of legislative power to affect the good order of social relations by setting standards or rules of behavior—the "police power." Typically, legislation lagged far behind the sweep of events moved by scientific and technological advances, and most efforts to deal by statute with hazards to life, limb, and economic efficiency were ad hoc and fragmented, only slowly shaping into patterns of policy. We shall note this aspect of affairs later, when we appraise the extent of social inertia or drift derived from responses to scientific and technical change.[43] Legislative powers of investigation were used more effectively. Legislative committee hearings provided a principal channel through which specialized scientific and technical information could affect general attitudes, expectations, and demands. Thus legislative processes of inquiry and deliberation helped to move new knowledge about disease and physical hazards toward expression in expansion of the law regarding public health and safety affecting workers and consumers.[44] The legislature's prime impact on events was through the power of the purse. Both state

42. Cf. Patterson (2), 12–23; Price (1), 165–169, 197–203; Snow, 55–65, 67, 74–76, 81–83, and Appendix, 4–5, 35.

43. Cf. Freund, Chap. III; Horack, 41–49, 53–56; Hurst (3), 93–101; Kapp, passim, but especially 50–56, 69–76, 82–85.

44. E.g., Hacker and Zahler (2), 57–58; Radin (2), 134; Sydenstricker, 629–630.

legislatures and the Congress made their most positive contributions to the roles of science and technology by spending public money to advance knowledge and skills in using knowledge. Within modest limits, state investments built up and showed continuity. But the great bulk of spending was by Congress.[45]

Congressional provision for scientific and technical advance was limited through the nineteenth century, curbed by distrust of any projects that did not appear to have immediate utility. In the first half of the century Congress made some efforts to give committees direct management of federal involvements in science, but it dropped this approach after 1860. From 1860 to 1900 few congressmen were informed enough to deal with scientific questions. The development of agencies and programs supporting science now went on typically by indirection, and thus without central planning. Commitments to substantive programs were made through riders attached to appropriations acts, and by this method a few interested and relatively knowledgeable congressmen, coached by professionals outside government and inside particular bureaus, moved against a prevailing situation of inertia. With the legislation creating the Bureau of Standards in 1901 and an irrigation program in 1902 under the Newlands Act, Congress began to show more capacity to support science directly.[46] But massive development came after 1940, as scientific and technical effort figured largely in World War II. The great scale of investment required for dealing with nuclear energy, electronics devices, and space exploration, along with expanding commitments in public health, made the federal purse power boom large in the course of scientific and technological advance and fostered growth of pressures both from interested agencies and interested private groups, forcing Congress to deal more forthrightly with the field than it had been accustomed. But Congress's dealings still lacked a center of coordination. The nineteenth-century tradi-

45. Baldwin, 559, 564, 569, 585; Nelson et al., 152, 155; Price (1), 34, 35, 36, 39–40.
46. Dupree, 233, 235, 273, 291, 380.

tion of fragmented specialization of concern among particular committees and bureaus had its mid-twentieth-century counterpart in the practical power wielded by Congress's Joint Committee on Atomic Energy, for example. By the 1960's, Congress showed unease over its failure to maintain a comprehensive consideration of priorities and planning among the various objects of federal expenditure for science and technology. Thus in the 1960's the House Committee on Science and Astronautics moved cautiously beyond attention to the space program toward more general appraisal of the federal government's involvement in scientific and technological change. But such effort was limited by jurisdictional jealousies among House committees, and the Senate long showed even less effort at coordinated appraisal than did the House. Such stirrings as occurred, however, were not entirely without product. A 1972 statute created the Office of Technology Assessment, "within and responsible to the legislative branch," charged broadly to assess public policy in regard to scientific and technological developments and available as a service agency to all committees of Congress. It was a bolder step than any yet taken to arm the executive to deal better with such matters.[47]

The specialized character of scientific and technological advance made the area potentially more open to executive than to legislative leadership. But the executive branch made as uneven a record here as the legislative. His own interest in science led Jefferson to set early precedents for concentrating policy leadership in this area in the executive; as secretary of state he drew an ill-advised report on weights and measures; as President he ex-

47. On the Joint Committee on Atomic Energy: Joseph P. Harris, 211–212, 236–237; Newman and Miller, 281; Price (2), 224–225, 226. On the House Committee on Science and Astronautics, compared with Senate action: N.Y. Times, Jan. 15, 1962, 10:3, id., March 23, 1962, 1:5, id., Aug. 31, 1964, 27:1. On the lack of policy coordination: Baldwin, 559, 560, 563, 572; Price (2), 216, 232–237, 277. On the Office of Technology Assessment: 86 Stat. 797 (1972); Beckler, 129; cf. Wiesner, 66, 67, 84. But cf. Price (2), 263, 264. See also N.Y. Times, June 9, 1975, 34:1.

erted himself more constructively to maneuver the Lewis and Clark expedition into being. But John Quincy Adams was the only other President who showed personal interest in public policy to promote scientific advance, and the only result of his effort was to demonstrate that it was too far ahead of the narrowly practical and state-centered concerns of the Congress of his time. From about the mid-nineteenth century on, the trend in the federal government—with analogous, though limited developments in some states—was to leave such attention as was given to science and technology to lower executive levels, tying effort to the particular missions of specialized bureaus or agencies. There was no top executive coordination of such efforts; each bureau fended for itself with the legislative branch, and outcomes depended primarily on the skill or political favor held by particular bureau chiefs. A short-lived exception, which served only to highlight the general rule, was the interest Theodore Roosevelt took in the conservation policies urged on him by Gifford Pinchot.[48] The prevailing attitude, as far as the matter came into awareness at all, seemed to be that declared in 1886 by the Allison Commission, a joint congressional committee that looked at the scientific work of various federal bureaus and, finding it good, rejected the idea of an over-all government department of science; the commission felt that "no such duplication of work or necessary connections of these bureaus with each other . . . makes such an establishment essential to their efficiency."[49]

More than any broader consideration of the problem, the exigencies of hot and cold war brought the most forthright efforts to create top executive provision for making policy on the federal government's involvements in scientific and technological affairs. During World War I the National Research Council was created,

48. In general: Dupree, 135, 137–138, 380–381; Perry, 56–60. On Theodore Roosevelt: Dupree, 247, 248, 251.

49. Dupree, 215, 229 (Allison Commission). On the rejection of a national department of science: Dupree, 293, 296; Price (2), 257, 258. Cf. N.Y. Times, June 19, 1961, 27:1 (continued disfavor for idea).

centralizing to an unprecedented extent the mobilization of information and personnel for war use. But this body lacked full-time administrative authority or funds, so its programs inevitably were controlled by the military services.[50] A handful of top scientists got the ear of President Roosevelt in 1940 and established for World War II a National Defense Research Committee, then in 1941 created a more powerful central science programming agency in the Office of Scientific Research and Development, which, because its director had immediate access to the President, wielded considerable policy-shaping capability.[51]

But this wartime effort left no clear legacy for peacetime coordination. Scientists and their allies in Congress sought to fill the gap by proposing creation of a top-level government research foundation whose director and successor board members would be selected by a board of directors made up of scientists and which would supervise allocation of research resources among government agencies and projects. President Truman vetoed a bill to this effect because he found it to invade presidential prerogative. In 1950, Congress created the National Science Foundation, with a director and a board named by the President; the measure conciliated the scientists by authorizing the foundation to make its grants with the advice of science panels selected by it. But Congress was unwilling to commit major spending on research and development to the foundation; principal funds continued to flow directly to more specialized operating agencies, and the foundation settled into a limited, though important, role as particular sponsor of funds for basic research unconnected to departmental or agency missions.[52]

In 1951 the Korean War brought again to the fore the President's need of counsel in coordinating federal research and de-

50. Dupree, 323, 324, 370–372.

51. Baldwin, 579; Penick et al., 10, 11; Price (1), 44, 45, 55, 57–58, 59–60, 61, and (3), 108.

52. Baldwin, 561, 572–574, 579, 580, 584; Price (3), 108; Schaffter, 7, 9, 11, 16.

velopment commitments; the result was creation of a Science Advisory Committee attached to the Office of Defense Mobilization.[53] In 1957 cold war urgency—the challenge of the Russians' first space satellite—pushed matters a step further; President Eisenhower named a special assistant to the President for science and technology and reconstituted the Science Advisory Committee as the President's Science Advisory Committee, both within the inner circle of White House advisers.[54] In 1959 the President created a Federal Council for Science and Technology, chaired by the special assistant, and including representatives of the principal federal agencies spending research and development funds; the council was designed to improve alignment of policy at operating levels.[55]

But the White House continued to enlarge its staff, and in this larger apparatus the scientific advisers found themselves shouldered aside, the more so because scientific scruples and scientists' concern with advancing knowledge did not always square with political and operational immediacies that tended to pre-empt White House attention. In 1962 by executive order having statutory authority, President Kennedy established an Office of Science and Technology (OST), chaired by the special assistant. Though the executive order tended more to institutionalize the provision of scientific and technical advice to the President, in creating a separate scientific panel it in effect put the scientists outside the inner White House circle.[56] From this point on, both the OST and the President's Science Advisory Committee rendered good service, but did not enjoy a commanding position

53. Beckler, 117; Schaffter, 194.

54. Beckler, 118, 119; Daddario, 138; Price (2), 243, and (3), 108; Wiesner, 78. Cf. N.Y. Times, Dec. 17, 1962, 1:2.

55. Baldwin, 583; Daddario, 138; Price (2), 243; Schaffter, 194; Wiesner, 80. Cf. N.Y. Times, Jan. 15, 1962, 10:3, id., Feb. 16, 1975, Sec. 1, 58:4.

56. Baldwin, 583, 584; Beckler, 115, 116, 120, 121, 122, 125, 127, 128, 131; Daddario, 135, 138; Price (2), 242, 243; Wiesner, 78, 79. Cf. N.Y. Times, Nov. 27, 1960, Sec. 1, 50:3, id., June 19, 1961, 27:1, id., March 28, 1962, 15:3.

over policy concerning science and technology, and, indeed, had
to share the field with a proliferation of other executive offices
or bodies, such as a Council on Environmental Quality, a Federal
Energy Office, and a National Aeronautics and Space Council.[57]
In 1973, President Nixon abruptly ended the post of science
adviser in the White House, abolished the Office of Science and
Technology, and accepted the pro forma resignations of the
President's Science Advisory Committee (PSAC), designating
the director of the National Science Foundation to take over the
civilian functions of the OST while its security functions went
to the National Security Council. The change, of course, was
disappointing for the development of a tradition of White House
coordination of policy affecting science and technology, but it
was not catastrophic, since for some time the special assistant,
the OST, and the PSAC had been of decreasing influence. Nor
was it the last word. Experience had shown that the National
Science Foundation was not well situated for its director to per-
form the strong coordinating role that the White House needed
on policy touching science and technology. In 1976, Congress reconstituted the Office of Science and Technology, under a director
with a small staff.[58]

The records of both Congress and the White House in dealing
with policy concerning science and technology show that this
area was specially difficult to bring under comprehensive survey
and judgment. Broader, more long-range treatment was needed.
Congress and the presidency were agencies specially adapted to
generalizing public policy, but because they were all-purpose
agencies, empowered to respond to the greatest sweep of community problems, their openness to such general roles made them
the targets of a bewildering volume and variety of pressures for
action. In this context, there was always a premium on disposing

57. Beckler, 123.
58. Beckler, 115, 127, 128, 129; Daddario, 138; N.Y. Times, Nov. 6, 1974,
24:1, id., June 11, 1975, 14:4, id., May 12, 1976, 48:6; Pub. Law 94–282,
May 11, 1976.

of the most immediately felt demands and on seeking the most immediately workable adjustments. The most profound problems posed by scientific and technological developments typically took a long time to show their implications and often called for subordinating to highly generalized values, wants, or needs what some particular parts of the society felt with sharp urgency. Thus there was a built-in inertia or drift to public policy on the social impacts of science and technology, which nearly two hundred years of experience with legislative and executive processes offered little to overcome.

There remained the judicial branch. But with their constitutional and traditional limitations to dealing with particular cases and controversies, courts were unlikely instruments for sweeping policy making in this field.[59] Moreover, the national and state governments affected scientific and technological change more and more through public spending; this was a domain peculiarly legislative, subject to little judicial control. From the late nineteenth century, state courts asserted authority to hold unconstitutional spending that could not reasonably be deemed to serve a public purpose. But the relatively modest state spending was typically for research and development tied to clearly established public purposes, auxiliary to state regulation or promotion in the fields of public health and promotion of economic productivity; and thus the public-purpose doctrine never significantly affected state policy in support of scientific or technological advance.[60] Since the United States Supreme Court would not recognize standing in a federal taxpayer to challenge federal spending under the general powers of Congress, the federal courts had no role to play in limiting or channeling federal expenditure in this or other areas of policy.[61] Judges made a great body of adjust-

59. Hurst (1), 180–183, 185.
60. Mills, 40, 282, 304.
61. Massachusetts v. Mellon, and Frothingham v. Mellon, 262 U.S. 447 (1923); cf. United States v. Butler, 297 U.S. 1, 58 (1936); Flast v. Cohen, 393 U.S. 83, 102 (1968).

ments to scientific and technological change in particular decisions at common law or under statute. But by its nature, this style of judicial activity did not involve master strokes of policy programming.

General Policy Concerning Social Impacts of Science and Technology

Public-policy dealings with science and technology in the United States fall into two periods; the break comes about the 1890's. Two features distinguish the periods. In the first, technology was far more prominent than science in setting the directions and pace of social change. After the 1890's the influential technology was often science-based and hence presented more intricate and subtle problems for public policy. In the years before the 1890's prevailing policy put law at the service of whatever expanded opportunities technology could create for profit seeking in markets of widening scope. From the 1890's on, public policy embodied questioning whether market-channeled technology was calculated to serve acceptable life values. Though in the years after the 1890's there was continued legal favor for and protection of nationwide markets, there also was a tendency to match broader markets with a growing amount of regulation by the national government.

Before 1890: The market sets the pace. Private market dealing functioned through the law of contract and property. Through most of the nineteenth century prevailing opinion accepted that it was in the general interest to let technological changes have the fullest play that contract and property law could give, to promote the greatest amount and diversity of private profit-seeking transactions. People valued diversity, but even more they prized volume in business; because technological change fostered an increasing volume of dealing, it was taken as a self-evident good.[62]

---

62. Boorstin (2), 411; Nelson et al., 88; Tribe, 14.

Examples could be multiplied as many times as the increase of business. Consider the law defining protectable titles. Men improved their techniques for getting logs out of the woods and moving them through sawmills into lumber; law responded by recognizing legally protected title in standing timber and in timber cruisers' field notes, as well as by creating statutory liens to protect claims of loggers and suppliers.[63] Barbed wire was invented and developed for mass production, and in consequence effective fee–simple titles were established on land that had been open range.[64] Development of waterpower and mining technology created profitable opportunities which the law recognized in water and mineral rights.[65] As new technologies fostered new areas and types of trade. businessmen devised new contract devices to serve expanding transactions. The sale of farm machinery on credit produced wider use of forms of chattel security. Manufacturers who sold durable goods through extended networks of dealers relied on the law of agency and turned to lawyers for new security devices such as trust receipts on stocks of goods entrusted to intermediaries.[66]

To the expansive potentials of contract and property law, we should add the flexibility that the law of business corporations proved able to supply in support of the industrial and commercial uses of new technology. Technology created business opportunities calling for promoters to muster and discipline capital on a scale that was impractical or at least cumbersome to accomplish by individual or partnership enterprise. The corporate device was not indispensable; Andrew Carnegie built and ran a massive steel works through a limited partnership.[67] But the corporation offered an instrument of such utility as to attract more and more

63. Hurst (4), 298–300, 391–402.
64. Burlingame (1), 172–178; Fred Cottrell, 203.
65. Friedman (3), 319; Hurst (4), 146, 154; Lake, 62, 72–74; cf. N.Y. Times, Jan. 15, 1967, Sec. 1, 64:3.
66. Benedict, 82–83; Boorstin (2), 422, 429–433, 434–442; Burlingame (4), 70, 71, 131; Friedman (3), 468–469, 474. Cf. Barger, passim.
67. Hacker (2), 357, 360, 387; Wall, 322, 360, 659–672, 718.

promoters. Relaxing initial jealousy and distrust of the corporate form, legislatures first granted special charters by the hundreds, then standardized the form in general incorporation laws. The underlying dynamics of this process lay largely in attractions created by technological developments; save for banking and insurance, the bulk of nineteenth-century corporation charters were for enterprises marked by sizable physical plant and the use of machinery.[68]

Policy makers did not feel that it was inconsistent with letting market processes have their head in applying technology to use law promotionally in aid of enterprisers' initiative. The Constitution sanctioned the grant of patents as a special form of property in aid of development of technical or scientific innovations. How often patent law was a prime stimulus to technological change is doubtful; patents often bred delaying, costly conflicts of claims, and a patent claim seems more often to have been a secondary weapon of business combat than a first mover of enterprise. Yet the principle remained that favor for market freedom in applying technology was not deemed to bar affirmative use of law in aid of the market.[69] Relaxation of early jealousy of grants of incorporation in favor of ready grant of the corporate franchise for technologically based enterprise carried the same policy implication.[70] The most forthright expression of the governing philosophy was in Hamilton's *Report on Manufactures,* urging bounties and a protective tariff to encourage machine industry. Hamilton wished to promote the maximum energy of private economic initiative, and he saw in the use of machinery the highest promise of multiplying the impact of such initiative. But he did not idealize the private market, which he found liable to timidity or inertia in the face of risks of new ventures; and he favored an energetic

68. Evans, 50, 66–69; Hurst (5), 56–57, 69–74; Kuehnl, 144–145.
69. U.S. Const., I, 8 (8); Boorstin (2), 58–61, 95; Burlingame (1), 175; Ferguson, 24; Hunter, 46; Jewkes et al., 3, 5, 106, 251, 253; Nelson et al., 161, 162; Price (2), 33; Schmookler, 146, 150, 156, 157; Struik, 259.
70. Hurst (5), 56–57, 69–74.

role for government in creating such devices as subsidies or tariffs to arm private risk takers against fear of foreign competition. Of critical importance to Hamilton's position, though, was promotion of the use of machine-based production for its promise of prodigious increases in over-all productivity. Hamilton would apply public power, in other words, only at points where its application promised high multiplier returns, and he saw machinery as fulfilling this key requirement. Congress did not adopt a substantial protective tariff for years after Hamilton's recommendation, and the Hamiltonian faith in the tariff was belied as it became an instrument of sectional, local, and industrial interest-group rivalries. But these wrangles never brought into dispute Hamilton's view that the tariff would serve public interest insofar as it fostered the use of machinery.[71]

Not the least tokens of society's acceptance of promotional use of law to advance science and technology were measures to help institutionalize the advancement of knowledge. As we have seen, the states early were generous in chartering philanthropic corporations to supply libraries, to operate academies, or—as in the case of the American Philosophical Society—to foster organized inquiry into scientific and technical matters. The federal government brought direct public action into play by organizing and financing exploration and by creating such service agencies as the coastal survey.[72]

Implicit in the readiness to let technological change express itself with the aid of contract and property law, and in law's promotional supports for increasing and using scientific and technical knowledge, was a policy no less real or weighty even though it found only glancing expression. This was, in effect, a presumption that adding to and using scientific and technical knowledge would serve the public good and hence should move ahead without check, let alone veto, from public policy. In law this

71. Alexander Hamilton, 4:70, 78, 83, 87, 89, 95–99. Cf. Hacker (1), 190, 307–309, and (2), 4, 7, 9, 27, 29–30, 33–37; Schattschneider, passim.
72. Notes 17–20, above.

attitude was consistent with popular acceptance of science and technology and their fruits. In scattered episodes, displaced workmen used violence against new machinery. But these were odd departures; the law never had to deal with substantial Luddite resistance to technological change.[73] Nor did nineteenth-century policy restrict the subject matter, timing, or pace of the uses of technology, nor the extent of natural resources (and only to a small degree the extent of human resources) consumed in applying technological capacities. The nineteenth-century willingness to give technology its head came close to a pure policy of laissez-faire—qualified by the acceptance of promotional uses of law to advance applications of scientific and technical knowledge.[74] This laissez-faire approach was a mixed product of calculation and drift. In part it represented unthinking acceptance of courses of behavior that (especially because they so largely involved skills gained on the job) fit this pragmatic, improvising culture so smoothly as to seem just "common sense." Thus, two generations of lumbermen wastefully exploited the Lake States forest under the spur of a developing technology, resting on naive faith that the forest offered in fact what it early appeared to offer, an "inexhaustible" resource; no spokesman appeared for the view that public policy should hold lumbermen to practices that would allow indefinite, sustained-yield production.[75] But there was deliberation in this approach, too. On the whole the law laid down deliberate policy that society should welcome maximum exploitation of technological competence. Indicative was the nineteenth-century development of the law of negligence. Law favored the active will, so that normally one who complained of hurt from another's actions carried the burden of persuading the court that the defendant's use of his land or machinery could

73. Barber, 210, 215; Burlingame (4), 37; Etzioni and Nunn, 195; Meier, 88, 89, 90; Morison (2), 10, 83, 89, 94, 121, 209, 210.
74. Hurst (4), 42, 43, 106, 113, 118, 206–207, 410, 442, 461; Nye, 259–262, 268–274, 276–282; Ogburn and Tibbetts, 127–130, 163–166.
75. Hurst (4), 67, 98, 107, 113, 119–120, 410, 461.

be fairly deemed against good order and subject to redress. Such was the ordinary standard applicable in the law of personal injury and of nuisance.[76] An analogous approach was taken in the ruling and the dicta of the Charles River Bridge case: the court would not imply in a toll-bridge franchise a statutory ban on the competition of a new bridge, and even less would it imply in canal or turnpike charters a ban on the competition of the new railroad, though the consequence might be the economic obsolescence of the older facility and the practical destruction of the capital investment it represented.[77] Again, calculated favor for free advance of scientific and technical knowledge showed in the doctrines that limited patent and trade secret rights, barring private preemption of use of laws of nature or of technical skills that others had gained independently.[78] The same underlying attitude was manifest when the law presumed the legality of duly formed contracts; presumably the law would enforce any new contractual arrangement for exploiting technological innovations (such as chattel security devices in aid of sales of the new farm machinery); the burden of persuasion was on one who claimed that the arrangement ran so counter to good social order that it should be denied enforcement.[79]

One substantial qualification on this nineteenth-century open-door policy on technological change was the slow development of a rudimentary law of public utilities. New technology made possible new forms of business that created relations of substantial dependence of those served on those who did the serving. At first these were relatively simple, local facilities—water supply, turnpikes, gristmills. But then came transport facilities of broader reach, marked especially in the case of the railroads by unprecedented concentrations of capital and complexity of organization.

76. Hurst (2), 19–20; Friedman (3), 262–264, 410; Levy, 319.
77. Charles River Bridge v. Warren Bridge, 11 Pet. 420 (U.S. 1837); Kutler, 93, 99, 160–164.
78. See notes 5, 6, above.
79. Corbin, 6A:4–6, 20–21; Friedman (1), 16, 111; Hurst (2), 12, 20.

These new enterprises typically flourished with the promotional help of law, not only in grants of incorporation, but also in grants of special privileges such as rights of way, use of the power of eminent domain, and the right to charge tolls. Thus assisted by public authority, the new enterprises tended to set the whole frame of dealings in small or large economic areas. From the outset the law took some account of the potentials for abusive power resident in these new situations; special-privilege franchises were qualified as to duration and imposed requirements that rates be reasonable and services be available fairly to all proper customers. Inadequate as the early provisions were, they foreshadowed the rise of elaborate public-utility regulation in the twentieth century, all at basis responsive to relations of superiority and dependence created by application of more sophisticated technology.[80]

Before 1890: Federal power matches the reach of technology. Most major themes in United States legal history have a federal component, for the potential of a continental nation persistently challenged the will and imagination of the people. Woven into the relations of public policy, market, and science and technology was the shaping of national law to help realize the possibilities of a national free-trade area and a national community opened up by technologies of transport and communications; looming up at the end of the century were the further promises and hazards of mass-production industries to exploit the business and cultural possibilities that national transport and communications networks sustained.[81]

When the framers of the federal Constitution gave Congress power to regulate commerce with foreign nations and among the several states, they were more concerned with political dangers attending commercial rivalry and retaliation among the states as to existing conventional trade than with the implications for ac-

---

80. Burlingame (1), 203–204; John Maurice Clark (1), 57–58, 119, 137, 183, 198–200, 285–288, 298–306; Hale, 401–402; Hurst (2), 63–65, 88–90.
81. Wabash, St. Louis & Pacific Ry. v. Illinois, 118 U.S. 557 (1886); Pensacola Telegraph Co. v. Western Union Telegraph Co., 96 U.S. 1 (1877).

commodating law to an expanding technology. But, as in so many other respects, the wisdom in their adoption of a broad constitutional standard served the public interest in ways they could not specifically foresee. Their expansive concept legitimated the national government's subsequent responses both to changing technology and to changing patterns of state policy threatening the promise of national markets. For the first, the sweep of the commerce clause warranted Congress and the Supreme Court in validating national regulation of successive new means of transport and communication, from sailing vessel to steamboat to railroad and—to anticipate the new century—to motor carrier, airplane, radio, and television.[82] In the second place, the commerce clause armed the national government with full capacity to strike down parochial threats to the broader currents of trade that new technologies could set in motion. The Court early seized the creative initiative. When New York granted a monopoly for steamboat operation on interstate navigable waters, Mr. Chief Justice Marshall in *Gibbons* v. *Ogden* (1824) led a unanimous Court in finding that the New York grant must fall because it conflicted with rights of free passage deemed granted under the federal coasting license statute.[83] Congress set the first legislative precedent for national rules affecting transport technology about mid-century with statutes providing for steamboat boiler standards and inspection.[84] In 1866, Congress picked up the lead suggested by the Court in 1824 in its treatment of the act licensing coastal vessels and declared free national rights of way for the new telegraph; in 1878 the Court enforced Congress's grant by invoking it to invalidate Florida's effort to give a statutory

82. Pensacola Telegraph Co. v. Western Union Telegraph Co., 96 U.S. 1 (1877); McCarroll v. Dixie Greyhound Lines, Inc., 309 U.S. 176 (1940); Evansville-Vanderburgh Airport Authority District v. Delta Airlines, Inc., 405 U.S. 707 (1972). Cf. Beveridge, 4:406–409, 411–412, 416, 426.

83. Gibbons v. Ogden, 9 Wheat. 1 (U.S. 1824); Hunter, 26, 27, 31, 32, 33, 44; Beveridge, 4:401, 402, 404, 405–406, 414–415; Warren, 1:598, 599, 612–616.

84. Burke, 100, 101, 107, 109, 112, 117–119.

monopoly of all telegraph business in that state to Florida corporations.[85] In 1886 the Court ruled that the spread of interstate
rail networks was incompatible with state regulation of the in-
state portion of interstate rail traffic, and in 1887, Congress responded with the Interstate Commerce Act, laying the foundation
for national regulation of interstate rail transport.[86]

Analogous to developments under the commerce clause was the
Court's extension of the Constitution's grant to federal courts of
jurdisdiction in admiralty. When the Court first considered the
matter in 1825, it read the framers' intent to be to incorporate
what the Court understood as the traditional English definition,
limiting admiralty jurisdiction to tidewater. By 1851 the intensive
use of the steamboat had dramatically increased carriage on the
inland, nontidal waters of the United States, especially since
steam power made it possible to carry substantial loads upstream.
Believing that the underlying policy of the grant of admiralty
jurisdiction was to make a uniform system of courts available to
all water traffic of national importance, the Court recognized the
change brought by expanded use of steam navigation and ruled
that the admiralty jurisdiction extended over all navigable waters
of the country. As with the developments under the commerce
clause, here too technological change provided the impetus for
fresh policy making, but the new policy was no mere reflexive
response; it embodied the idea that national lawmaking should
help to realize the possibilities for a national market and community offered by science and technology.[87]

The Constitution also gave Congress power to tax and spend to
provide for the general welfare of the United States. At the outset

---

85. 14 Stat. 221 (1866); Pensacola Telegraph Co. v. Western Union
Telegraph Co., 96 U.S. 1 (1877); cf. Richmond v. Southern Bell Telephone
& Telegraph Co., 174 U.S. 761 (1899); McCloskey, 124.

86. Wabash, St. Louis & Pacific Ry. v. Illinois, 118 U.S. 557 (1886);
McCloskey, 125, 126; Warren, 2:633.

87. The Propeller Genesee Chief v. Fitzhugh, 12 How. 443 (U.S. 1851),
overruling The Thomas Jefferson, 10 Wheat. 428 (U.S. 1825); Friedman
(3), 229; Hurst (3), 34–35, 42, 56, 74–75; Warren, 2:239–240.

of the national government there was basic dispute whether this authority was merely auxiliary to other powers granted to Congress (a position urged by Madison) or an independent authority in Congress to spend whenever it reasonably could decide that the object of the spending would advance the well-being of the people of the country (the position taken by Hamilton). Federal spending to increase scientific and technical knowledge—as in Jefferson's ingenious support of the Lewis and Clark expedition and in the support of the coastal survey—often could be considered aid to another specific power, such as that of providing for national defense or regulating interstate commerce. However, the persistence of federal spending for various research and development activities tended to establish legislative and executive precedent that it was in the national interest to promote the advance of knowledge, without showing a tie to some immediate, operational mission. Thus impulses generated by scientific and technical effort helped add content to another head of federal power.[88]

After 1890: Matter-of-fact idealism. A different temper of policy concerning social changes bred by science and technology showed itself from about the turn of the century. The nineteenth-century record came to seem relatively simple compared with the many-phased demands made on law by a growing diversity of interests in the twentieth century.

Long-term experience with scientific and technological developments had two effects on general opinion that tended to generate fresh demands for legal action. First, people gained increasing confidence in their ability to grasp cause-effect relationships and to turn this knowledge to account in manipulating experience. Matters that once had appeared to present simplistic moral judgments (of "good" or "bad"), or to turn on simplistic religious faith (obedience to "the will of God"), or to work according to

88. See United States v. Butler, 297 U.S. 1, 58 (1936). Cf. Dupree, 14, 15, 26, 30, 32, 40–42, 48–49, 60; Penick et al., 2–5; Price (1), 7, 14, 15, 20.

unanalyzed common sense (the "laws" of supply and demand) now appeared to present matter-of-fact issues of choice of workable means in relation to chosen ends. What counted was learning that we could do something about given situations and finding efficient ways to use ordered knowledge to improve things. This attitude was made manifest in the change of the law dealing with industrial accidents. At common law an employer's duty to pay his employee for injury suffered on the job depended on appraisals of the moral quality of will involved; the employer was liable if he negligently failed to provide a safe place to work, but the employee might not recover if he had assumed the risk, or if he were guilty of contributory negligence, or if he were injured by the negligence of a fellow servant. The workmen's compensation acts swept away this array of concepts in favor of liability based on a finding that the injury in fact arose out of the employment. The new doctrine recognized that accidents were actuarially predictable costs of production that insurance could cover. The outcome was to substitute matter-of-fact engineering of a social relation for moralistic judgments on it.[89]

That public policy tended to express more matter-of-fact judgments on social arrangements did not mean a lack of moral impetus back of policy. To the contrary, attitudes developed from more experience with the fruits of science and technology represented often a new moral dynamic for lawmaking. Lord Bryce shrewdly sensed a new temper in public policy when he observed toward the end of the nineteenth century that the more people learned how to manipulate affairs, the more they felt the sight of preventable evil to be a reproach.[90] Consider the moral underpinnings of the matter-of-fact workmen's compensation scheme

89. On workmen's compensation: Friedman (3), 422–425, 587–588. Cf. Barber, 62, 64; Fred Cottrell, 201; Hays, 122–127, 134–137, 265; Huxley, 8; Price (2), 271, 274, 275, and (3), 105, 107; Whitehead, 3. On the shift from morality to empirical analysis: Charles E. Rosenberg, 4, 5, 121, 128, 213. On the stress on environment more than on morality: McKelvey, 99, 112; Charles E. Rosenberg, 215–216, 229, 230.

90. Bryce, 2:591.

and the concurrent adoption of factory safety legislation. From more objective perceptions of cause-effect relationships grew an enlarged sense of public interest, as people began to see that conduct affected broader ranges of human concerns than they formerly had identified. Safety precautions could cut on-the-job accidents; consumers of goods and services should pay the fair cost of such precautions, else the consumers were subsidized by the workers, who must shoulder built-in risks of production. Moreover, loss from on-the-job accidents fell not only on the injured worker, but on the community which must suffer loss in its work force and somehow pay the costs of rehabilitating the injured individual and caring for his dependents; insurance could help spread these costs over those who benefited from the production of which the accident was an incident. Thus, sharper perception of cause-effect relations, developed out of increasing science-and-technology-based manipulation of affairs, generated political pressures for more rational and humane arrangements, given form, however inadequately, in factory safety laws and workmen's compensation.[91]

After 1890: Law and the acquisition of knowledge. In the nineteenth century scientific and technical advance were taken for granted as a natural outpouring of human creativity. The twentieth century showed more calculation in providing for additions to knowledge. As we have seen, it was mainly in the twentieth century that public and private decision makers took the boldest measures to institutionalize research and development. Public policy long had favored commitments of assets for philanthropic purposes; within this context twentieth-century donors obtained legal sanction for creating great private research foundations. Industrial laboratories were originally the creation simply of private entrepreneurial initiative, but they developed further with the aid of favoring provisions of corporation income tax

91. Commons, 141–143, 156–159; Friedman (3), 422–425, 587–588. Cf. Barber, 66; Berle, 80, 86, 99, 128, 158; Compton, 17; Lampard, 4; Morison (3), 167–169; Price (2), 194–196; Struik, 229–236; Tribe, 7, 8, 10, 14; Whitehead, 114.

laws. The states and the federal government, and especially after 1940 the federal government, by the scale and continuity of their spending on research and development affirmed acceptance of a strong positive role in advancing knowledge, most pointedly when in 1950, Congress created the National Science Foundation.[92]

Entwined with the growing institutionalization of research and development were two strands of policy—competing demands of basic and applied research and tensions between demands for social control over disseminating or applying knowledge and assertions that spreading and using knowledge were activities that should enjoy the law's protection as civil liberties.

Specialists recognized that advance of knowledge depended on research that probed the farthest reaches of cause and effect within scholars' capabilities. But in this often narrowly pragmatic culture there was insistent common demand that to justify spending assets—especially public assets—we should see close-to-hand operational results. Because this demand pressed so hard on elected officials, the law's validation of private research foundations was far more important for the advance of science than was suggested by comparing the rather limited resources of such foundations with the more massive spending done by public agencies. This gave particular poignancy to issues raised in the 1960's when Congress, properly seeking to curb abuse of foundations for private profit, imposed taxes and regulations that threatened to trench upon foundations' capacity to allocate assets for true scientific effort.[93] In the great increase of federal research and development spending of the mid-twentieth century, scientists and some public policy makers repeatedly warned that basic was losing in competition with applied research, to the great hazard of long-term growth of knowledge. Here lay the special meaning of the creation of the National Science Foundation and the continuing efforts to obtain for it larger appropriations, against the competition of particular-mission-focused efforts of the Depart-

92. See notes 22–28, 35–41, and accompanying text, above.

93. Baldwin, 563, 574; Penick et al., 133–134; Price (1), 37, 38, and (3), 104; Weaver, 194–197; Wiesner, 73–74; Wolfman, 29, 30, 38.

ment of Defense, the agencies concerned with nuclear energy and space, and the National Institutes of Health. In the late twentieth century the course of this competition for funds between basic and applied research provided a major test of the capacity of legal processes to care for a long view of public interest.[94]

In the nineteenth century people took for granted broad freedom to apply technology, while science remained too remote from everyday life to lead policy makers to raise issues of the scientist's freedom to inquire. There was so little thought, let alone conflict, over these matters, however, that nineteenth-century freedom was a precedent of dubious strength when issues of freedom of research and development became acute in the twentieth century.[95] The twentieth-century strains on the civil liberty of science first arose from tensions with religious belief. Problems concerned the dissemination or use rather than the acquisition of scientific knowledge. Early in the century fundamentalist Protestant sects objected to teaching Charles Darwin's theory of evolution, and a few states legislated against such instruction. Values of civil liberties finally won a substantial victory as the Supreme Court ruled that a state violated First Amendment protection of free speech, embodied in Fourteenth Amendment due process of law, when it penalized disseminating scientific theory in order to protect religious sensibilities.[96] More profound was another tension be-

94. For general criticism of priority given applied science: N.Y. Times, July 8, 1960, 1:2, 7:3 (Committee on Science and Promotion of Human Welfare, Am. Ass'n for Adv. of Sci.); id., Oct. 16, 1963, 24:1 (president, National Academy of Sciences); id., Dec. 29, 1963, Sec. 1, 22:1 (Am. Ass'n for Adv. of Sci.); id., Jan. 30, 1966, Sec. 1, 74:5 (annual report, director, National Science Foundation); id., Feb. 16, 1975, Sec. 1, 58:4 (report, Federal Council for Science and Technology). Cf. Baldwin, 571, 572, 573, 574, 576, 579, 582, 587; Daddario, 136, 140; Dupree, 373, 374, 375, 377; McCamy, 50, 65, 68, 70, 73, 77; Nelson et al., 154, 155, 167; Perry, 189–197; Price (1), 37, 60, 61, 62, and (3), 99, 100, 103; Wiesner, 70. On the problem in industry: Jewkes et al., 147; N.Y. Times, Dec. 10, 1961, Sec. 1, 24:1.

95. Price (2), 90–94.

96. Epperson v. Arkansas, 393 U.S. 97 (1968); cf. Scopes v. State, 154 Tenn. 105, 289 S. W. 363 (1927). See Lederberg, 595.

tween research and development and religious belief that began
to be expressed from about the 1960's on. Science began to probe
with increasing success into the genetic bases of life, and possibilities loomed of creating life in the laboratory, or of doing
genetic engineering on human beings. Scientists also began to use
the human fetus as a research subject. As the century moved into
its last quarter, it appeared that public policy would be brought
to grapple with possible legal limits on the extent to which research and use of its products might deal with shaping human life.
Moreover, as psychological research progressed, with new techniques of studying human attitudes and emotions, issues arose as
to whether the law should forbid the student or the technician to
invade certain domains of human privacy.[97]

Political values also gave rise to secular tensions between research and development and social controls. After 1940 massive
federal spending for research and development linked to national
defense led government to impose classified, secret status on important areas of inquiry and use of data. Leading research universities finally had to confront this problem, and after a period
of drift moved toward the decision that it was inconsistent with
their social mission to do classified research in their laboratories;
government must get its classified research by contract with such
nonacademic enterprises as the Rand Corporation, or must do it
itself. This resolution by no means settled all problems. Apart
from limits put on nonacademic contract research, individual researchers' personal and professional standing was seriously implicated in determinations of eligibility to deal with classified

97. On genetics: Barber, 72, 73, 210, 215; Tribe, 598; N.Y. Times, Nov.
29, 1959, Sec. IV, 11:7; id., Feb. 2, 1962, 1:5; id., March 30, 1962, 22:1;
id., July 17, 1965, 6:5. On use of animals and persons in scientific research:
Lewis, 53–54, 56, 59–61, 63–64; N.Y. Times, March 15, 1975, 20:2. On
privacy: Griswold v. Connecticut, 381 U.S. 479 (1965); Eisenstadt v. Baird,
405 U.S. 438 (1972); Cavers, 9; Ruebhausen and Brim, 87, 91, 92; N.Y.
Times, Jan. 1, 1962, 33:2; id., Oct. 4, 1964, Sec. 1, 120:3; id., May 15, 1966,
23:5; id., July 28, 1966, 24:1; id., July 27, 1966, 33:5.

materials, and the general advance of knowledge could be hampered by the existence of islands of classified data. Classification was open to abuse to serve political ends or bureaucratic vested interest, and in the 1970's it is an open question whether effective external checks against abuse can be devised. But in a cold war atmosphere, clearly in the late twentieth century research and development will continue to be limited in the name of national security in ways that have no nineteenth-century precedent.[98]

Another area of conflict over free use of science and technology arose in the twentieth century primarily from problems of maintaining domestic security. Lie detectors and electronic surveillance equipment armed national and local police with new means of gathering evidence for detecting and prosecuting crime. As far as new techniques presented simple issues of credibility, courts were reasonably equipped by experience to deal with them; thus judicial skepticism over the extent of subjective judgment entering into reading lie-detection data tended to confine use of that technique to private security measures, apart from public prosecutions. Surveillance techniques implicated both courts and legislators because they created issues under the Fourth Amendment (limiting search and seizure without warrant) as well as presenting matters for legislative balancing of interests between public security and the privacy of individuals. The tendency of the Supreme Court's reading of the Constitution, and Congress's sense of a balance of public interests, was to refuse full discretion to the executive to use the new surveillance possibilities that technology provided, but rather to insist that surveillance be subject to check by the courts, which might impose some barriers to government's probing.[99]

98. Barber, 91, 180; Compton, 25, 27, 31; Conant, 13–16, 30; Jewkes et al., 77; Gellhorn (1), Chaps. II, III, V; Grodzins, 220–228; Palfrey, 70, 71; Perry, 203–207; Price (1), Chap. IV, especially 99, 100, 106, 112, and (2), 137, 141.

99. United States v. United States District Court of the Eastern District of Michigan, 407 U.S. 297 (1972); Amsterdam, 356–357, 365, 382–388; Cavers, 9; Ruebhausen and Brim, 83, 84, 87.

After 1890: Reassessment of market freedom to apply products of science and technology. Technological developments brought into question key elements relied upon in the nineteenth century to make the market a major institution of social control. Hence public policy moved toward enlarging government planning or regulation at the expense of market freedom. The dynamic of the nineteenth-century market was supplied by the innovating will of managers of economic enterprise—the Patrick Tracy Jacksons, the Peter Coopers and Abram Hewitts, the Andrew Carnegies, and their numberless smaller counterparts in factories, farms, and mercantile houses.[100] Twentieth-century public policy found three main reasons why the society no longer could afford to give such free rein to entrepreneurial will in the market to weave the products of science and technology into the common life.

First, the classic market worked through one-to-one dealings (seller confronting buyer), on the assumption that such focused dealings could encompass all factors to be reckoned with. Of course, this grossly oversimplified reality, even in the first half of the nineteenth century, as we are reminded by Patrick Tracy Jackson's leadership in developing the first railroad to be chartered in New England.[101] But it was an assumption which common opinion was willing to accept as part of the legitimation of the market. In the twentieth century, people began to realize that technological change often set in motion broader chains of cause and effect than the immediate calculations of market dealers took into account; public policy began to consider benefits and costs accruing to others than the parties in market transactions. This new assessment produced tardy concern for legal regulations against industrial pollution of air and water. Scientific and technical advances underlay multiplied uses of chemicals in processing goods, foods, cosmetics, and nostrums; new regulations putting a burden of proof of safety on the producer reflected

100. Cochran and Miller, 183–188; Hacker (2), xxxiii–xxxvi, 62–63, 195–198, 230, 347–353; Kirkland (2), 50–53; Tocqueville, 2:155–156.
101. Hunt, 1:570.

increasing worry about damage to the health of laborers, consumers, and third parties from hazards unforeseen even by conscientious enterprisers. Rising gross national product put heavier demands on such nonrenewable natural resources as petroleum, spurring debate whether we were allowing the market irrevocably to reduce our future options.[102]

Second, the classic market worked on assumptions that eliminated worry over abuses flowing from gross imbalance of power among bargainers; a multiplicity of dealers would assure that no significant disparities could appear and that the best available information would flow through many channels to everyone. But twentieth-century technology fostered large concentrations of assets, tighter factory discipline, and resort to more and more specialized knowledge unavailable or unintelligible to many dependent on the new products. Pressures generated by these circumstances created an extended and elaborated law of public utilities (notably affecting the new electric power industry), more and more licensing of occupations in which the professional's or craftsman's special skill put the customer at great disadvantage (reaching from medical specialties to certification of television repairmen), and the creation of laws fostering and protecting collective bargaining in industry (as much to enforce standards of fairness in factory discipline as to adjust bargaining power over wages and hours). This area of policy was marked by confusing cross-currents of interests. Policies adopted in the name of achieving more fairness in bargaining position could be used as a cover for building the practical power of one party. Occupational licensing laws were mixed with a good deal of fence-me-in purpose, to restrict competition among the regulated group at greater cost to their customers. Public-utility law restrictions on price and

102. Cavers, 11, 12; Ciriacy-Wantrup, 5–7, 15–17, 231–242, 253–265; Kapp, Chaps. 4, 5, 6, 10; Christopher Stone (1), 450. On the flow of developing policy regarding the burden of proof as to the acceptability of technological innovations, see, e.g., N.Y. Times, Nov. 18, 1959, 38:7, and Nov. 30, 1959, 39:8; id., July 26, 1960, 28:3; id., Jan. 11, 1963, 1:5; id., Dec. 19, 1974, 1:8.

service competition among railroads, truckers, and airlines like-wise could hinder rather than foster the most rational develop-ment of the technical capacities of one of the regulated interests to the competitive advantage of another. Trade unions could use their legally protected bargaining power to limit technological changes they saw as threatening jobs, without regard to cost savings to those served. Thus, there was a darker side to almost any aspect of this new concern of public policy with redressing imbalances of power created by new technology. But by the later twentieth century it has become plain that people too much fear the balance-of-power problems stemming from technological change ever to go back to the simpler nineteenth-century faith in the market as corrective.[103]

In a third respect the twentieth century changed its estimate of the market as a sufficient instrument to channel scientific and technological change into the general life. The market was an institution of cooperation as well as of competition. Some sharing or reciprocity must be achieved, however imperfectly, else parties would not conclude a deal. In the nineteenth century, fragmented cooperation in allocating resources, presented in countless sep-arately bargained transactions, was assumed to produce accept-able over-all results. But the impact of technology created broader areas of interdependence in social living, notably through the need to concentrate larger pools of assets, through technologies of transport and communication that broadened and diversified markets, and through the technologically based growth of cities. Public policy gradually reflected felt needs for more comprehen-sive, planned patterns of cooperation and integration in dealing with problems largely created by technology. It did so, for ex-ample, in the resources law gave to regulating use of the auto-mobile—by preventive measures concerning highway safety,

103. Dulles, Chap. XV; Kohlmeier, Chaps. 1, 20; Penick et al., 196–208; Tribe, 15, 24–25. Cf. West Coast Hotel Co. v. Parrish, 300 U.S. 379 (1937); Eastern Railroad Presidents Conference v. Noerr Motor Freight, Inc., 365 U.S. 127 (1961).

traffic control, and automobile construction, by financial responsibility laws, and by the large investment of civil and criminal law in dealing with personal injuries incident to use of the automobile. In zoning and land-use control laws, in increased public spending and regulation affecting sanitation, recreation, police and fire protection, public policy responded to needs for more highly organized cooperation created by the growth of cities. Sophisticated industrial technology called for larger scales of asset accumulation, and communications technology facilitated creation and operation of broader markets for raising investment capital and trading in corporate securities; the development of tighter legal controls of capital markets was in substantial part a response to these technologically based requirements for more reliable patterns of interdependent action.[104]

Science and Technology as Contributors to Social Inertia

In one aspect there was profound irony in directions the society took largely under the influence of scientific and technological change. This culture put high value on creative will, or at least on active will. We attested the value we put on such capacity to manage affairs by the extent to which we institutionalized the advancement of knowledge and by the scope the nineteenth century gave to entrepreneurial will in translating technology into social use and effect. Yet, in important respects, the uses we made of science and technology worked to create deep, subtle constraints on creative will, by helping the growth of ill-perceived, unplanned, unchosen attitudes and social arrangements that operated to forestall or block the conscious shaping of public policy.

Challenges to the law's monopoly of force. A prime function claimed for law in this society was that law should maintain in itself a monopoly of force. This monopoly is legitimate as long as

104. Frederick R. Anderson, Chaps. I, VIII; McKelvey, viii, 3, 5, 7, 13, 17, 30, 31, 34, 45, 76, 81, 82, 111, 113; Price (1), 9, 10; Charles E. Rosenberg, 2, 4, 6, 7–20, 57–58, 70–71, 73, 74, 184, 186, 198–199; Tribe, 15.

it is exercised within constitutional limitations. Within that frame, legal agencies alone either should possess and use force in ordering social arrangements or should effectively determine and supervise delegations of functions of force to nongovernment agents. But products of science-and-technology-based change steadily put under dangerous pressure law's efforts to maintain its legitimate monopoly.[105]

Two salient problems arose on the domestic front. The manufacture of firearms was one of the first areas of successful large-scale production of goods. In the nineteenth century the conditions of the frontier and of a largely rural people made private possession of guns an accepted practice.[106] Building on this tradition, but in their own context, a predominantly urban population in the mid-twentieth century showed disturbingly wide ownership of private weapons. Legal controls lagged far behind this practice. The Second Amendment had guaranteed the right of the people to bear arms, but it did not pose a barrier to maintaining the law's proper monopoly of force. The Supreme Court ruled that the Constitution simply meant to preserve the capacity of the states to maintain their militias as part of the federal balance.[107] Lawmakers found no urgency about gun-control laws in the nineteenth-century situation; individuals needed guns for peaceful uses—hunting for food, protecting farm stock—and where the force of the law often was distant and thinly spread, it was easily accepted that private firearms were needed for self-defense. In the twentieth century the peaceful functions of private arms decreased, though new recreational uses developed; and in an urban setting private arms—notably, the handgun—proved to disturb rather than to keep the peace. Yet the nineteenth-century tradition was available, to be borrowed by patriotic ideologues and

105. Hurst (3), 274–296, 301–309.
106. Boorstin (2), 34–35; Burlingame (2), Chap. 19.
107. United States v. Miller, 307 U.S. 174 (1939). See also, Stevens v. United States, 440 F. (2d) 144, 151 (6th Cir. 1971); Cases v. United States, 131 F.2d 917, 922 (1st Cir. 1942), cert. denied, 319 U.S. 770 (1943); United States v. Tot, 131 F.2d 261, 266 (3rd Cir. 1942), rev'd on other grounds, 319 U.S. 463 (1943). Cf. Feller and Gotting, 46.

to find new uses in ugly racial tensions. In the background, too, was the nineteenth-century inheritance of faith in the active private will and of willingness to let the products of new technology find their social place through a relatively unregulated market. In the later twentieth century private firearms have played too large a part in dangerous urban crime to be ignored; an increasing number of state laws set some limitations on the sale and possession of arms, and federal law limited interstate shipment of some types of weapons. But potent ideological lobbies have opposed effective controls, and as late as the 1970's high controversy swirls about the subject, while technology still makes handguns readily and cheaply available to an extent that makes the policing of the cities problematical.[108]

Urban technology unwittingly generated a more subtle, potentially more dangerous threat to the law's command of force than private possession of firearms. The United States developed into a high division-of-labor society, characterized by reliance on intricately organized facilities to provide transport, communication, energy, and water. These essential service systems embody key points at which a relatively few individuals—striking workmen, for example, on a subway system or skilled technicians at electric generating or transmission plants—can exert great leverage on the lives of millions of other people. The public and the policy makers have been slow to respond to this new vulnerability of urban living. As of the 1970's, the law's most focused response has been in fostering or seeking to compel processes of collective bargaining, mediation, or arbitration specially geared to key-point industries. Experience is not encouraging in using legal compulsion in this type of situation; technological realities put stubborn limits on law's practical capacity to assert its monopoly of force.[109] It seems to be only good fortune that in this setting public order has yet confronted little challenge from third-party

108. National Commission on the Causes and Prevention of Violence, Chap. VII; Zimring, 735–737; N.Y. Times, Oct. 9, 1975, 18:1.

109. Fleming (1), 200.

saboteurs. The high hazards posed to the order of city life by a sudden, widespread, accidental blackout of electric power in the northeastern United States in 1965 underlined the gravity of the potential challenge. Technological skill could prevent and help cope with accidents; dealing with intentional disruption of key services is another matter.[110]

From the American Civil War on, the technology of national warfare grew steadily more destructive, but until the atom bomb the havoc brought by national rivalries at least seemed capable of limitation. Hiroshima opened a new chapter of legal history. The possession of a legitimate monopoly of force heretofore could be treated as an attribute of national legal order, but the hazards of nuclear fallout did not respect national boundaries. Stubborn facts created by the science and technology of nuclear energy dictated the need to contrive some effective international monopoly of force to supplement national legal order. But at the end of the first nuclear power generation the destructive threat of nuclear arms still far outdistances effective efforts at international arms control.[111]

Challenges to constitutionalism. The constitutional ideal dictated that power always be justified by criteria of utility and responsibility, in some material degree defined and enforced by others than the immediate powerholders. This meant that power must be justified by efficiency (utility), but that efficiency was not enough; it must be measured always with reference to ends consistent with and fulfilling decent individual life in society (responsibility). Advances in science and technology, however, tended to breed fascination simply with practical capacity to manipulate people and events. Thus scientific and technological developments have carried a subtle cultural threat to the constitutional ideal, that the people would become accustomed to

110. See N.Y. Times, Nov. 15, 1965, 36:6; id., Dec. 15, 1965, Sec. 4, 6:4; cf. id., Nov. 18, 1965, 1:4 and Nov. 15, 1965, 42:1.

111. Cf. Lapp, Chaps. 6, 9, 14, 15; Newman and Miller, Chaps. 3, 11, 12; Roberts, passim.

turning means into ends, exalting their capacity to bring things about at the expense of concern for the purposes of action.[112]

Science and technology provided means enormously to increase the practical powers of physical and psychological compulsion held by government. The practical effectiveness of the constitutional ideal depends on the existence of some effective division between official and private power; indeed, a function of that aspect of constitutionalism embodied in the idea of substantive due process of law, which holds that public power may be used only for public purposes, is to guard the relative autonomy of private areas of thought and action from which individuals can mount efforts to exert external check on official power. But various products of scientific and technical development have tended steadily to erode the relative capacities of private ability to withstand official might. The growth of the technology of arms gave twentieth-century government overpowering force against the people, compared with early nineteenth-century years when the frontiersman's or farmer's rifle could match the militiaman's. In this setting the tradition of civil control of the military has taken on a new urgency, but by late twentieth century the tradition is under unprecedented potential tension.[113] Another aspect of the shift of power toward government has been government's increased, technology-based capacity to invade the privacy of individual lives, to police or intimidate private political action through electronic surveillance machinery and computerized data banks, and to exert pressure on radio and television news and commentary through regulation of technical access to these channels.[114]

112. Hurst (3), 31, 68–69, 74–75, 91, 122–130, 184, 205, 239, 242.
113. Id., 311–314; cf. Huntington, Chaps. 4, 12, 13; Millis, Mansfield, and Stein, Chaps. 2, 4, 9; Louis Smith, Chaps. II, XIX.
114. On electronic surveillance: note 99, above; cf. Olmstead v. United States, 277 U.S. 438 (1928); Nardone v. United States, 302 U.S. 379 (1937), 308 U.S. 338 (1939); Goldman v. United States, 316 U.S. 129 (1942); On Lee v. United States, 343 U.S. 747 (1942); Fellman, 141–146. On regulation of access to the air waves: Ashmore, 13–24, 105–111; Georgetown Law Journal, 111–130, 163–175.

Science and technology contributed largely to rise in the material standard of living in the United States, especially from the last quarter of the nineteenth century on. Relative distribution of wealth and income probably did not shift a great deal, but absolute standards of health and material well-being rose substantially. The fruits of science and technology thus contributed to an idolatry of rising gross national product to which an energetic, striving, middle-class culture was already much disposed. This course of events sharpened the point of Tocqueville's prescient warning from the 1830's that this people—so bound up in enjoying increasing access to more and more broadly shared material goods—would more and more begrudge giving their energies to public affairs. By fostering the growth of immediate material satisfactions, science and technology encouraged privatization of life, to the detriment of attention to commonwealth values. The overshadowing demonstration of Tocqueville's point was the nineteenth-century readiness to give free rein to the market, working through the law of contract and property, to determine the translation of technological change into the general life, and the tardy, grudging attention given in the twentieth century to the costs and benefits of uses of technology external to the situations of immediate contracting parties. In this respect, indeed, preoccupation with means has tended to exclude from public-policy processes a due concern for ends.[115]

Challenges to long-term direction of affairs. Science might take broad and long views, but technology often thrived on the success of firing-line improvisations and successive adjustments in operating practices. Technology thus tended to put the society under a tyranny of countless, accumulating small decisions, preoccupying people's attention to the point that they lagged in attending to the directions to which their day-to-day activities were committing them.[116]

115. Tocqueville, 2:95–97. Cf. Hurst (2), 7, 71–73, 84, and (3) 56, 69, 84, 115–116, 121–130, 224–225, 239, 243–249; Maritain, 223; Morison (3), 167–169, 170, 171, 174, 175.
116. Tribe, 7, quoting Alfred E. Kahn, The Tyranny of Small Decisions:

Mass use of the automobile provided a major example of this mindless drift moved by technological change. Following the nineteenth-century pattern, for several critical decades twentieth-century inertia allowed the automobile to weave its way into social life through the market. Unregulated mass use of the automobile fostered the sprawling growth of cities and suburbs, encouraged great public expenditures on highways with scant attention to rational ordering of priorities among objects of public spending, built up dangerous dependence of the general economy on employment in producing, selling, and servicing motor cars, and created substantial new problems of policing traffic and adjusting the costs of traffic accidents. In these and other respects public policy consistently trailed behind social changes brought by the motor car, instead of intervening at points when more considered choice might have given calculated direction to its use.[117]

Technological development in many other ways spurred the growth of cities, again without plan, creating whole new sources of problems that were belatedly brought to law. Technology fostered unprecedented concentration and organization of assets for industrial production and commercial distribution, promoting centralization of economic activities that brought people into urban ways of life. The developing technologies of transportation and communication first encouraged growth of cities and later growth of suburbs that robbed central cities of tax resources and public leadership. From the early nineteenth century on, the growth of city living regularly outpaced deliberate public policy making in provision of municipal services, in rational land-use controls, in development of legislative and administrative apparatus adequate to the complexity of social adjustments de-

---

Market Failures, Imperfections, and the Limits of Economics, KYKLOS: International Review for Social Sciences 19, 23 ff. (Fasc. 1, 1966).

117. Kouwenhoven, 215–220; Lerner, 96–97, 120, 867–868; McKenzie, 464–467; Morris, 379–401; Ogburn and Tibbitts, 141; Willey and Rice, 172–180.

manded by an urban way of life. Technology gave us the practical capacity to build cities faster than we were able to govern them.[118]

One could multiply examples of areas of social experience in which the pace, variety, and depth of changes largely based on uses of the products of science and technology outran our capacity for directed intelligence in social relations. As with the automobile and the city, research and development often set in motion currents of events that in their larger outlines and total effects were not perceived or were tardily perceived, and were not deliberated, planned, or chosen. A great deal of experience attested that legal processes could be used to considerable effect for bringing issues of social choice over the threshold of awareness, to definition, debate, and calculated decision. In however fumbling fashion, we used law to create policies for disposing of a vast public domain, promoting national systems of transport and communication, and creating a working federalism. But experience also attested that it was a close question in any given area of social life whether either a formless drift of events or the accumulated weight of narrowly operational decisions would prevail over the setting of larger, more deliberately planned courses of social development. The impact of science and technology and their fruits both created this tension and profoundly affected failure or success in its resolution. Herein lies, therefore, a major area of challenge for the study of legal history.

118. William Anderson, 61–64; Gulick (2), 69–72, 74–78; McDougal, 216–228; McKelvey, 76, 81, 82, 111, 113; McKenzie, 481–492, 495–496; Reeve, 168–203.

CHAPTER IV

Consensus and Conflict: Market, Corporation, and Government

Through the country's national history those most influential in making public policy prized creative, active will as the prime factor giving meaning and dignity to life. The only value ranked higher was that of constitutionalism—that individuals should exercise will responsibly, to ends that would enrich individual life experience. So high was the prizing of energetic will that recurrently it threatened to engulf the constitutional ideal and to make the expression of will in action an end in itself.

Active will confronted two external challenges. It might be overborne by the implacable, impersonal facts of the physical and biological setting of life, and it might be denied or frustrated by the swamping variety, detail, and complexity of social relations, customs, and habits, or by the accumulated weight of social experience. A great deal of United States legal history is a clear effort to use legal processes to overcome these challenges to using creative will to shape life in society.

Another article of faith figured critically in public-policy responses to the challenges of the physical-biological and the social environments. This was the conviction—readily adopted in an improvising, middle-class culture, continually taught by the people's experience of opening up a raw, new continent—that growth in production of goods and services was the most efficient lever we had on our situation and a prerequisite to achieving less tangible, more ideal values. This premise, as the previous chapter suggested, meant that until well into the twentieth century there was almost unquestioned acceptance of the judgment that public policy should foster and protect increase in technological and scientific command of physical and biological circumstances, to the end particularly of maximizing production of goods and services in the market. This bias of policy took on its full dimensions only over time and with some fumbling and lack of direction; in particular, public policy earlier was more prominent in fostering private effort to advance science and technology than in moving government into strong, positive roles. But only by the mid-twentieth century did opinion show substantial questioning of these lines of economic growth. Before then such limitations as marked the record were more the product of limits of knowledge or limits of experience in affirmatively using government's powers than of conflict over the worth of using law to advance the capabilities of science or technology.

People were confident that economic growth also was a prime lever for affecting social situations. This belief made uses of law to affect allocation of economic resources a major theme of public-policy history. Because of the diversity of interests and experience in play in the social setting, we confront here less clear agreement on ends and means than marked the record of policy toward science and technology. Thus to examine salient aspects of the record on resource allocation calls for examining more closely the ideas of consensus and conflict in public policy making.

Consensus and Conflict

Formal products of legal processes—the common law, statutes, and administrative decisions and rules together with informal practices that cluster about them—add up to a formidable body of evidence of values held by some individuals or groups. The evidence is solid because using legal processes involves substantial costs in money, time, energy, and courage, so that people do not invoke law lightly. On the other hand, it is often ambiguous for what it shows of agreement or disagreement among various interests. Because law typically has held only marginal influence compared with the whole array of institutions and ideas functioning in the society, to be effective legal processes often must enjoy broad-based consent or at least substantial acceptance for what they do. But legal processes also offer leverage to individuals or groups that are determined to have their way against those of less conviction or effectiveness, whether by adroitness and skill in litigation or by bargains struck in legislative trade-offs. Thus, consensus and conflict are not simple phenomena, especially where law allocates economic resources, benefits, and burdens. One task for legal history is to identify the varied types of situations of consensus and conflict represented in public policy.

Law sometimes has expressed the wants of relatively small groups, fulfilled against a background of indifference on the part of most people. There are two common types of such situation, distinguished by different intensity of the interests pressing for or against action. One type is game laws. Through most of the nineteenth century only law dealing with trespass to land affected hunters. But settlement and the growth of a recreation industry began to press harder on stocks of game. As part of a general conservation movement, legislatures began to limit hunting seasons and hunters' bags. Setting these limits was of acute concern to hunters and resort owners, but the bulk of the population was indifferent, or at most concerned only that there be some regular, rational procedure for settling matters among those immediately affected. Thus the hunting laws reflected the focused desires and intent of only a small part of the population, though they usually represented some real consensus of the values of that part. More difficult to appraise were situations in which focused selfish interests fought each other in a public arena, most likely in a contest to obtain or to block legislation immediately favorable to one and disadvantageous to the other. Typical was the clash between truckers seeking legal authority to carry larger and more profitable loads and railroads seeking to block such authorizations in order to protect their own worsening competitive position. This type of situation became more and more common as growing diversity of the economy produced growing diversity of competing special interests. This specialization of interests also made it more difficult in a given instance to identify where public interest lay and made it easier for general opinion to stand indifferent or ignorant regarding broader interests at stake in the clash of particular claimants to the law's favor. In both types of situation a consensus in any broad meaning existed only in a procedural sense: that the general—and generally indifferent or unknowing—public accepted the idea that legislative, judicial, or administrative processes would resolve the particular matters of substance at issue. Regarding focused, adverse interests that contended with each other, the legal outcome could only be called a consensus of the victors.[1]

Continuity and growth of stable bodies of law could provide convincing evidence that some broad consensus of values existed. Thus the steady course of state and federal laws providing more and more schooling and more and more highways from the 1920's into the 1960's attested general popular acceptance of certain priorities in allocating public moneys. Similar evidence of widely held values exists in the twentieth-century expansion of regulatory statute law on a variety of matters involved in market operations, including industrial safety, pure foods, and issuing and trading corporate securities.[2]

Of course, laws regulating private profit seeking potentially might express broadly shared values, and yet weak or faithless administration might convert their operating substance to serve selfish interests of the regulated persons. Thus sophisticated observers saw that the Interstate Commerce Act might be turned to the railroads' advantage. The fact that the statute was on the

1. On hunting laws, see e.g., Wis. Stats., 1973, Section 29.174; Bittenhaus v. Johnston, 92 Wis. 588, 66 N.W. 805 (1896); State v. Herwig, 17 Wis. (2d) 442, 117 N.W. (2d) 335 (1962). On collisions of special interests: Daniel v. Family Security Life Insurance Co., 336 U.S. 220 (1949); Eastern Railroad Presidents Conference v. Noerr Motor Freight, Inc., 365 U.S. 127 (1961); Buchanan and Tullock, 284–295.

2. Horack, 41.

books would assure the general public that something had been done to curb railroad abuses. Meanwhile, railroad officials would learn how to influence those administering the law and could do so more easily because general opinion was lulled into complacent confidence that the new law had solved the problems. This skeptical analysis was commonly advanced by critics of the twentieth-century administrative process. The analysis itself deserved some skeptical appraisal. Administrative lawmaking was not always the clear captive of one special interest, but was sometimes an arena for the play of diverse interests among the regulated groups, as between motor carriers and railroads. Administration was not static. Antitrust enforcement dwindled to insignificance in the peak years of business influence on the federal government in the 1920's, only to be brought to sustained, professionalized activity pioneered by Thurman Arnold in the late 1930's; following years in which its principal activity was limited to policing advertising frauds, the Federal Trade Commission moved into vigorous use of its broadened authority to proceed against mergers under the Celler-Kefauver Amendment of 1950. As in the regulation of natural gas, businessmen sometimes conspicuously failed to get the favorable treatment they wanted from administrators, and the regulatory situation might well be too cloudy on the merits to make possible dogmatic judgments of where the public interest lay. Though administrative performance sometimes might be mistaken or bungling, the long-term careers of the Federal Reserve System and the Securities and Exchange Commission showed that agencies could achieve substantial working independence of regulated interests, as the governing statutes intended.[3]

Law sometimes reflected the force mustered by a relatively small lobby whose sustained, aggressive effort carried it to a legislative victory against other interests that, because of their

3. Cary (1), 61–66, 67–68; Hofstadter, 231–235; Hurst (7), 207, 208, 219, 230; Kolko (1), 58–60, 283–285, and (2), 3–6, 35–41, 45, 57–63, 233; McCraw, 165, 170, 179–183; Wiebe, 48–50.

diffuse character, lacked capacity to persuade legislators. A common example was the array of twentieth-century laws licensing entry to various occupations. Enacted for the declared purpose of protecting consumers, such laws in substance often were designed to erect barriers against competition for the benefit of restricted classes of sellers. A kindred type of regulation was federal and state law designed to protect independent retailers against price competition of chain stores by barring sales of loss-leader items below cost or by forbidding manufacturers to grant discriminatory prices to large outlets. Again, the legislation represented a consensus, but all one could say with sureness was that it was a consensus of a relatively small part of the population, arguably against the interest of a diffuse, unorganized body of consumers.[4]

Law might achieve an artificial consensus of values by forcibly excluding from the value calculus those who would reject or contest it. This was the nature of slavery. Enslaved blacks were not legally recognized persons. Since they were thus ruled out of the law's consideration as independent claimants on the legal order, their dissent to the system did not count in law; rather, the law of slavery stood as a consensus of whites in slaveholding states. In substance, though not in form, the position of Indians vis-à-vis whites was similiar. A long record of military action and of broken treaties attested that the Indians were not counted in determining the prevailing consensus on land titles and legally protected uses of land; favor for fee-simple title was broad in the nineteenth century, but it was an evaluation made by and for whites, and not with the consent of Indians. From this viewpoint, one of the most significant themes in legal history was the tendency to enlarge the definition of those who were persons in law.[5]

Thus there are various criteria by which to estimate the presence or absence of consensus in the background of particular uses

4. Friedman and Macaulay, 307; Gellhorn (2), 106–125, 140–151.
5. Howard Jay Graham, Chap. 4; Handlin (1), 16–22, 37–46; Kelly and Harbison, 301–304; Rose and Rose, 29–34.

of law. A given state of the law showed the existence of shared values by those who obtained a particular legal outcome. This was at least a consensus of victors, who might be many or few. In this aspect the law on the books typically represented a prevailing, but not necessarily a pervasive agreement on values. The moral or political legitimacy of the prevailing consensus might be questioned because of those who lost or were left out or because of the basis on which they lost or were left out. Legitimacy was important in the country's political history, but even if one might question the legitimacy of the prevailing consensus, its reality in fact remained as part of the total social situation.[6] Again, law had uses that did not involve an alignment of victors versus losers, but rather presented decisions on which there was either broad, positive agreement or at least an acceptance through indifference by those who did not have a close-felt interest at stake. Such was the instance of legal definition of hunting seasons. An example of another type of broad consensus is the keep-to-the-right rule of the road, on which there was indifference as to the particular rule adopted, but common desire for some rule by which individuals could hold reasonable expectations of others' conduct.[7]

The example of the keep-to-the-right rule suggests a still broader category—that in which people used law to resolve conflicts arising within a framework of consensus. Consensus and conflict often existed together, particularly in dealings with economic interests, because the rising curve of material productivity not only made possible but promoted high division of labor and increasing diversity of economic wants and needs. But it was not a condition limited to economic expression. The country's growth involved varied strands of immigration and internal migration, differences in sectional experience, a protean use of private associations learned from the need to muster collective effort first to overcome scarcity of resources and later to offset the imper-

6. Buchanan and Tullock, 284, 295; Dahl and Lindblom, 294–299, 302–306, 325–329; Truman, 353–357, 391–394, 508–515.
7. Freund, 248–260; Patterson (1), 51, 275–280.

sonality of a big society and the weight of public and private concentrations of power. Such factors accustomed this people to accept cultural, religious, and political, as well as economic diversity, as norms of social experience. The experience of diversity bred the practice and expectation of bargaining out differences. The bargaining temper sought institutional frameworks and integrating ideas that would allow individuals and groups to move from particular differences to broader grounds of accommodation or at least to a working resolution of conflicts.

A mingling of agreement and dispute typically occurred where law legitimated or fostered a social institution other than law. Thus the First Amendment reflected a broad consensus favorable to a diversity of churches and to the idea that government should leave to religious sects a large autonomy. But if members of a religious denomination fell into serious quarrel among themselves, law would intervene to enforce observance of the church's own rules of fair procedure for handling disputes.[8] Again, the law of contract and property reflected a broad nineteenth-century consensus on the social utility of the market. But within that consensus law provided doctrine and procedures by which individuals could resolve particular disputes over contract performance or the validity of titles.[9]

Where law embodied general integrating ideas about public policy, there could be wide sharing of the basic concept, coupled with dispute over what the concept called for in particular activity. As I have noted, this society had, through the nineteenth and the first half of the twentieth centuries, a broadly shared faith that a rising material standard of living would make for a better society. Within that broad area of agreement, however, people brought to law a variety of conflicts over the most just or effective ways to implement the idea—as in contests between rival claimants to public subsidies for building railroads and in

8. Chafee, 1023–1026; Zollman, Chaps. VII, VIII.
9. Hurst (4), 289–294, 297–301, 326–328, 333–342; Patterson (1), 54, 56, 95, 454–455, 520.

battles over the tariff. In this area it was often peculiarly hard to say that law served "public" interest except to see that special interest should achieve its resolution within certain legal processes and subject to the requirement that public authority assent to the particular resolution. Such an outcome at least required that private power pursue its ends within procedures set by other than the private powerholders. But general opinion would not settle for this procedural minimum, if it became convinced that individuals or groups were pursuing private interest in ways that deeply imperiled achievement of a rising standard of living. At that point acceptance of conflict within consensus broke down because the ultimate basis of consensus was called into question. Thus, for all its frailties, antitrust law did outlaw as unfair such business tactics as predatory price cutting or unlawful railroad rebates, which were radically inconsistent with the productive functioning of the market. Again, through the nineteenth century public policy left policing of standards of honesty and safety in sales of food and drugs largely to the inadequate remedies available in common-law actions by aggrieved individuals. But a broad and demanding opinion could see that the result was so serious as to endanger health and safety to an extent that threatened the desired advance in the standard of living. At that point legislation introduced more positive public regulation to create more exacting terms on which the interplay of public and private interest should proceed. Special interest often found ways to warp the new administrative processes to its advantage. But its room for maneuver was substantially less in the twentieth than in the nineteenth century.[10]

One might attack at its roots the idea that law ever expressed a true consensus of values and find either naive or hypocritical those who claim the contrary. Because law dealt so much with resolving group conflicts, the argument might be that wherever one found resort to law there must be broad-scale conflict rather

10. Blair, Chap. 14; John Maurice Clark (1), 212; Corwin Edwards, 157–179; Hacker and Zahler (2), 57–58; Kaysen and Turner, 18, 20.

than agreement on values. But on at least two counts this sweeping conclusion did not follow. First, individuals made large use of law to attain by collective action a capacity to achieve results that individual effort could not bring about. Thus we taxed and we spent tax-derived funds to provide social capital in highways and schools and in government-supported science and technology. Conflict occurred over particular applications of such spending policies, but the steady growth of the service functions of government attested to a substantial underlying consensus behind such programs.[11] Second, the presence of the criminal law as part of legal order was a reminder that law must deal with particularized individual or group deviance from social norms. Probably such deviance would occur in any social order, whatever its organizing principles, but this fact did not negate the reality of social norms by which we measured deviance in a given society.[12]

Those skeptical of the reality of consensus also might point out that, because law embodied organized force, possession of the legal apparatus was inherently a standing temptation for selfish interests to capture the law for their own purposes at the expense of injustice to others. Law did foster a good deal of injustice—in tax laws that favored the rich, in criminal law enforcement that bore harder on the poor or on blacks than on middle-class whites, in use of law to repress peaceful criticism of the social system, in illegal actions of government agencies. One might read these facts to mean that such consensus as law reflected was never more than a consensus among oppressors. But the record denied so simplistic a reading. The large and increasing use of law to provide such broadly shared benefits as a clean water supply and other protections of public health ran counter to an interpretation that identified all of legal order with oppression. In the working character of this high division-of-labor society, care for social capital inherently loomed large among functions of legal order.[13] More-

11. Bator, 18–35; Fabricant, 56–57, 60, 62–64, 66, 73–74, 77–79.
12. Hurst (3), 285–294; Robinson, 154; Julius Stone (1), 565–568.
13. Goodrich, Chap. 8; Johnson and Krooss, Chap. 13; Charles E. Rosenberg, 227–234.

over, the ideal of constitutionalism included a politically potent standard of criticism of wrongful use of legal order. To help implement the constitutional ideal the legal order favored dispersed private associations and embodied a sharing of powers among separate legal agencies—factors that produced substantial bases for resisting oppressive uses of law. Taken in itself, such resistance showed conflict rather than agreement on values. But in the background was substantial agreement on a sufficiently open style of social organization to provide resources from which to challenge abuse of legal power.[14]

Finally, we should note that the existence of either consensus or conflict required that people be aware that they confronted an occasion for making value choices. Activity might go on, or some particular state of facts might exist, but these would produce no determination of public policy until people perceived the activity or the situation as a subject for legal action. Thus the state of knowledge was a prime determinant of the presence of policy issues. Before people knew of the action of bacteria in milk there was neither consensus nor conflict over treating milk to eliminate organisms that might cause disease. When knowledge spread of the bacterial origin of disease and of the efficacy of pasteurization to eliminate the danger, consensus rapidly emerged on legal requirements for safety of the milk supply.[15] Too, the context of facts often must develop to some point of felt competition of interests before people confronted either an occasion to effect agreed-upon values or to disagree about what the situation called for. In days of sparse and widely separated settlements, no issue arose over contamination of water from deposit of industrial waste in streams. The emergence of a public-policy issue waited upon growth in competing demands for the use of streams to bring about a problem of scarcity of satisfactions, which in turn created

14. E.g., Humphrey's Executor v. United States, 295 U.S. 602 (1935) (administrative tenure); National Association for the Advancement of Colored People v. Button, 371 U.S. 415 (1963) (private association); United States v. Nixon, 418 U.S. 683 (1974) (limits of executive privilege).
15. Hurst (3), 93–101; Charles E. Rosenberg, 213–220, 226–234.

a public-policy conflict. An activity might go on for some time—the selling of untreated milk, the dumping of sawdust into a river—without entering the field of public-policy choice because people lacked the knowledge or the pressure of competing wants necessary to make them perceive that they faced an occasion for using law one way or another. Unlike the case of the blacks or the Indians, such a situation did not spell consensus by suppression of competing interests; rather, we deal here with states of social relations that had not emerged as occasions either for consensus or for conflict.[16]

Against this background, we can note some principal forms of consensus and conflict expressed in law in the United States. Some outstanding instances of broad agreement concerned aspects of the society about which much of its activity was organized. Substantial public-policy agreement existed on legitimating and supporting key institutions. Save for the massive exception of the Civil War, public acceptance of the legitimacy of government continued, especially of its claim to hold a monopoly of legitimate force. The country had relatively little occasion to call into play the law of treason or related law concerning subversion of government. Laws on subversion for political advantage were abused, as in proceedings under the Sedition Act of 1798, but the long-time trend was to legitimize peaceful political opposition.[17]

A general consensus supported First Amendment values on religion. No drive emerged to establish a single national church or to penalize dissenters for the benefit of a national church; such qualified religious establishments as state laws provided disappeared early in the nineteenth century. Social class lines were drawn to a considerable extent according to religious differences, and there was episodic violence of the socially dominant Protes-

16. Hurst (4), 464, 455, 542, 577; see Marshall, J., in State ex rel. Owen v. Donald, 160 Wis. 21, 124, 141, 151 N.W. 331, 365, 371 (1915), and Winslow, C.J., id., 160 Wis. at 158–159, 151 N.W. at 377, 378.

17. Hurst (3), 274–284, and (6), 260–267; James Morton Smith, 21, 50, 94, 117–118, 120, 122, 176–179, 186, 263–265.

tants against Catholics. But no great battles had to be fought on the general principle of separation of church and state; the diversity of the country's population created basic agreement on religious toleration. The mid-twentieth century brought lively controversy over direct or indirect public financial aid to parochial schools. These disputes were socially divisive and were hard fought in the courts, but were marginal to roles of church and state.[18]

The monogamous family was fostered and protected by general agreement in the law and in social practice. The reality of this consensus was dramatized by legal action against Mormon polygamy.[19]

People shared an overwhelming confidence that the general good was served by allowing large play to changes brought about by advances in scientific and technological knowledge, especially through market processes. This remained, as we have seen, a matter of sturdy consensus until about mid-twentieth century.[20] The market was an institution that received much of law's favor and support. I postpone further consideration of this to the next portion of this chapter.

Substantial consensus existed also in the realm of general integrating ideas centering about values of the striving, business-oriented middle class. Of course, middle-class values did not govern the whole of society, especially when immigration brought great numbers of individuals from a peasant background in Europe. But the prevailing patterns of public policy were set mostly in a middle-class mould. One salient example was the broadly shared confidence that bargaining could resolve all clashes of interest, however deep they ran. It was deeply engrained in this society that public policy should move by incre-

18. Ahlstrom, Chaps. 34, 50; Beer, 137–170; Howe, Chaps. I, III, V. Cf. Zorach v. Clausen, 343 U.S. 306 (1952); Lemon v. Kurtzman, 403 U.S. 602 (1971), and Tilton v. Richardson, id., 672 (1971).

19. Reynolds v. United States, 98 U.S. 145 (1878).

20. Chap. III, above, notes 62–80, and accompanying text.

mental stages through the bargaining out of particular differences. Except for the Civil War the country's politics never embraced a significant drive for radical change in the institutions of power, though political polemics sometimes borrowed the colorful language of class war. Thus in the late nineteenth-century free-silver controversy, agrarian politicians depicted an irreconcilable conflict between the common man and a ruling plutocracy. But when gold supplies increased about the turn of the century, providing the basis for more generous credit, the farmers showed themselves for the small businessmen that they were, and talk of class antagonism dwindled away.[21]

Consensus was not complete; the society was riven by real differences. As I have noted, the most serious conflicts of values involved suppressing or ignoring certain interests, rather than acknowledging their claims to a place in a pattern of legal adjustments. The country achieved apparent consensus by ruling some major groups out of the calculus of consent, notably the Indians, the blacks, and women. Not until the mid-twentieth century did these excluded interests begin to achieve some significant success in bringing their claims to the fore. When this happened, the country became uneasily aware of the gulf that past policy had maintained in the society between the prevailing white, male, middle-class ethic and these disregarded groups. Yet it was significant of the potential of legal processes for exerting leverage on affairs that major efforts were made to use the law to redress even gross imbalances of power.[22]

This was an impatiently opportunistic society, which sought quick and increasing satisfactions, often with scant regard for the impact of current policy on unborn generations. Neglect of the future suppressed or ignored interests that cut across class, racial, or sex-determined lines, affecting everyone who would

21. Chap. I, above, notes 51–64, and accompanying text.
22. Cf. Brown v. Board of Education, 347 U.S. 483 (1954); Gomillion v. Lightfoot, 364 U.S. 339 (1960); South Carolina v. Katzenbach, 383 U.S. 301 (1966).

come later. One of the most important roles open to law was to provide leverage for those gifted with foresight, who could define future problems and speak for present choices that would keep options open for generations to come.[23]

Most of the visible conflict that combatants consciously pursued went on within accepted frames of social institutions. This was characteristic of the market in relation to law.

Consensus and Conflict in the Market

Through the nineteenth and into the early twentieth centuries no institution bulked larger than the market for organizing and adjusting social relations. By the market I mean the existence of sustained patterns of private exchange of goods and services for money-measured profit. Usually markets did not exist by legal fiat, though law in effect created some markets, as by providing for sales or grants of public lands in the nineteenth century. Normally the market was a product of business practice and custom, to which law was auxiliary. Nonetheless, law rendered important support to market processes.[24]

First, law provided substantial autonomy for private exercise of will in the market. At the outset of national history and for some decades the principal traded commodity was the land. State constitutions and statutes ratified practical reality by declaring that there should be no feudal land tenure in this country; the fee simple absolute should be the norm of title. The policy of the national government in disposing of the public domain in the nineteenth century powerfully reinforced the preference for fee-simple title. Between about 1827 and 1848, Congress made a brief experiment in withholding from sale lands bearing minerals and granting only limited licenses to mine. But the general demand was imperative for fee-simple titles to all parts of the

23. Hurst (3), 230–232, and (4), Chap. XI; Christopher Stone (1), 450.
24. Walton Hamilton, 6–7, 26, 31; Polanyi, Chaps. 16, 17; Williams, 138–149.

public domain. The mining-lease program collapsed in the face of widespread fraud in entering land at government land offices. To keep the federal government as perpetual landlord of parts of the public domain in the Mississippi Valley would require a far greater investment in public land administration than Congress was prepared to finance or general opinion to support. Not until settlement pushed to the semiarid regions of the West did the United States effectively withhold fee-simple title and pursue a policy of granting only limited licensing for grazing and mining.[25]

A fee-simple title meant that the holder enjoyed a wide range of discretion in deciding how to use the land he owned. In the nineteenth century this discretion was qualified by common-law nuisance doctrine, but the qualification was marginal. Not until the twentieth century did law substantially limit the freedom of the holder in fee simple. Responding to problems of urban environment, policy makers devised zoning laws and then laws seeking to prevent uses of land that polluted air and water.[26] Responding to problems of uncertain agricultural markets, twentieth-century law witnessed the development of government programs inducing farmers to withhold land from production or influencing their choice of crops.[27] But both zoning and crop-control laws still left substantial decision-making capacity in the owner of the fee.

Other nineteenth-century legal doctrine conferred a substantial autonomy on private will in the market. The law of contract presumed that every trading agreement was consistent with social interest. Law thus put on one who wished to escape the obligations of a deal the burden of proof that such antisocial consequences would attend fulfillment of the contract that law

25. Clawson and Held, 57–60, 85–87, 95–101; Hurst (4), 26–30; Lake, Chap. 2.
26. Babcock, 115–125; Kapp, Chaps. 5, 6; Murphy (1), 183–186.
27. Benedict, 332–335, 347–355, 375–381, 388–396; Wickard v. Filburn, 317 U.S. 111 (1942).

should refuse to enforce it. In the twentieth century the range and complexity of economic regulatory law grew, multiplying grounds on which argument could be made that public policy should be deemed to bar certain contractual arrangements. But the basic bias of policy remained as it had been set in the nineteenth century: presumptively the field was open for private ingenuity to contrive new forms of dealing; one who would erect barriers to contract innovations must be able to show particular grounds in law to warrant the limitation.[28]

Late in the nineteenth century the Supreme Court's development of substantive meaning in the due process clause of the Fourteenth Amendment gave a constitutional underpinning to market autonomy. Substantive due process meant that policy makers must respect distinctions between what was of public concern and what was of private concern only. The market existed in and by the exercise of private will in trade and therefore specially benefited by the public-private distinctions the Court drew in the name of substantive due process. Matters stood so between the 1880's and the early 1930's. A majority of the Court epitomized this constitutional doctrine when in 1923 in *Adkins* v. *Children's Hospital* it declared, "Freedom of contract is the rule and restraint the exception." By this test, if a statute on its face limited private contracting activity, the statute did not enjoy the benefit of the ordinary presumption of constitutionality; instead, the proponent of the statute carried a heavy burden of persuading the Court that there was compelling reason for the regulation. But from the mid-1930's on the Court repudiated this doctrine and ruled that the ordinary presumption of constitutionality applied on behalf of economic regulatory laws. This change did not end market autonomy; by and large most legislation continued to be consistent with substantial freedom for trading in the market. But the change did mean that market autonomy was not henceforth a preferred value; statutes reg-

28. Corbin, 6A:4–6; Hurst (2), 12, 20.

ulating dealings in the market would be upheld as long as the Court could find that reasonable legislators could believe that a given regulation would serve public interest by means reasonably adapted to the end.[29]

Law fostered the market by favoring trade as such, and thus recognized and sanctioned the imperative demand of the people to bring land into trade. This was a contribution of particular significance before 1850 when land was the most common and valuable item in exchange relations. The fee-simple title included ready transferability as a key attribute. Law helped create other tradeable items. By providing a regular system for defining units of land the public lands survey promoted trade in land. The creation of recording acts also furthered this objective. Law favored trade by recognizing new subjects of traffic when it accepted standing timber or mineral or water rights as tradeable items.[30] Freedom of incorporation greatly increased tradeable goods in the shape of stocks and bonds; particularly under the liberal incorporation acts that became standard about the turn of the century promoters gained power to multiply types of corporate securities.[31] In the rules against perpetuities and against accumulation law frowned on property arrangements that indefinitely tied up titles, denying them transferability.[32]

The energies and ambitions of businessmen could not be satisfied with a market formed solely for present exchange; to achieve greater variety and scale of transactions called for arrangements that looked to the future for full performance. Contract and property law provided a basis on which traders could erect reasonable expectations of future fulfillment of promises.

29. Adkins v. Children's Hospital, 261 U.S. 525, 545, 546 (1923), overruled in West Coast Hotel Co. v. Parrish, 300 U.S. 379, 400 (1937). Cf. Nebbia v. New York, 291 U.S. 502 (1935); Ferguson v. Skrupa, 373 U.S. 726 (1963).

30. Hurst (4), 27, 28, 176, 368, 378; Lake, 62–63, 72–74.

31. Robbins, 14–20, 36–38; Sobel, 128–130, 150–153, 158–171, 237–246, 254, 324–328.

32. Friedman (3), 211, 222, 369.

As businessmen formed continuing relationships, however, proportionally they came to rely mainly on informal adjustment of interests when conflict or difficulty arose; traders who valued their continuing relationships were not likely to endanger them by bringing lawsuits. Thus in mid-twentieth century contract law probably was less important to the market than it was in times when transactions were more likely to be single dealings not woven into continuing patterns between contracting parties.[33]

But at least two lines of future-looking contract doctrine continued to have vitality into the twentieth century. Business transactions that involved postponed performance typically required the use of credit. Lawyers' ingenuity went into devising reliable forms of security for credit, with a good deal of invention as the terms of business grew more sophisticated. Thus the law recognized trust receipts for goods held for sale by middlemen. It sanctioned security arrangements in fluctuating stocks of raw or semifinished materials. Lawyers and courts adapted the real estate mortgage or trust deed to the uses of corporation bond issues floated under trust indentures.[34] Again, maximum use of the market required that traders feel confidence in the validity of the titles they exchanged. To this end law developed its special favor for the bona fide purchaser in the market, who cut off competing equitable claims on goods, land, or securities that were traded.[35]

Only the most crude and limited markets worked by barter. For extensive market dealing businessmen needed a definite and reliable system of money. Law could not—at least not for long—create effective money simply by legal fiat; what traders would accept as tokens to settle trading transactions depended not only on the law's definition of money but also on how people perceived the money stock in relation to the whole flow of trans-

33. Macaulay, 55.
34. Cravath, 153; Skilton (1), 221, 403, and (2), 359; Stetson, 1.
35. Casner, 3:325–327; Friedman (3), 235–238, 468–471; cf. Fletcher v. Peck, 6 Cranch 87 (U.S. 1810).

actions. Law facilitated a wider reach of market transactions by various contributions it made to a working system of money.

Law provided authoritative definition of media of exchange. It authenticated metal coinage and later adopted standard forms for paper currency. The biggest change in this respect was the product primarily of business custom in the use of checks drawn on bank deposits. Though law did not create deposit-check money, the law of negotiable instruments provided the basic assurance of regularity and the basic definition of the incidents of issue of such money that helped to make deposit-check money acceptable in commerce.[36]

Law created the quality of legal tender in the money supply and could do so effectively regarding its own processes; the federal Constitution defined the states' legislative competence to declare what tokens courts should accept as payments that legally would complete a transaction. Moreover, the legal tender quality of given tokens might help make them more acceptable in trade. But, again, at basis the practical acceptability of any money tokens depended on how people saw the relations between the stock of money and the volume and pace of transactions in real goods and services.[37]

The most ambitious uses of law to affect the market by creating a system of money were those measures that undertook to regulate the quantity and timing of money flow relative to the quantity and timing of business transactions, and the quality of credit underpinning deposit-check money. The first major effort at this kind of money management came in the years from about 1824 to 1832 in which Nicholas Biddle managed the Second Bank of the United States so as to give it somewhat the role of a central banker, adjusting the flow of currency and deposit-check money to seasonal changes in the flow of raw materials and finished goods. After President Jackson vetoed renewal of the bank's charter the country had no central bank until Congress created

36. Hurst (7), 38, 50, 55–56, 59, 61, 72, 82.
37. Id., 40–45.

the Federal Reserve System in 1913. Even then it was not until the 1950's that the Federal Reserve Board and its Federal Open Market Committee launched sustained efforts to regulate the quality and supply of money by buying or selling government securities so as to affect the general flow of business to avoid costly fluctuations of business activity or extremes of deflation or inflation.[38]

Control of the money supply carried the potential for accomplishing radical shifts in holdings of wealth in the society. It was significant of the deep attachment to market dealings among broad segments of the public as well as among lawmakers that political history showed profound distaste for manipulating the money supply in order to shift power among social classes. By mid-twentieth century acceptance was general that the Federal Reserve Board and its Federal Open Market Committee should use monetary policy to temper swings of the business cycle. But this meant using control of the money supply simply to make the market work more smoothly, without abrupt curtailments of credit and without inflationary or deflationary excesses. Earlier the free-silver movement went down to defeat because too many voters saw it as a use of money controls to change class alignments. And in the depression of the 1930's, President Franklin Roosevelt never elected to use the massive money-creating power Congress gave him by the Thomas amendment to the Agricultural Adjustment Act, designed to sanction redistribution of wealth as well as social and political power. Money was to be the servant of the market; it was not to dispossess the market.[39]

Many of the conflicts that people brought to law existed within the accepted frame of market dealings. From the late eighteenth century into the depression of the 1930's the prevailing consensus accepted market processes as major means for allocating economic resources. Though bitter disputes sometimes occurred among market participants, they generally stayed within the as-

38. Id., 78–85.
39. Id., 85–91.

sumptions of a market-oriented society. No significant political force was mustered for substantial changes from the market orientation until the mid-twentieth century. The principal exception to this pattern was the creation of the law of public utilities.[40]

Creditor-debtor tensions showed themselves in legal battles over statutory moratoriums on enforcing creditors' rights and in recurrent contests over managing the money supply and determining the costs of credit. To some extent these were differences between parts of the country that were dominantly raw-materials producers as against those that were financial centers; the raw-materials producers wanted cheap credit by enlarging the money supply, while eastern financial circles wanted to restrict government's issues of currency and to obtain higher interest rates. Industrialists ambitious for expansion now and again joined farmers in seeking to increase the money supply and hold down interest rates.[41]

Growth in the scale of enterprise meant tighter work discipline and mustering larger numbers of workers under particular management. Disputes over wages, hours, and conditions of labor mounted, but on the whole did not take on the color of class war. As labor struggled to organize, its objective was typically to strike more favorable bargains within the context of the market. Management opposition to unions in effect denied workers means to use market bargaining, and out of this confrontation grew a record of serious, widespread violence. For a long time the balance of power in legislative halls opposed labor's effort for effective legal redress; the law's defaults here allowed continuation of violence on the labor-management front. Foreshadowed by the Railway Labor Act of 1926, in 1935 the National Labor Relations Act finally brought law into play to foster and protect collective bargaining. After an inaugural period

40. Hartz, Chap. 9; Hurst (2), 88, 89; Lowi, Chaps. 1, 2, 3; Truman, Chap. 16.
41. Feller, 1061; Hale, 197–209; Hurst (7), 80–81, 87–91.

of continued battling, management generally accepted the new regime, and the new law helped substantially to reduce violence in labor relations. The change wrought here was perhaps the single most striking instance where the use of law moved from a condition of deep-seated conflict to one of consensus within the frame of which limited, generally peaceful conflict could go on.[42]

The consumer was a factor in market bargaining whose voice rarely was raised in influential demands on the law through the nineteenth century. The twentieth century witnessed efforts to use law—especially to use the administrative process—to get for the consumer his money's worth within the frame of regulated market dealing. The new emphasis showed in regulation of public utilities and of the purity of foods and the safety of drugs. Acute problems continued in achieving effective leverage for interests that typically were diffuse and unorganized. But, as in the case of labor relations, policy makers sought solutions within the frame of market bargaining, trying to use administrative regulation partly to arm the consumer with better information for his own protection, and partly to use the specialized will and knowledge of administrators to do the bargaining individual consumers were unequipped to do for themselves. This was a bargaining process because typically the regulated groups engaged in a good deal of maneuver and persuasion for their own interests vis-à-vis the administrators. Indeed, regulated groups showed so much capacity to look out for themselves that by mid-twentieth century critics had become disenchanted with the administrative process, seeing a tendency for regulated groups to enter into what amounted to working partnerships with the regulators.[43]

Market-determined values never occupied the whole range of public policy. Indeed, the very existence of government attested

42. Dulles, Chaps. IX, X, XV; Fleming (2), 126–136, 148–152; Perlman, Chap. V.

43. Hacker and Zahler (2), 56–57, 446–448; Kohlmeier, Chaps. 1, 19; McCraw, 179–183; Wiebe, 48–50, 66.

that some important social concerns could not be bargained out
for profit in the market. Significant areas of policy consensus and
conflict were defined by nonmarket values. The classic example
was provision by government of services that were too diffuse
in impact to be handled administratively by market bargains—
provisions for national security in a world of warring nations
and for public health and safety, for mass education, and for
general road systems. The hold of the market on public-policy
tradition meant continuing controversy over defining areas of
service where government action should be primary. If there
was no dispute on public provision of police and fire protection,
there was, for example, ample dispute over public subsidies to
railroads and then to airlines and motor carriers.[44]

In the twentieth century concern with conservation of natural
resources, or at least with their more efficient use, emerged. In
the nineteenth century the market was allowed to use resources
without substantial check; if exploitation of a resource returned
a profit, measured by money gain in the market, the activity was
assumed to be in the general interest. The reality of resource
scarcity began to be felt in a more crowded twentieth-century
society. Some opinion leaders now began to urge that we needed
to calculate our use of resources by a "real"—a tangible goods—
measure and not just by a money calculus that operated on the
assumption that the profit calculations of private dealers in the
market would embrace all the terms of dealing that society needed
to consider.[45] A prime symbol of desired change from a money
to a real calculus was the Environmental Protection Act of 1970,
requiring that before a government agency sanctioned action that
might affect the environment it must prepare and file an environmental impact statement.[46] Growing federal and state regulation

44. Dahl and Lindstrom, 385–393; Fabricant, 3–9, 140–155.
45. Ciriacy-Wantrup, 54–55, 70, 252–259; Hurst (4), 36, 40, 44, 50, 59,
85, 94, 111–112, 119, 122, 124, 128, 135, 220–221, 262–263, 410, 541,
602–603; Kapp, 228–231.
46. 83 Stat. 852 (1969); Frederick R. Anderson, Chap. IV.

of air and water pollution, enacted and enforced amid considerable dispute, also bore witness to a new concern with nonmarket values. The market worked too much by short-term reckonings; the new emphasis in public policy was to exercise care to keep the society's options as open as possible for the benefit of future generations.[47]

The market also brought to issue problems of the conservation of human resources, deriving from the narrowness and short-term characteristic of the market's money calculus. Public policy developed to build some of the costs of industrial accidents into the costs of production through workmen's compensation. After stubborn controversy, the states commonly barred child labor, rejecting the harsh impersonality of a short-term money calculus of labor costs. In one important dimension the legal protection of collective bargaining qualified the impersonality of the labor market by providing the framework within which union-management contracts protected individual workers against arbitrary imposition of plant discipline. In such respects law broadened the implications of the declaration of the Clayton Act (1914), "That the labor of a human being is not a commodity."[48]

Twentieth-century public policy also profoundly qualified the autonomy of market processes by acting to lessen the human costs of shifts in the general course of business. As markets enlarged their reach and became more and more interlocked, more and more people became subject to the impact of inflation and deflation, unemployment, and disturbance of credit. In proportion to their elaboration, market processes made greater numbers of individuals vulnerable to basic unsettlement of their life expectations, and hence made the society more vulnerable to widespread unrest and loss of morale. Particularly from the mid-1930's on, the legal order showed a broadening range of responses to such market-borne vulnerability—by providing unemployment insur-

47. Ciriacy-Wantrup, 39, 251–253, 256–257, 265; Gulick (1), 31, 142, 163, 196, 211; Christopher Stone (1), 486.
48. Brodie, 161; Brandeis, 197; Dulles, 201, 202, 262, 269, 283; cf. 38 Stat. 730 (1914), section 6.

ance, by fiscal and monetary policy designed (however imperfectly) to moderate swings of the business cycle, by insurance of
bank deposits, and by enlarged welfare services.[49]

Public policy continued to rely heavily on the market as a resource allocator. But concern arose that market processes were
not capable of maintaining themselves against private power so
concentrated as to be able to overawe or at least to manipulate
the market. The use of the corporate form of business enterprise
facilitated the concentration of assets that gave rise to this new
concern.

Consensus and Conflict Concerning
the Business Corporation

The changing technology of industry together with the use of
the corporation brought fundamental changes in the role of the
market from the 1880's on. In old and new industries new technology invited larger concentrations of capital than the country
had seen before. The corporate form of business organization
not only helped to muster capital on the scale suggested by technological change, but also provided facilities for concentrating
capital and its management beyond the point dictated by technology alone.[50]

By the late 1880's use of the corporation had passed through
three stages that left the device readily available for a new style
and size of business enterprise. From the late eighteenth century
into the 1850's formal public policy jealously guarded the grant
of corporate status for doing business. Incorporation in itself
facilitated group action, and the greater power resident in organized as compared with individual effort was distrusted.
Moreover, the bulk of early charters went to men who wanted
more than corporate status. They wanted, also, franchises permit-
ting them to engage in activity the law forbade to the general

49. Heller, Chap. II; Rostow (1), Chaps. 12, 13, 14; Herbert Stein, 457–
468.
50. Blair, 255–285.

population—franchises to build dams on navigable streams, for example, or to set up banks empowered to issue paper currency. Apart from balance-of-power considerations, the grant of corporate status plus the grant of special-action franchises ran counter to strong egalitarian sentiment; the law here was enabling groups to do things or to enjoy privileges not open to individuals. Resultant doubts about the corporation were expressed formally by the early insistence that promoters obtain a special statutory charter for each business enterprise that sought corporate status. Policy makers' distrust of the business corporation as a threat to the self-regulating market appears in the fact that even though legislatures insisted on passing separately on each application for a charter, they were willing to enact general incorporation acts for nonmarket, philanthropic undertakings, such as libraries or religious bodies.[51]

The special charter era lasted in form in the states into the 1870's, but most of substance had departed from it long before then. From about the 1840's state legislatures granted almost all applications made to them for special charters for ordinary business purposes. Little was "special" about these charters in most fields; for the general run of enterprises the special charters settled into stable patterns, conferring about the same powers and imposing about the same regulatory conditions on all grantees. As state legislatures enacted hundreds of special business corporation charters, a growing consensus grew to see the corporate device as simply a handy, utilitarian instrument for doing business, which the community welcomed. Some dwindling political polemic continued against charters for conferring privileges that ran counter to egalitarian sentiments. But the true basis of objection was not to the grant of corporate status in itself, but to those charters that were accompanied by grants of special-action franchises.[52]

From about the mid-nineteenth century, legislatures began to

51. Hurst (5), 14–30, 134.
52. Id., 28–46.

recognize the substance of public policy by enacting general incorporation acts for broadly defined categories of business enterprise under which promoters could obtain a corporate franchise by meeting standard statutory terms. The earlier tradition of wary distrust of corporate bodies showed in regulatory provisions embodied in the general incorporation acts, such as those that limited the life of the corporation, required payment in of certain capital to protect creditors, and defined the allowed purposes of corporate action. The first generation of general incorporation acts simply offered promoters an option; if businessmen still chose to seek incorporation by special legislation, they might do so. Many continued to obtain special charters to avoid regulatory provisions in the general acts. But from the 1870's on state constitution makers forbade further issue of special charters, and the general acts became the exclusive means of acquiring corporate status. Again, a consensus appears from the face of legislation, which was substantially the same in all states, that businessmen properly should enjoy the utility of the corporate form, but under some restrictions designed to keep corporate business within limits consistent with maintaining a free market.[53]

A new phase of public policy toward the business corporation opened in 1896 when New Jersey and soon afterward Delaware adopted general incorporation laws more generous in their terms for the interests of promoters and management. Particularly important for its bearing on the market was the grant of authority to a corporation to hold the shares of other corporations. Moved by desire for the revenue from chartering fees, New Jersey and Delaware set off a competition among states to offer charter terms more and more favorable to corporate entrepreneurs at the expense of protection of investors or the general public. In the course of this development general incorporation laws dropped most of the regulatory provisions contained in the general acts of the late nineteenth century. Now more than ever the corpor-

53. Id., 56–57.

ate device facilitated massing capital under management discipline. Promoters used the new style of general incorporation statute to aid creation of larger enterprises and to give management maximum freedom of maneuver in building firms of unprecedented size.[54]

By the second quarter of the twentieth century all economically important states had adopted corporation laws drawn to give the greatest scope for managerial discretion. By this time the evident prevailing consensus was that corporation law should not provide significant regulation of corporate power in behalf of interests other than those of management. Such regulation as existed in a regime of large-scale business corporations would be accomplished mainly under law other than that of corporate organization. State and federal laws forbade combinations in restraint of trade, for example. Federal bankruptcy law was specially adapted to corporations. State statutes of varying scope regulated the issue and sale of corporate shares. Federal regulation of corporate finance centered on the Securities Act of 1933 and the Securities Exchange Act of 1934. The National Labor Relations Act, though applicable to all employers in interstate commerce, was particularly important as it bore on large-scale corporations.[55]

At mid-twentieth century public policy thus emerged with a patchwork of consensus and conflict that left unresolved questions of the political and social legitimacy of the big business corporation. The issue of legitimacy was real and urgent. Great practical power over resource allocation and over the social and political values it affected had come to rest in modern corporate management. The constitutional ideal, a stubbornly enduring part of the country's political tradition, insisted that all forms of private and public power should be accountable to others than the powerholders. But trends in corporation law and practice worked against effective external accountability of management in the big company. The board of directors should exercise

54. Cary (2), 664–670; Hurst (5), 45, 69–75.
55. Hurst (5), 90–104; cf. Cary (2), 696–705.

knowledgeable scrutiny of the managers. But key members of
the board were likely to be from management ranks, in practice
management nominated directors drawn from outside the operation, and these outside directors found it increasingly difficult
to obtain and master the information needed for independent
judgment on the quality of management's conduct of affairs.[56]
Information costs bore even harder on ordinary stockholders,
whose scattered numbers and limited commitments to the enterprise raised almost insuperable practical obstacles to mustering effective challenge to management. As his distance increased
from the working policies of the company, the ordinary stockholder's concern focused simply on assured receipt of dividends
and the hope of capital gain; as long as management maintained
some reasonable satisfaction of these limited demands, the stockholder showed himself unlikely to inquire further into the
corporation's operations; if he became sufficiently dissatisfied,
he would sell his shares, and though a declining market for the
company's shares could provide some stockholder-generated
pressure on management, it was a residual, last-resort discipline.
Moreover, insofar as stockholder concern impinged more directly
on management's conduct—as it might in the case of large holders
who kept some contact with top managers—that concern most
likely would measure corporate performance only by ordinary
market calculus. The market calculus measured important functions of the enterprise, but, given the political and social as well
as economic influence resident in modern large-scale firms, the
general society had reason to seek accountability in terms that
might reach beyond conventional business accounting.[57] The
growth of regulatory statutes and the administrative controls
they provided gave tangible evidence of felt needs to impose on
the big corporation accountability in terms that reached beyond
the market. But these government regulations developed in an

56. Hurst (5), 105–106; Livingston, 67–69; Christopher Stone (2), 125–
133, 145.
57. Hurst (5), 82–104; Livingston, Chap. 2; Christopher Stone (2), 47–
48, 81–82.

ad hoc fashion and did not express a clear or coherent philosophy of corporate responsibility.

Some claimed to find in the development of corporate management the grounds of its own legitimacy. In this view, the large corporation had ceased to be the individualized creation of some masterful captain of industry and had taken on the continuity and momentum of an institution. The institution now served needs of various constituencies—its shareholders, its labor force, its suppliers and customers, the ultimate consumers of its products, and the general community insofar as the community depended on the corporation's fulfilling its role in the general social division of labor. This institutional setting, the argument ran, schooled modern management and influential shareholders to make decisions that would serve the continuity of the enterprise rather than the opportunistic gains of the moment and that would strike fair balances among the claims of the varied groups affected by the corporation's activity. Management had become a profession, like law or medicine, and the sense of professional responsibility to social function would discipline its use of power.[58]

The thesis had some plausibility to the extent that twentieth-century big business management took on characteristics of bureaucracy. But the scope of the legitimizing role claimed for management was little short of that traditionally held by the legislative branch of government—to hear and judge competing claims of a broad range of interest groups and to seek equitable adjustments among them. The boldness of the claim threw into sharp relief the fact that the thesis did not meet the basic criterion of the constitutional ideal, that powerholders be subject to external checks. Over the years there was little development in the specific content of public policy to warrant the claim that broad interest balancing was accepted as a proper role of corporate management or controlling shareholders. The law did

58. Berle, Chap. III; Hurst (5), 105–107.

sanction some charitable giving by corporations, justified both by the corporation's social responsibilities and by its own enlightened self-interest. But no other development gave clear legal recognition to claims made for the corporation's self-justifying social roles. On the contrary, the tendency was to enlarge legal regulations of corporate labor practices, the safety of corporate products, the honesty of corporate advertising, the integrity of corporate financial arrangements, to an extent that showed that the general society was not prepared to accept management as self-legitimizing.[59]

Apart from legal controls, nineteenth-century public policy relied on competition in the market as an external curb on inefficient or abusive use of private economic power. As the development of the big business corporation weakened the checks directors or stockholders might exercise on corporate management, emphasis turned more to market discipline. But the rise of big business posed threats to the integrity, or indeed the existence, of processes of competition that pointed to the need of law to protect the market against subversion. A specialized response was the Interstate Commerce Act (1887). Of broader reach was the Sherman Act (1890).

Consensus and Conflict Concerning Antitrust Law

The whole of antitrust law is much too large to be brought within the compass of this chapter. But we can grasp some key aspects of antitrust policy by centering on the Sherman Act and the Clayton and Federal Trade Commission Acts (1914) and by emphasizing main lines of policy developed between 1890 and 1941. Antitrust policy history is useful particularly for examining consensus and conflict in all their variety. On the one hand, the record shows broadly shared wants—to an important extent inconsistent with each other—and on the other hand, it shows the

59. Hurst (5), 107–108; Katz, 181.

leverage that could be exerted by relatively few persons operating against a background of general indifference or ignorance.

The most striking characteristic of the principal antitrust statutes was their breadth. Mr. Chief Justice Hughes observed, "As a charter of freedom, the [Sherman] Act has a generality and adaptability comparable to that found to be desirable in constitutional provisions."[60] The statute declared simply, "Every contract, combination in the form of trust or otherwise, or conspiracy, in restraint of trade or commerce among the several States, or with foreign nations, is hereby declared to be illegal." With like simplicity it also laid penalties upon "every person who shall monopolize, or attempt to monopolize, or combine or conspire with any other person or persons, to monopolize any part of the trade or commerce among the several States, or with foreign nations."[61]

The act of September 26, 1914, created a Federal Trade Commission. The statute devoted the bulk of its provisions to broadly phrased grants of power to the commission to investigate "the organization, business, conduct, practices, and management . . . and . . . relation to other corporations and to individuals, associations, and partnerships" of corporations engaged in interstate commerce other than banking or transportation. It also declared unlawful "unfair methods of competition in commerce" and empowered the commission to proceed against such unfair methods by cease-and-desist orders ultimately enforceable by recourse to the federal circuit courts of appeals.[62]

The Clayton Act (October 15, 1914) seemed to depart from this pattern of generality by forbidding specified practices, including price discrimination, tying contracts and exclusive dealing arrangements, intercorporate stock acquisitions, and interlocking directorates. Specifically, the act dealt only with a limited

60. Hughes, C.J., in Appalachian Coals, Inc. v. United States, 288 U.S. 344, 359–360 (1933).
61. 26 Stat. 209 (1890).
62. 38 Stat. 717 (1914).

range of business practices relevant to the concentration of economic power. And, except in the ban on interlocking directorates, in effect the act returned all its specific prohibitions to the realm of general standard by making them apply only where the effect might be "to substantially lessen competition or tend to create a monopoly in any line of commerce."[63]

History was of limited help in fleshing out these statutes, especially the two enacted in 1914. When it referred to tying clauses, price discrimination, and other specified particulars, the Clayton Act used terms born of its own day. The Federal Trade Commission Act created a new agency and a new function when it broadly granted the commission powers to investigate current business practice. On its face, and in the intent of its sponsors, the statute deliberately skirted a historic common-law concept when it forbade "unfair methods of competition." The common law had developed doctrine against "unfair competition," but clear-cut precedent under this head ran only against palming off one's goods as those of another. Far from invoking such practice as history might offer, the language of the Federal Trade Commission Act was designed to cast free from historical limitations.[64]

At first view the Sherman Act seemed to draw some precision from history. Contracts in restraint of trade and monopoly were terms familiar to English common law and legislation. Perhaps when Congress used the familiar words it merely gave federal courts the authorization they needed—since there was no federal common law—to enforce doctrines well marked in the English inheritance. In the congressional debates preceding the Sherman Act some speakers indicated that this was Congress's intent and said little more to indicate the content of the policy adopted. But in fact the English concepts were so different from the situation that faced the United States in 1890 as to give the familiar-

63. 38 Stat. 730 (1914).
64. Cf. Hughes, C.J., in Schechter Poultry Corp. v. United States, 295 U.S. 495, 531 (1935); see Blaisdell, 17–23; Letwin, 277.

sounding words little relevance. English common law developed a precise but limited notion of a contract in restraint of trade. The seller of a business might agree that he would not after the sale compete with his buyer; one working for another might agree that after the employment ended he would not compete with the employer for the favor of established customers. But this doctrine concerned small-scale dealings, where restraint of competition was an incident of another and primary purpose. Moreover, in the general view taken after 1800, the common-law doctrine was wholly passive in effect; the common law did not declare that it was a crime or a tort to make a forbidden type of restraining agreement, but only that the law would refuse to lend its aid to enforce the agreement, if the agreement were found to limit competition more broadly than was fair to the interests of the parties or the public.[65]

The English inheritance of doctrine against "monopoly" simply opposed the grant by the crown to private persons of exclusive rights to make or trade in given articles; it was directed not against privately contrived concentration of economic power, but merely against government creation of private empire. True, from the thirteenth through the sixteenth centuries other statutes sought to preserve simple bargaining relations between sellers and ultimate consumers in fairs or markets. But by 1890 conduct that these old laws forbade under the names of forestalling, regrating, and engrossing had become commonplace, approved practices in a more complicated distribution system that included manufacturers, wholesalers, jobbers, and retailers.[66]

Previous United States developments helped little to put definite content into the Sherman Act's words. Andrew Jackson fought renewal of the charter of the Second Bank of the United

65. See Taft, circ. j., in United States v. Addyston Pipe & Steel Co., 85 Fed. 271, 282–283 (6th cir. 1898); Letwin, 39–52, 77–84; Stocking and Watkins, 260–261; Thorelli, 17–20, 50–53, 181, 183–185, 200–201, 228, 229.

66. Letwin, 19–39; Oppenheim, 10–12; Thorelli, 20–26.

States in terms that provided an American analogy to the classic
English policy against government grants of monopoly.[67] Mr.
Chief Justice Taney spoke in the same tradition in the Charles
River Bridge case, when he declared that special statutory
franchises must be strictly construed to preserve the public interest in development of new enterprise.[68] But up to 1890 the law
in this country had little to say about concentrated economic
power created by private effort. A scattering of late nineteenth-
century state statutes regulated "natural monopolies," as in the
operation of grain elevators at key junction points. In 1876 in
Munn v. *Illinois* a majority of the Supreme Court sustained such
regulation, but in terms that soon were used to restrict the significance of the ruling to classic public utilities.[69] Between 1848 and
1890 about a score of reported decisions in the United States
dealt with various kinds of agreements that directly sought to
restrain trade, without the historic excuse of being ancillary to the
sale of a business or a contract of employment. But, though most
of these decisions found the questioned agreements to be illegal,
it was impossible to spell out of the courts' opinions any unified
doctrine. Moreover, neither the decisions nor most of the theoriz-
ing in the courts' opinions fitted the uncompromising ban of the
Sherman Act on "every" contract in restraint of trade. If some
members of Congress thought that the words of the Sherman
Act invoked a more definite common-law doctrine than in fact
existed, congressmen did not spell out what they thought this
doctrine was. At the most, reliance on the common law could
serve to warrant more flexibility in antitrust policy than the
unqualified words of the Sherman Act alone indicated. The
sweeping terms of the statute necessarily implied a delegation
of power to the courts; reliance on an ill-defined common law

67. Hurst (7), 166, 167, 169; Meyers, 17–19, 22.
68. Charles River Bridge v. Warren Bridge, 11 Pet. 420 (U.S. 1837) 1;
cf. Kutler, 15–16, 43–44.
69. Munn v. Illinois 94 U.S. 113 (1876); cf. Nebbia v. New York, 291
U.S. 502 (1934); Kelly and Harbison, 508, 511, 710–714; McCloskey, 127–
128, 156.

to add content to the statutory terms underlined the readiness to delegate power to the judges.[70]

Events in Congress leading up to the passage of the Sherman Act contributed little to develop the content of antitrust policy. The dangers and abuses of great economic power concentrated in private hands stirred public opinion and political response in the last quarter of the nineteenth century. First a few states passed what proved to be fruitless statutes against monopoly, until policy makers came to see that the problems demanded national attention. But up to 1890 attention went mainly to the money supply, the tariff, and the regulation of railroads. In each of these areas of controversy people expressed their fear of "monopoly," but in terms special to these particular problem areas; from these disputes no coherent philosophy or program for ordering the general economy emerged. Presidents Grover Cleveland and Benjamin Harrison in messages to Congress mentioned the threat of aggregations of power outside the areas of money, tariff, and railroads, but neither chose to apply pressure for action. Antitrust planks in both major party platforms in 1888 showed no evidence of being more than part of the usual dragnet for votes. There was no flood of petitions to Congress, nor did the press show sustained interest in the general subject to account for enactment of an antitrust law in 1890. The press paid almost no attention to the course of the congressional debate or the enactment of the statute. Consideration in Congress was marked by general denunciations of the trusts, but otherwise most of the discussion went to shaping a bill that would be within Congress's constitutional authority. The value of the debates was limited further because most of the discussion related to a bill substantially different from the one Congress finally passed. The Senate first debated a bill sponsored by Senator John Sherman and reported by the Finance Committee. This became entangled in a number of confusing amendments, and on the third attempt

70. Letwin, 79–85, 96–97, 174–177; Thorelli, 41–48.

it was referred for reworking not to the original committee but to the Senate Judiciary Committee. The Judiciary Committee reported out the bill that passed, and this went through both houses with relatively little discussion.[71]

The statute's ambiguous origin was prophetic of the first years of its administration. The tepid interest of press, public, and Congress raises the question why an antitrust law was passed at all in 1890. There was the continuing spark of agrarian revolt; Congressman John H. Reagan (Texas) and Senator John J. Ingalls (Kansas) were pressing for specific bans on or regulations of obnoxious business practices. Senator Sherman was conscientious and had a strong party sense, which perhaps made him feel that the Republican party should show that it was not solely concerned with tariff protection for big industry. Once the movement had gained some momentum, it was politically difficult to stop it by direct attack; everyone was against "the trusts." Plainly, however, influential senators were not ready to enact a detailed specification of forbidden business practices. A retreat into generalities sanctioned by common-law tradition was a way out of the immediate difficulty.[72]

Despite its generality and the lack of an informative history, the Sherman Act was not without significant effect on the state of the law. (1) Congress formally acknowledged an ideal of free competition, however ill-defined. Thus Congress set up a rallying point for demands that henceforth would exert some continuous, if uneven, pressure on government. (2) The Sherman Act determined that government had a positive duty to do something to maintain free competition. It was not enough that courts withhold enforcement of illegal agreements; criminal and civil actions were to be brought by government against the offenders, and the statute provided treble damages to induce private suitors to use the right of action it gave them. We must not exaggerate

71. Letwin, 85–95; Thorelli, 169–210.
72. Letwin, 54–59, 70, 85–97; Morison and Commager, 2:144; Stocking and Watson, 256–260, 263–264; Thorelli, 160–163, 226–230.

the emphasis on the public cause of action in the thinking of 1890; that was a period of high individualism, and Congress apparently thought that the private suit would be an effective instrument of enforcement. However, the act did depart strikingly from the common-law pattern in providing for criminal prosecutions, and even more so in authorizing the government to seek civil relief. (3) The Sherman Act provided the authority policy makers felt was necessary to allow federal action against restraint of trade. This decision marched with the times; the problems of industrial and financial concentration were outstripping the capacities of the states. (4) By its form—a direct, if vaguely defined command, enforceable by courts—the Sherman Act put the shaping of antitrust policy into the hands of prosecutor and judge. This was so natural to the times as hardly to amount to a conscious choice. Only three years before, Congress had created the first great federal administrative agency; the untested Interstate Commerce Commission could not be expected already to have set a new pattern for economic regulation. This initial reliance on the combination of prosecutor and judge had lasting effect in determining what attitudes and professional initiative and skill would control the development of antitrust policy. The lawyer, rather than the politician, economist, or administrator was to have the deciding voice. Both consensus and conflict typically would show themselves within quite narrow and specialized circles of interest in antitrust policy.[73]

No one paid much attention to antitrust policy for about eight years after passage of the Sherman Act. There was a scattering of random prosecutions, including one successfully brought against a labor union's activities. The tone of the times was set by Attorney General Richard Olney's unabashed refusal to prosecute under a law he thought to be ineffective. Then the rise of a great merger movement began to arouse public concern. Congress reacted first by creating the Industrial Commission of

73. Hurst (2), 92; Letwin, 93, 94, 96, 100–102; Thorelli, 229, 571, 587–589.

1898 to find facts and make recommendations on national economic problems, including the concentration of power in private hands. In 1900–1901, Congress considered recommendations made by the Industrial Commission, along with other proposals to strengthen the Sherman Act. The stumbling block was the Supreme Court's ruling in 1895 in a Sherman Act prosecution brought against the sugar trust. Manufacture was a local matter, said the Court, and a combination of manufacturers had only indirect effect on interstate commerce; the Sherman Act was not intended to apply to such combinations, and if it were so intended, the clear indication was that the Court would hold it unconstitutional. In the debate in 1900–1901, Congress was unable to work out any strengthening amendments that would fit within the sugar trust decision. As a practical matter, only a fresh prosecuting effort and a responsive Court could clear away this obstacle to further antitrust policy making. At this point vigorous executive action entered the picture. Encouraged by President Theodore Roosevelt, the Department of Justice cast off the discouragement the sugar trust decision had laid on prosecution and brought suits that gave the Court a chance to reconsider its earlier attitude. In 1904 and 1905 the Court accepted the opportunity and in substance repudiated the narrow approach it had taken under the commerce clause ten years before.[74]

This was Roosevelt's most significant contribution to the legislative level of antitrust policy. From his first regular message to Congress in 1901 through his insurgent campaign for the presidency in 1912 he put antitrust policy to the front of his legislative program. Indirectly he affected the course of policy by helping to build popular acceptance for some significant legal controls on

74. United States v. E. C. Knight Co., 156 U.S. 1 (1895); cf. Addyston Pipe & Steel Co. v. United States, 175 U.S. 211 (1899); Northern Securities Co. v. United States, 193 U.S. 197 (1904); Swift & Co. v. United States, 196 U.S. (1905). On the Industrial Commission of 1898: Hacker and Zahler (2), 22–23, 27, 32–33; Lynch, 387–388.

big business, giving that concept almost the sanctity of a constitutional principle. But he never applied to antitrust policy the
skill he showed in pressing Congress on other matters. Perhaps
his successful fight for a modest beginning at more effective rate-
making powers for the Interstate Commerce Commission ex-
hausted his energy. Perhaps, with his shrewd grasp of the limits of
public opinion, he may have decided that the railroad battle had
used up the effective stock of public interest. He characteristically
wavered between an urgent sense of the need for change and a
worried concern lest political processes too much disturb working institutions. The lack of an assured theory of action concerning business concentration also may have limited his zeal.[75]

Building on public and professional economic discussion of the
preceding decade, the 1912 campaign brought the first explicit
consideration of the premises of antitrust policy. When Congress
passed the Sherman Act, and for at least ten years thereafter, the
ideal of free competition was so taken for granted as to be little
discussed. In 1912, Theodore Roosevelt resolved his wavering
between reform and the status quo by preaching that modern
big business was big mainly because it was efficient and that the
proper approach to it was not to try to break it up, but to license
it under strict federal control. This approach already had found
some expression in Congress and among economists. After some
hesitation, Woodrow Wilson rejected this solution and made
free competition an explicit goal of policy. He found his program
in the idea of preventive action, striking early at practices destructive of competition. As President, Wilson assigned high
priority to antitrust legislation and exercised his influence to
achieve the bargaining compromises necessary to produce the
Clayton Act, with its catalogue of forbidden business practices.
But he reserved his most vigorous action for the companion bill
to create a Federal Trade Commission. Under the bill first put
through the House with the President's approval, the new com-

75. Blum, 87–105; Roosevelt, 427–430.

mission was to be simply a fact-finding body. In this form the measure aroused no controversy and easily passed the House. By the time it reached the Senate, however, the President had been persuaded by his advisers that effective prevention of undue business concentration called for a commission vested with regulatory powers. Congress already had strong advocates of such a body, but Wilson's decision to support the idea was decisive of the shape of the legislation. In its new form the bill provoked vigorous debate, but passed with the regulatory provisions intact a few weeks before Congress adopted the watered-down Clayton Act. The President's new-found reliance on the regulatory commission vested with power to prohibit "unfair methods of competition" probably explained his readiness to give ground on the Clayton Act.[76] The Federal Trade Commission did not fulfill the hopes of its sponsors. Torn by internal dissension and headed by men who did not hold a strong anti-trust point of view, for years the commission largely confined itself to dealing with false advertising. Only after 1950, when Congress enacted the Celler-Kefauver bill amending the Clayton Act to extend its ban on mergers that might substantially limit competition, did the commission become a major force in anti-trust enforcement.[77]

In the 1920's the growth of trade associations stimulated suggestions for relaxing antitrust policy. Lawyers, business leaders, and trade association bureaucrats argued that trade associations opened the way to a new kind of competition in which business itself would police undesirable practices. To these advocates, what was undesirable mainly seemed to be aggressive price competition. The principal official support for relaxing antitrust

76. Blum, 116–121; Letwin, 277; Link, 417–418, 423, 427, 433, 434, 438, 440–444; Mason, 402–404.

77. On the indifferent record of the FTC: Marver H. Bernstein, 49, 222, 225; Corwin Edwards, 301–303; Green, 321–333; Hacker and Zahler (2), 333. On the Celler-Kefauver Amendment: 64 Stat. 1125 (1950); Brown Shoe Co. v. United States, 370 U.S. 294, 312–323 (1962); Mueller, 146–147, 158.

policy to give scope to trade associations came from the Department of Commerce under Secretary Herbert Hoover. Hoover did not support price fixing through trade associations, but he believed that cooperative action by business could improve efficiency and raise the level of competition. He recommended that cooperating organizations be authorized to submit their plans to some federal agency for approval so that their good work would not be hindered by doubts of its validity under the antitrust laws.[78]

The idea of relaxing the antitrust laws to give scope for "stabilizing" activity of trade associations persisted in a different social context when depression fell on the country in the 1930's. In the fall of 1931 the Senate Committee on Manufactures held hearings on establishing a national economic council. Business leaders told the committee that if trade associations were free of antitrust restraints, they could render valuable service in curbing abrupt swings of the business cycle. This idea was embodied in the National Industrial Recovery Act (NIRA) of 1933, under which industries were to draw "codes" for their own governance, with their own code authorities, to enforce standards of fair competition. Government would supervise and pass on the codes and their administration. Implicit, again, was the idea that fair competition would bar aggressive price cutting.[79]

The NIRA represented a preference for an immediate chance at market stability over the long-term benefits of competition. But the decision reflected no broad, integrated policy, as was apparent in the unresolved conflicts disclosed by the face of the statute. It declared the policy of Congress to be to promote full use of productive capacity of industries and to remove obstructions to the free flow of commerce. At the same time it stated the policy of promoting united action of producer groups to

78. Arthur R. Burns, 73–75; Hacker and Zahler (2), 259–260; Joan H. Wilson, 98–102, 110, 120, 152–154.

79. Hacker and Zahler (2), 381, 401–403; Hawley, 19–34.

eliminate unfair competitive practices and conceded that production might have to be "temporarily" restricted. The President must find, as a condition of approving any industry code, that it was not designed to permit monopolies or oppression of small firms. But the statute also made a sweeping declaration that any action complying with the provisions of the act or of a code established under the act should be exempt from the antitrust laws.[80]

A measure of economic improvement restored the country's nerve. With increasing vigor liberals and small businessmen attacked the National Industrial Recovery Act as a device promoting concentration. In 1935 the Supreme Court held the act unconstitutional, in part as an undue delegation of legislative power. This eased the administration's retreat from an increasingly embarrassing position. The rapid collapse of public and political support for the NIRA showed that there was not yet any broad consensus for substantial departures from the competitive ideal symbolized by the Sherman Act. On the other hand, the impetuous, opportunistic enactment of the NIRA and the popular enthusiasm that supported its early days showed that the foundations of antitrust policy were uncertain. After forty years antitrust policy had not evolved into a reasonably definite and coherent set of ideas with a firm base in popular understanding and acceptance. The point was made, again, in 1938 by the facility with which the administration and supporting opinion changed emphasis on enforcing the antitrust laws.[81]

The country suffered an economic relapse in 1937. Now President Franklin Roosevelt accepted the theory that economic ills were due largely to rigidity of prices in fields controlled by a few great companies. Rigid prices, the argument ran, limited purchasing power and blocked smooth market adjustment of

80. 48 Stat. 195 (1933); Hawley, 35–52, 72–90; Oppenheim, 29–32.
81. Schechter Poultry Corp. v. United States, 295 U.S. 495 (1935); cf. Arthur R. Burns, 512–521; Hawley, 91–129; Morison and Commager, 2:601–604.

supply and demand. Following this tack, the President authorized the start of the most ambitious antitrust campaign ever undertaken by the Department of Justice. The drive met with substantial public approval.[82]

Antitrust enforcement first took on separate status in the Department of Justice with the creation of the Antitrust Division in 1903. But for years Congress provided little resources for the division, while successive Presidents applied no pressure for more generous treatment. In Theodore Roosevelt's time the Antitrust Division numbered five lawyers and four stenographers. From 1914 to 1923, years of a great surge of business mergers and general economic growth, the division staff averaged eighteen lawyers, and never more than twenty-five. In 1933 the division had only fifteen lawyers. By 1938 for the first time it employed as many as fifty lawyers, but the increase of staff traced mainly to the division's handling of cases arising under the administration's early recovery legislation.[83] In 1939 the division jumped to two hundred lawyers and half a dozen economists, pursuing for the first time a large, planned course of antitrust enforcement under the leadership of Assistant Attorney General Thurman Arnold. The 1939 point of growth represented a new and lasting level of commitment of resources to antitrust enforcement. For the first time major antitrust effort in the Department of Justice was professionalized and given permanent, substantial status. Even so, we must not exaggerate the extent of change. The greatly increased budget of the Antitrust Division in 1940 was only about as much money as was then given, simply for research and fact-finding, to the Bureau of Labor Statistics or the Bureau of Agricultural Economics. In 1940 the Antitrust Division was allocated about $1,250,000, compared with $5,470,000 for the Securities and Exchange Commission, $3,990,000 for the Maritime Commission, $3,254,000 for the Railroad Retirement Board, and

82. Green, 67–68; Hawley, 386–419; Hofstadter, 228–229; Mueller, 156, 158.

83. Arnold (2), 170–171, 184, 212, 276–277; Hamilton and Till, 24.

$3,189,600 for the National Labor Relations Board. Each of these agencies dealt with areas of regulation highly specialized in comparison to the field of the Antitrust Division. Indeed, the latter had to use its budget not only for enforcing the antitrust laws, but also to discharge duties with which it was charged under some thirty other acts of Congress. Nonetheless, the greater commitment to antitrust enforcement made in 1939–1940 marked a turning point. World War II interrupted Arnold's campaigns, but after the war the Antitrust Division continued to build on the enlarged base he had erected.[84]

Using the opportunities afforded them by government prosecutors or private plantiffs, federal judges, not Congress, made the bulk of particular antitrust policy. With rare exceptions—notably the Robinson-Patman Act of 1936 on price discrimination—Congress was content to leave the matter, and no compelling public opinion pressed Congress to shoulder more responsibility.[85] This pattern poses problems in identifying areas of consensus and conflict in antitrust policy. Conflict was inherent and conspicuous, within relatively narrow bounds, in a body of public policy fashioned mainly by litigation. But it was conflict between small bands of professionals—primarily between government prosecutors on the one hand and business leaders and their lawyers on the other. Once we move outside the circle of litigious combat, estimates of opinion and attitudes rapidly become vague. Businessmen believed in competition as an abstract ideal, but feared its specific application; thus there was in the background a general business sentiment critical of zealous antitrust enforcement.[86] Yet the ideal of a competitive market protected under the antitrust laws was a general article of faith in the society, evidenced by the fact that, except for the short-lived experiment

84. Arnold (3), 70, 171, 276; Corwin Edwards, 296–297; Hamilton and Till, 23, 24, 25, 34, 40; Hofstadter, 230–235.

85. Cf. 49 Stat. 1526 (1936) (Robinson-Patman Act).

86. Arnold (3), 35–36, 207–229; Bowen, 66, 108; Eells, 120–123, 249, 251–258; Galbraith, 184–197; Sutton et al., 168, 189.

under the National Industrial Recovery Act, no one mustered enough political strength to make a serious effort to repeal or drastically to modify the Sherman Act. Measured by the demonstrated limits of political practicality, there appeared a consensus in favor of, or at least accepting of, the broad delegations of power by Congress to government prosecutors and the courts. In 1950, Congress bore witness to this consensus when, in one of its rare interventions, it amended the Clayton Act still further to extend the delegation of powers by authorizing broader preventive action against any merger that might substantially lessen competition in any line of commerce in any section of the country.[87]

The matter was not so simple because general opinion included other articles of faith that might work against determined efforts by government to break up big enterprise or to prevent its creation. Up to the 1970's prevailing opinion has held that general welfare is served by a rising material standard of living based on steady increase in gross national product. General opinion has associated rising productivity with large-scale business enterprise. There have been diverse, strong currents of criticism of big business: that it had too much power in the market, squeezing out smaller enterprise; that it harmed consumers by keeping up prices; that it wielded too much power over government; that it showed lack of consideration for workers or for maintaining employment. But broad currents of opinion also relied on big business to create jobs and to foster mass production and distribution that would make goods and services more readily available to more people. The criticisms were broad-based enough to support particular extensions of government regulation, but there was no evidence that they added up to potential support for antitrust action vigorous enough drastically to restructure an economy built around operations of large-scale firms. Certainly the critical climate was not

87. Hawley, 456–494; Hofstadter, 228–235; Mueller, 166–175.

sufficiently threatening to bring forth any broad-scale effort between the United States Steel Company decision in 1920 and the Celler-Kefauver Amendment of 1950. More vigorous Federal Trade Commission action under the 1950 statute pointed up the principal element of uncertainty in the forecast—whether the vigor and staying power in the new, professionalized atmosphere of antitrust policy dating from Thurman Arnold's pioneering regime of 1938–1941 were strong enough to encourage the antitrust specialists to give a new lead and to hope that general opinion might ratify it.[88]

The general outlines of judge-made antitrust law were consistent with cautious regard for the ambiguities in public opinion regarding big business. For the present purpose it suffices to note two central aspects of the policy that judges hammered out—the place of intent and the place of power in the market as determinants of the legality or illegality of business conduct.

One point of doctrine was clear. An explicit agreement among competing firms to fix prices or to divide territory was a violation of the Sherman Act, whether or not the parties could argue that their purpose was consistent with the general welfare and regardless of arguments that the prices agreed on would produce only a reasonable return on investment. To make out a violation the government need not prove that the participants in the agreement had practical power to dominate the market. The unquestionable acceptance of this tight doctrine reflected a prevailing judgment that it was socially desirable that participating firms not be allowed to pool their efforts to end such competition as existed in a market. Within this definition, there was consensus on the desirability and importance of free markets.[89]

Monopoly or power in the market approaching monopoly was

88. Fisher and Withey, 20–25, 29, 34, 36, 43, 60, 66, 106. Cf. Hofstadter, 212–221, 225–228.

89. United States v. Trenton Potteries Co., 273 U.S. 392 (1927); United States v. Socony-Vacuum Oil Co., 310 U.S. 150 (1940). See Arnold (2), 310–314; Mueller, 142–143.

rare. Early decisions left uncertain the legal significance of proving that a firm held a dominant position in the market. The government won a decree for dissolution of Standard Oil (1911), but the Court said that the Sherman Act forbade only conduct that amounted to "an undue restraint" on commerce, and the Court so emphasized proof of predatory competitive methods by the defendant as to cloud the importance attached to the defendant's relative power in the market. In 1920 the Court refused a decree to dissolve the United States Steel Company, ruling that "the law does not make mere size an offense or the existence of unexerted power an offense." Because the defendant controlled about 50 percent of the industry, the decision could be appraised as catastrophic for efforts to prevent the merger and concentration movement. Later, however, the Supreme Court endorsed stricter doctrine. Where the defendant in fact dominated a market, and did so by intentional effort to hold and increase its market share, a violation of the Sherman Act existed, though the result was not the product of predatory tactics, nor of a specific intent to monopolize. But there would be no unlawful monopoly, if this had been thrust on the defendant by operation of forces outside its deliberate seeking. Again, the judges' conclusions spelled a consensus, but this time one of some ambiguity. Size in itself was not to be condemned, but only size procured by deliberate business policy.[90]

By the mid-twentieth century important markets in the United States were characterized by the presence of a few firms (four to eight, say) which together held the bulk of trade in their market. So general a condition of oligopoly was not familiar in 1890 and was emerging only gradually by 1914. Thus the legislative history of the key antitrust statutes gave little guidance for

90. Standard Oil Co. v. United States, 221 U.S. 1 (1911); United States v. American Tobacco Co., 221 U.S. 106 (1911); United States v. United States Steel Corp., 251 U.S. 417 (1920); United States v. Aluminum Co. of America, 148 Fed. (2d) 416 (2d cir., 1945); United States v. Griffith, 334 U.S. 100 (1948). See Mueller, 143–146; Stocking and Watson, 271–276, 288–296.

dealing with the problems of such markets. The issue here was typically one of intent, rather than of market power; at least, once the relevant market was defined—a point that could produce sharp controversy in itself—there was usually little to disagree about in measuring defendant firms' share of that market. Without resort to explicit agreement to limit competition, four dominant firms were likely in practice to behave with mutual regard to what each was doing. The fact that the market behavior of each paralleled that of its fellows was not in itself proof of an antitrust violation; perfect competition would tend to produce the same parallelism. On the other hand, competitors constantly were tempted to collude to fix prices, especially in highly concentrated industries. The Court allowed violations to be proved by circumstantial evidence. If other firms showed a continued pattern of following the pricing lead given by one firm, or if there was a continued pattern of parallel action in many details of marketing policy among firms of sufficiently diverse character to make such similarity of behavior unlikely save for collusive gains, a violation might be made out, even without proof of exertion of power to exclude others from the market. Yet the decisions were cautious; by and large, judges accepted oligopoly as the norm of twentieth-century markets, and the government did not press for further breakup of the handful of firms that made such markets. Again, consensus was ambiguous. The law would attack the monopolistic tendency of a handful of firms that indicated deliberate concert of action by the detail with which their respective marketing policies coincided. But antitrust policy did not reflect any sustained effort to use law further to fragment such markets.[91]

What stood out most sharply after nearly three generations of antitrust policy was that antitrust law neither had prevented nor

91. Interstate Circuit, Inc. v. United States, 306 U.S. 208 (1939); Federal Trade Commission v. Cement Institute, 333 U.S. 683 (1948); Theater Enterprises, Inc. v. Paramount Film Distributing Corp., 346 U.S. 537 (1954). See Kaysen and Turner, 25–41, 110, 111, 114–115; Mueller, 13–18, 85–96.

corrected the existence of large concentrations of market power in private hands. The few attempts at "trust busting" had not created markets of broadly dispersed competition. Size of firms was more critical than was overt collaboration among firms in determining the working character of markets. Whether it was the product of merger of competitors, or of vertical integration of operations from handling raw material to turning out finished product, or of the giant accumulation of diverse enterprises under one control, concentration was in practice a more fundamental threat to the balance of power than any number of agreements in restraint of trade. Concentrated power hung together; agreements among broadly dispersed competitors tended to fall apart under the stress of immediate self-interest or the pressure of newcomers. Agreements could be broken up by injunction; concentrated power presented daunting problems of dissolution, with fears for the unsettling effects of breaking up a pattern of industry. Concentrated power tended to grow by accretion. It built by plowing back the returns from its control of the market, so that ambition for power could more easily fix the course than if the business had to seek capital in the open market. Concentrated power thus tended to widen its reach, so that it became sensitive not only to events in its own industry, but to those in related industries; it made a favorable atmosphere for inter-industry treaties. Restrictive agreements in their nature involved too little group discipline, too much leeway for the ambitions of particular firms, to allow such sweeping growth. Concentrated power was apt to represent so broad a spread of interests and resources that, within wide limits, it could afford to disregard or subordinate profits to power politics and grow for the sake of growth. Alliances among independent firms could not mobilize resources of such weight.[92]

Thus, sound instinct was behind the main stress that the first generation of antitrust effort put on attacking concentrated

92. Kaysen and Turner, 25–27, 41, 100–111; Mueller, 11–20, 84–106.

power. But the attack faltered and never was pressed to the point of thorough breakup of private empire—the 1911 decisions still left oil and tobacco in control of a few great aggregations of wealth—and from 1920 to 1941 on the whole antitrust enforcement turned away from the concentration problems and gave most of its attention to agreements in restraint of trade or to trade practices deemed to limit efficient service to consumers. Not until the 1960's did antitrust enforcement, better grounded in the enlarging amendment to the Clayton Act of 1950, again emphasize mergers. But, over-all, enforcement tended to put aside the concentration issue and to content itself with seeking to establish administrative control of the operations of oligopolistic markets. The general run of antitrust enforcement effort after 1938 seemed sustained more by ideas about what economic structure or conduct would be conducive to economic efficiency than by concern for the social and political balance of power. A realistic appraisal could not ignore the balance-of-power dimension of antitrust policy; it figured in the creation and tenacious endurance of the legislation of 1890 and 1914. Indeed, a complete policy needed to embrace both economic and political aspects of private power in the market. Some men saw both aspects. Louis D. Brandeis appraised trusts or monopolies as "inefficient both economically and socially." Organizations like United States Steel were, he thought, too big to be efficient in production and distribution of goods, and those that were not too big for efficiency were often "too large to be tolerated among the people who desire to be free." If he had to choose, Brandeis would prefer the political (balance-of-power) values over the economic criteria of efficiency. His estimate did not prevail in the general course of antitrust enforcement. It was not rejected in a clear-cut debate between political and economic priorities, but rather was lost to sight in an opportunistic, unplanned course of action by those charged with enforcing the antitrust laws.[93]

93. On Brandeis: Mason, 354, 360. On activity after 1950 against mergers: Mueller, 146–155.

What stands out as most basic in the record is the lack of well-defined, comprehensive, sustained planning of public action affecting concentration of private economic control. This was not simply a defect of policy under the Sherman Act and its fellows, but a general failure to relate broader ranges of government activity to the structuring of private economic power. Corporation tax laws favored internal growth of large enterprises through retained earnings, incidentally lessening the discipline exerted by investment capital markets. Extension of public-utility-style regulations limited competitive innovations and competition in price and services, as in oil or the airlines. Government contracts tended to go to big concerns in a measure that furthered their power in the market. By underwriting the risks of scientific and technical venture in nuclear energy, electronics, and space efforts, government created a favorable environment for expansion of big business into new product and service fields. The point was not a lack of good ground in public interest for some government action in such matters, but that so much was done without clear definition and decision regarding the consequences for the overall balance of power in society. As with more focused aspects of antitrust law, so in the more general reaches of policy, there was a matter more fundamental than the state of consensus or conflict—the realistic definition of goals about which to rally agreement or opposition.[94]

Consensus and Conflict Regarding Government as Resource Allocator

This discussion has centered on the market as a prime resource allocator and on problems posed for the existence of the market by use of the corporation and by the related concentration of private economic power. Reality warrants this emphasis, for throughout the country's history the market continued to be the principal private institution for channeling the uses of economic

94. Adams and Gray, 52–54, 71, 75–95, 115–116, 163.

resources. But, to keep a proper perspective, we must not forget that political processes early played an important role in allocating resources and that policy makers tended to enlarge the goals and the impact of public intervention. The second chapter sketched this dimension by portraying the development of the legislative power of the purse and its analogues. The third chapter noted the growing role of government in directing resources to the advancement of science and technology. Even though its prime attention is given to the market, the present chapter has found it necessary to give weight to government's resource-allocating activities in support of the market, as in efforts to moderate swings of the business cycle.

To relate law and the market realistically to the general course of public policy, we need especially to note that legal history witnessed increasing resort to law to promote nonmarket values. Laissez-faire was never the dominant emphasis of the country's public policy; even in the nineteenth century we used law in varied ways both to foster and to regulate market behavior, but in the twentieth century lawmakers became more concerned with objectives that lay substantially outside market calculations.[95]

The resource-allocating goals of government in the nineteenth century centered on promoting growth of national markets and increasing the volume and pace of transactions. The dominant character of policy regarding disposal of the public domain was to underwrite development of bulk transport facilities and of a family farm economy. The tariff sought to foster the growth of industry as well as to protect the profits of the favored interests. Different groups contended over monetary policy, but all of them —farmers, merchants, bankers, industrialists, laborers—commonly wanted government to wield its influence over the money supply to promote and protect their respective concerns with doing business.[96]

Market-oriented goals remained important in the twentieth

95. Auerbach (1), 516–532; Hurst (2), Chaps. II, III.
96. Hurst (2), Chap. I, and (7), 76–85.

century over a wide range of resource allocations by government, from fiscal and monetary measures to affect the business cycle, to tax laws drawn to encourage capital investment, to government loans to subsidize the management of farm surpluses.[97] But in the twentieth century public-policy direction shifted toward major new emphasis on nonmarket values.

Three lines of policy stood out as particularly important. Cold war fears and the arms competition with Russia meant that government withdrew large resources from the civilian economy for defense spending and foreign military aid. Of course, such spending had significant bearing on markets; defense goals sometimes could not be distentangled from goals of maintaining domestic purchasing power and manufacturing activity as hedges against depression. But the basic objectives were more concerned with the international balance of power than with the state of the economy.[98]

Second, in the twentieth century unprecedented concern developed for providing constructive social capital—in the forms, notably, of education and promotion of scientific and technological advance—and for care of functional requisites of a livable society apart from demands of the market, particularly for the physical and biological environment, with special reference to policy affecting use of nonrenewable resources. In these domains the market tended to create more than to solve problems; accordingly, government moved into stronger resource-allocating and regulatory roles.[99]

Third, the very success of a market-oriented economy in increasing the supply of goods and services sharpened people's concern with patterns of the distribution of wealth and income; the society's demonstrated potential for raising the general material base of living tended to increase expectations brought to

97. Rostow (1), Chaps. 12, 13; Herbert Stein, 454–468.
98. Bator, 30–31; Mosher and Poland, 12–14, 24–26, 30, 40–41, 103–116.
99. Bator, 21–22, 26–28, 34, 35, 36; Mosher and Poland, 116–127; Solo, 265–276.

bear on public policy. Market processes had led in bringing about a substantial absolute rise in the material standard of living for a large part of the population, but by mid-twentieth century it was plain that these processes were not significantly changing the relative distribution of wealth and income and that only law would accomplish substantial change. Again, as with defense spending, policy goals overlapped; provision of greater social services, such as unemployment insurance and social security payments, helped to sustain and even out purchasing power for smoother operation of the market economy. But the deeper drives of politics appeared to lie in the search to achieve the non-market goals of income-transfer programs, as these sought to protect human dignity and to foster a more humane quality of life. As of the 1970's, public policy has accomplished little fundamental shift in the distribution of wealth and income. Partly this has resulted from lack of skill; enough administrative blundering and waste have occurred in carrying out such modest redistributive programs as law-makers adopted to show that we have a lot to learn about how to manage complex affairs. Partly, and more basically, lack of impact has derived from lack of will; the country's middle-class political tradition still contains idealism, but those in a broad spectrum of middle-range ambitions as well as those in top brackets still cling to privilege. Yet the promise of the new directions looks toward greater rather than less impact of government resource-allocation powers, for objectives outside the market calculus.[100]

100. Bator, 11–16; Heilbroner (1), 76–87.

Retrospect

For reasons rooted in the functional requisites of a going society (notably the need to deal with scarcity of satisfactions), and in the particular values developed in this society (especially the unfolding and tenacity of the constitutional ideal), a realistic history of law in the United States must relate law to institutions and ideas derived largely from outside the law. Thus we need to study the social history of law, and not merely appraise its history as a self-sufficient institution.

Nonetheless, law has made itself felt as a distinctive institution. Law has developed values specially defined and implemented through legal processes, such as the standards of due process and equal protection. Law also has generated vested interests in some values or procedures and in some ways contributed to the uncritical custom and habit and narrowly focused or short-term decisions that formed large parts of social experience. Thus, though we ultimately strive to view law in relation to other-than-legal currents in the society, the starting point for study of legal history is the presence of separate legal institutions.

The formal structure of the major legal agencies has been relatively stable over the country's lifetime; the principal exceptions were the rise of standing committees to dominate the legislative branch and the expanding delegation of powers by legislatures to executive and administrative offices. More changeful and more influential in determining the impact of the major legal agencies was the development of the kinds of authority committed to them and of the characteristic working capabilities and limitations that accompanied these endowments of power.

Given our inheritance from the Parliamentary Revolution, the character and fortunes of the legislative branch provided the framework of legal order within which judicial, executive, and administrative authority took shape. From the late nineteenth century the legislative role grew to overshadow lawmaking by judges, save as courts asserted authority to pass on the constitutionality of statutes. In the twentieth century, the most significant competition for policy-making position went on between legislatures and executive and administrative officers. The legislative branch continued to hold a great potential of authority, especially by its right to control the public purse and its powers of investigation. But, partly because of the complexity of the service and regulatory demands that the growth of the society made on government and partly because of defaults of leadership, legislators have delegated more and more discretion to executive and administrative officers, without keeping firm checks on their delegates. After some seventy-five years of this course, the prime issue over the character of government power is whether the legislature can muster the will, courage, and skill to use its potential capacity to call executive and administrative authority to account.

When we turn from law's own structure and processes to its interplay with the rest of society, at first sight we confront a bewildering variety and density of detail; there seems almost no important sector of experience that has not had some legal dimension. This study suggests that we can begin to find some order in law's social involvements by noting that these fall into three large categories.

First, law worked in relation to other social institutions. Typically, law did not create these other institutions, but legal processes helped to legitimate them, to offer them supporting services or protection, and to regulate in some measure their relations to individuals, groups, and other institutions.

Second, legal processes helped bring under examination, debate, deliberation, and decision a great range of values by which people sought meaning and effectiveness in their social relations.

Institutions alone did not create social coherence; shared ideas about ends and means did not all fit neatly into some institutional framework. But even so they enlarged people's capacity to communicate, exchange, cooperate, and adjust their affairs. A pattern of middle-class values formed one particularly important cluster of integrating ideas implemented by law. These assigned high priority to creating constitutional order, to providing diverse outlets for creative will, to promoting a firm economic base for erecting noneconomic goals, and to advancing the quality of individual life. The central dynamic of this middle-class outlook was the prizing of active will, which found varied expression in uses of law to help individuals deal with the physical and biological setting (through science and technology) and with the social setting (as in public policy affecting the market and the business corporation and legal action concerning the relations of market and corporation).

Law's third type of involvement with the general life of this society carried an element of paradox. Within the constitutional ideal, and measured by the functions it was most obviously structured to fulfill, law was a means to enlarge rational and fair order in social relations. Law did not hold a monopoly on this role; other institutions also sought to bring more desired regularity into experience. But achievement of calculated order stood particularly high in the priorities set by legal processes. This pursuit carried critical human values, for people found that their individuality and their capacity for fruitful association stood constantly under threat of being overwhelmed by the infinite, chancy variety and dense detail of events. Apart from ordered development of scientific and technical knowledge, legal processes offered probably the most potent collective instrument against this threat of chaos. And —again, apart from the realms of science and technology—in its formal output of statutes and legislative records, executive and administrative orders and rules, and judicial opinions, law contained probably the largest body of deliberately defined and chosen values in the society. There is a more profound meaning in linking "law and order" than common usage gives to that familiar coupling.

But legal processes enjoyed no exemption from limits of the human condition or constraints of the culture of which they were part. They, too, worked within limits of knowledge, limits of energy, imagination, and courage, limits set by broadly shared habits and preoccupations of thought, emotion, and action. Thus law achieved only partial gains for broad and long-term direction of affairs, against the tendency of short-run calculations, unplanned cumulation of events, or sheer drift or inertia to predominate in the flow of social experience. With considerable effect we used law to promote and support growth and use of scientific and technical knowledge. But out of these same developments we learned a fascination with operational skills that threatened to exalt means over ends. Habituation to market bargaining as a major institution of social control inclined us to let uses of scientific and technical knowledge flow wherever exercises of contract and property rights might carry them, little checked by the narrow accounting set by traditional tort or nuisance law. We used law to provide supporting services and protection for the market and to make the corporation more readily available to muster and manage aggregations of capital. But public policy lagged badly behind the tendency of large-scale corporate enterprise to subvert market discipline. By the second half of the twentieth century the result of this lag of public policy behind the pace and range of private will and ambition was to raise unresolved questions of the social legitimacy of both the market and the big business corporation—a matter of serious concern, given the key roles those two private agencies had come to play in shaping the society.

Institutions, ideas, and inertia thus provide concepts through which we can considerably enlarge our perception of law's various involvements with life in society. Two other, related concerns bulk so large in the record as also to give form and content to the social history of law. These are concerns with achieving justice and with expressing consensus or finding principled resolution of conflict. A sensible division of labor assigns to the philosopher examination of the potentials for achieving justice through law and to the historian examination of working measures of justice and injustice in fact embodied in law. Legal history thus must deal with the search for rational, fair, and correct application of public policy norms, with successes and failures in adjusting sharply focused (special) interests and broadly shared (general) interests, and with contention over those criteria for allocating benefits and burdens (such as race, sex, and wealth) that raise the most piercing questions of acknowledging or denying dignity to individual life. Conflict resolution through law, of course, involves issues of justice and injustice, most acutely when dominant interests have imposed an artificial consensus by excluding weaker sectors (Indians, blacks, women) from the policy calculus. But legal processes also facilitate and express broad sharing of values, including provision of procedures for handling conflict within consensus, as through the legal framework of the market. The reality of conflict does not negate the existence of consensus; legal history must take account of both.

The social history of law is so intricately woven into the whole fabric of social experience as almost to defy a neat and final cataloging. But these five categories—institutions, ideas, inertia, the pursuit of justice, and the balancing of consensus and conflict—can provide ample occupation for legal historians. The range and diversity of the quest promise rewards in the excitement of piercing through confusing or opaque detail to see better the reality of the law and of the society of which it is part.

Sources Cited

[Official action documents are cited in full in the footnotes.]

Aaron, Henry. Inventory of Existing Tax Incentives—Federal. In Tax Incentives: Symposium Conducted by the Tax Institute of America, November 20–21, 1969, p. 39. Lexington, Mass.: D.C. Heath, 1971.

Adams, Walter, and Horace M. Gray. Monopoly in America: The Government as Promoter. New York: Macmillan, 1955.

Ahlstrom, Sydney E. A Religious History of the American People. New Haven: Yale University Press, 1972.

Allard, Robert E. See Winters and Allard.

American Political Science Association, Committee on American Legislatures. American State Legislatures, edited by Belle Zeller. New York: Thomas Y. Crowell, 1954.

Amsterdam, Anthony G. "Perspectives on the Fourth Amendment," 58 Minnesota Law Review 349 (1974).

Anderson, Frederick R. NEPA in the Courts: A Legal Analysis of the National Environmental Protection Act. Baltimore: The Johns Hopkins University Press, 1973.

Anderson, William. Political Influences of the Metropolis. In The Metropolis in Modern Life, edited by Ernest M. Fisher, p. 57. Garden City, N.Y.: Doubleday, 1955.

Andrews, F. Emerson. See Glenn et al.

Angly, Edward. See Jones and Angly.

Arnold, Thurman W.
  (1) "Trial by Combat and the New Deal," 47 Harvard Law Review 913 (1934).
  (2) The Bottlenecks of Business. New York: Reynal & Hitchcock, 1940.
  (3) The Folklore of Capitalism. Garden City, N.Y.: Blue Ribbon Books, 1941.

Ashmore, Harry S. Fear in the Air. New York: W. W. Norton, 1973.

Auerbach, Carl A.
  (1) "Law and Social Change in the United States," 6 U.C.L.A. Law Review 516 (1959).

(2) Comment on Robert L. Heilbroner, The Roots of Social Neglect in the United States. In Is Law Dead?, edited by Eugene V. Rostow, p. 307. New York: Simon & Schuster, 1971.

Auerbach, Carl A., Lloyd K. Garrison, Willard Hurst, and Samuel Mermin. The Legal Process: An Introduction to Decision-Making by Judicial, Legislative, Executive and Administrative Agencies. San Francisco: Chandler, 1961.

Babcock, Richard F. The Zoning Game: Municipal Practices and Policies. Madison: The University of Wisconsin Press, 1966.

Bailey, Stephen Kemp. Congress Makes a Law. New York: Vintage Books, 1950.

Baldwin, Gordon Brewster. "Law in Support of Science: Legal Control of Basic Research Resources," 54 Georgetown Law Journal 559 (1966).

Bancroft, George. The Office of the People. In The Shaping of the American Tradition, edited by Louis M. Hacker and Helene S. Zahler, 1:366. 2 vols. New York: Columbia University Press, 1947.

Barber, Bernard. Science and the Social Order. Glencoe, Ill.: The Free Press, 1952.

Barger, Harold. Distribution's Place in the American Economy Since 1869. Princeton, N.J.: Princeton University Press, 1955.

Barrett, Edward L., Jr. Criminal Justice: The Problem of Mass Production. In The Courts, the Public and the Law Explosion, edited by Harry W. Jones, p. 85. Englewood Cliffs, N.J.: Prentice-Hall, 1965.

Barth, Alan. The Loyalty of Free Men. New York: Pocket Books, 1951.

Bator, Francis M. The Question of Government Spending: Public Needs and Private Wants. New York: Harper & Brothers, 1960.

Beckler, David Z. "The Precarious Life of Science in the White House," 103 Daedalus 115 (1974).

Beer, Thomas. The Mauve Decade. Garden City, N.Y.: Garden City Publishing Co., 1926.

Benedict, Murray R. Farm Policies of the United States, 1790–1950. New York: The Twentieth Century Fund, 1953.

Berger, Raoul. Executive Privilege: A Constitutional Myth. Cambridge, Mass.: Harvard University Press, 1974.

Berle, A. A. The American Economic Republic. New York: Harcourt, Brace & World, 1963.

Bernstein, Irving. Turbulent Years: A History of the American Worker, 1933–1941. Boston: Houghton Mifflin, 1971.

Bernstein, Marver H. Regulating Business by Independent Commission. Princeton, N.J.: Princeton University Press, 1955.

Beveridge, Albert J. The Life of John Marshall. 4 vols. Boston: Houghton Mifflin, 1916–1919.

Bikle, Henry Wolf. "Judicial Determination of Questions of Fact Affecting the Constitutional Validity of Legislative Action," 38 Harvard
Law Review 1 (1924).

Blair, John M. Economic Concentration: Structure, Behavior and
Public Policy. New York: Harcourt, Brace, Jovanovich, 1972.

Blaisdell, Thomas C., Jr. The Federal Trade Commission: An Experiment in the Control of Business. New York: Columbia University
Press, 1932.

Blum, John Morton. The Republican Roosevelt. Cambridge, Mass.:
Harvard University Press, 1954.

Blum, Walter H., and Harry Kalven, Jr. The Uneasy Case for Progressive Taxation. Chicago: The University of Chicago Press, 1953.

Boorstin, Daniel J.
   (1) The Americans: The National Experience. New York: Random
   House, 1965.
   (2) The Americans: The Democratic Experience. New York:
   Random House, 1973.

Bowen, Howard R. Social Responsibilities of the Businessman. New
York: Harper & Brothers, 1953.

Brandeis, Elizabeth. Migrant Labor in Wisconsin. In Labor, Management and Social Policy, edited by Gerald G. Somers, p. 197. Madison: The University of Wisconsin Press, 1963.

Brandt, Lillian. See Glenn et al.

Brim, Orville G., Jr. See Ruebhausen and Brim.

Brodie, Abner. The Adequacy of Workmen's Compensation as Social
Insurance: A Review of Developments and Proposals. In Labor,
Management and Social Policy, edited by Gerald G. Somers, p.
161. Madison: The University of Wisconsin Press, 1963.

Brown, Ray A. "The Making of the Wisconsin Constitution: Part II,"
1952. Wisconsin Law Review 23.

Bruchey, Stuart. The Roots of American Economic Growth, 1607–
1861. New York: Harper Torchbooks, 1968.

Bryce, James. The American Commonwealth. New edition, 2 vols. New
York: Macmillan, 1913.

Buchanan, James M., and Gordon Tullock. The Calculus of Consent:
Logical Foundations of Constitutional Democracy. Ann Arbor: The
University of Michigan Press, 1962.

Burchard, John Ely, ed. Mid-Century: The Social Implications of
Scientific Progress. Cambridge, Mass.: Technology Press of M.I.T.,
1950.

Burke, John G. Technology and Government. In Technology and Social
    Change in America, edited by Edwin T. Layton, Jr., p. 99. New
    York: Harper & Row, 1973.
Burlingame, Roger.
    (1) Engines of Democracy: Inventions and Society in Mature
    America. New York: Charles Scribner's Sons, 1940.
    (2) March of the Iron Men: A Social History of Union Through
    Invention. New York: Charles Scribner's Sons, 1940.
    (3) Backgrounds of Power. New York: Charles Scribner's Sons,
    1949.
    (4) Machines That Built America. New York: New American
    Library, Signet Key Books, 1955.
Burns, Arthur Robert. The Decline of Competition. New York:
    McGraw-Hill, 1936.
Burns, James MacGregor. Congress on Trial. New York: Harper &
    Brothers, 1949.
Campbell, Angus, Philip E. Converse, Warren E. Miller, and Donald E.
    Stokes. The American Voter. New York: John Wiley & Sons, 1960.
Cardozo, Benjamin N. The Nature of the Judicial Process. New Ha-
    ven: Yale University Press, 1921.
Carstensen, Vernon. See Curti and Carstensen.
Cary, William L.
    (1) Politics and the Regulatory Agencies. New York: McGraw-
    Hill, 1967.
    (2) "Federalism and Corporate Law: Reflections Upon Delaware,"
    83 Yale Law Journal 663 (1974).
Casner, Andrew J., ed. American Law of Property: A Treatise on the
    Law of Property in the United States. 7 vols. Boston: Little, Brown,
    1952.
Cavers, David F. Law and Science: Some Points of Confrontation. In
    Law and the Social Role of Science, edited by Harry W. Jones, p.
    5. New York: The Rockefeller University Press, 1966.
Chafee, Zechariah, Jr. "The Internal Affairs of Associations Not for
    Profit," 43 Harvard Law Review 993 (1930).
Chamberlain, Joseph P. Legislative Processes, National and State. New
    York: D. Appleton-Century, 1936.
Chamberlain, Lawrence H. The President, Congress and Legislation.
    New York: Columbia University Press, 1947.
Chardin, Teilhard de. The Future of Man. New York: Harper & Row,
    1964.
Chayes, Abram. The Modern Corporation and the Rule of Law. In

The Corporation in Modern Society, edited by Edward S. Mason, p. 25. Cambridge, Mass.: Harvard University Press, 1960.

Christman, Henry. Tin Horns and Calico. New York: Henry Holt, 1945.

Ciriacy-Wantrup, S. W. Resource Conservation: Economics and Policies. Berkeley: University of California Press, 1952.

Clark, John Maurice.
(1) Social Control of Business. Chicago: The University of Chicago Press, 1926.
(2) Economic Institutions and Human Welfare. New York: Alfred A. Knopf, 1957.

Clark, Victor S. Manufacturing Development during the Civil War. In The Economic Impact of the American Civil War, edited by Ralph Andreano, p. 41. Cambridge, Mass.: Schenkman, 1962.

Clawson, Marion, and Burnell Held. The Federal Lands: Their Use and Management. Baltimore: The Johns Hopkins Press, 1957.

Cleaveland, Frederic N. Science and State Government: A Study of the Scientific Activities of State Government in Six States. Chapel Hill: The University of North Carolina Press, 1959.

Cochran, Thomas C.
(1) Railroad Leaders, 1845–1890: The Business Mind in Action. Cambridge, Mass.: Harvard University Press, 1953.
(2) The American System: A Historical Perspective, 1900–1955. Cambridge, Mass.: Harvard University Press, 1957.
(3) Did the Civil War Retard Industrialization? In The Economic Impact of the American Civil War, edited by Ralph Andreano, p. 148. Cambridge, Mass.: Schenkman, 1962.

Cochran, Thomas C., and William Miller. The Age of Enterprise: A Social History of Industrial America. New York: Macmillan, 1943.

Cohen, Morris L. Literature of the Law-Science Confrontation. In Law and the Social Role of Science, edited by Harry W. Jones, p. 135. New York: The Rockefeller University Press, 1966.

Commager, Henry Steele. See Morison and Commager.

Commons, John R. Myself. Madison: The University of Wisconsin Press, 1964.

Compton, Karl T. The State of Science. In Mid-Century: The Social Implications of Scientific Progress, edited by John Ely Burchard, p. 13. Cambridge, Mass.: Technology Press of M.I.T., 1950.

Conant, James B. Modern Science and Modern Man. New York: Columbia University Press, 1952.

Converse, Philip E. See Campbell et al.

Corbin, Arthur Linton. Corbin on Contracts. 8 vols. St. Paul, Minn.: West, 1962.

Corwin, Edward S.
(1) The Impact of the Idea of Evolution on the American Political and Constitutional Tradition. In Evolutionary Thought in America, edited by Stow Persons, p. 182. New Haven: Yale University Press, 1950.
(2) The President, Office and Powers, 1787–1957. 4th revised edition. New York: New York University Press, 1957.

Cottrell, Fred. Energy and Society: The Relation between Energy, Social Change, and Economic Development. New York: McGraw-Hill, 1955.

Cottrell, Leonard S., Jr. The Interrelationships of Law and Social Science. In Law and the Social Role of Science, edited by Harry W. Jones, p. 106. New York: The Rockefeller University Press, 1966.

Cravath, Paul D. Reorganization of Corporations. In Association of the Bar of the City of New York, Some Legal Phases of Corporate Financing, Reorganization and Regulation, p. 153. New York: Macmillan, 1930.

Crèvecoeur, J. Hector St. John. Letters from an American Farmer. New York: Fox, Duffield, 1904.

Curti, Merle. The Growth of American Thought. New York: Harper & Brothers, 1943.

Curti, Merle, and Vernon Carstensen. The University of Wisconsin. 2 vols. Madison: The University of Wisconsin Press, 1949.

Cushman, Robert E. "The Social and Economic Interpretation of the Fourteenth Amendment," 20 Michigan Law Review 737 (1922).

Daddario, Emilio Q. "Science Policy: Relationships Are the Key," 103 Daedalus 135 (1974).

Dahl, Robert A., and Charles E. Lindblom. Politics, Economics and Welfare. New York: Harper & Brothers, 1953.

Davidson, Kenneth M., Ruth Bader Ginsburg, and Herma Hill Kay. Sex-Based Discrimination. St. Paul, Minn.: West, 1974.

Davis, Kenneth Culp. Discretionary Justice: A Preliminary Inquiry. Baton Rouge: Louisiana State University Press, 1969.

Davis, Otto A., M. A. H. Dempster, and Aaron Wildavsky. On the Process of Budgeting: An Empirical Study of Congressional Appropriations. In Nine Papers on Non-Market Decision Making, edited by Gordon Tullock, p. 63. Charlottesville, Va.: Thomas Jefferson Center for Political Economy, University of Virginia, 1966.

Dempster, M. A. H. See Davis et al.

Dicey, A. V. Lectures on the Relation Between Law and Public Opinion in England during the Nineteenth Century. London: Macmillan, 1914.

Dickerson, Reed. The Interpretation and Application of Statutes. Boston: Little, Brown, 1975.

Dodd, Walter F. State Government. 2d edition. New York: Century, 1928.

Doob, Leonard W. Public Opinion and Propaganda. New York: Henry Holt, 1948.

Douglas, Paul H. Ethics in Government. Cambridge, Mass.: Harvard University Press, 1952.

Dulles, Foster Rhea. Labor in America. New York: Thomas Y. Crowell, 1949.

Dupree, A. Hunter. Science in the Federal Government: A History of Policies and Activities to 1940. Cambridge, Mass.: The Belknap Press of Harvard University Press, 1957.

Edelman, Murray. New Deal Sensitivity to Labor Interests. In Labor and the New Deal, edited by Milton Derber and Edwin H. Young, p. 157. Madison: The University of Wisconsin Press, 1957.

Edwards, Corwin D. Maintaining Competition: Requisites of a Governmental Policy. New York: McGraw-Hill, 1949.

Edwards, Newton. The Courts and the Public Schools. 3d edition. Chicago: The University of Chicago Press, 1971.

Eells, Richard. The Meaning of Modern Business: An Introduction to the Philosophy of Large Corporate Enterprise. New York: Columbia University Press, 1960.

Etzioni, Amitai, and Clyde Nunn. "The Public Appreciation of Science," 103 Daedalus 191 (1974).

Evans, George Heberton, Jr. Business Incorporation in the United States, 1800–1943. New York: National Bureau of Economic Research, 1948.

Fabricant, Solomon. The Trend of Government Activity in the United States Since 1900. New York: National Bureau of Economic Research, 1952.

Feller, A. H. "Moratory Legislation: A Comparative Study," 46 Harvard Law Review 1061 (1933).

Feller, Peter B., and Karl L. Gotting. "The Second Amendment: A Second Look," 61 Northwestern Law Review 46 (1966).

Fellman, David. The Defendant's Rights. New York: Rinehart, 1958.

Fenno, Richard F., Jr.

(1) The Power of the Purse: Appropriations Politics in Congress. Boston: Little, Brown, 1966.

(2) Congressmen in Committees. Boston: Little, Brown, 1973.

Ferguson, Eugene S. Technology as Knowledge. In Technology and Social Change in America, edited by Edwin T. Layton, Jr., p. 9. New York: Harper & Row, 1973.

Fine, Sidney. Laissez Faire and the General-Welfare State: A Study of Conflict in American Thought, 1865–1901. Ann Arbor: The University of Michigan Press, 1956.

Fisher, Burton R., and Stephen B. Withey. Big Business As the People See It. Ann Arbor: The Survey Research Center, Institute for Social Research, 1951.

Fisher, Louis. Presidential Spending Power. Princeton, N.J.: Princeton University Press, 1975.

Flack, Horace E. The Adoption of the Fourteenth Amendment. Baltimore: The Johns Hopkins Press, 1908.

Fleming, R. W.

(1) The Search for a Formula. In Emergency Disputes and National Policy, edited by Irving Bernstein, Harold L. Enarson, and R. W. Fleming, p. 200. New York: Harper & Brothers, 1955.

(2) The Significance of the Wagner Act. In Labor and the New Deal, edited by Milton Derber and Edwin H. Young, p. 121. Madison: The University of Wisconsin Press, 1957.

Fordham, Jefferson B. See Read et al.

Frankfurter, Felix. The Commerce Clause Under Marshall, Taney and Waite. Chapel Hill: The University of North Carolina Press, 1937.

Franklin, Benjamin. The Writings of Benjamin Franklin, edited by Herbert Henry Smyth. 10 vols. New York: Macmillan, 1905.

Frantz, Laurent B. "Congressional Power to Enforce the Fourteenth Amendment Against Private Acts," 73 Yale Law Journal 1353 (1964).

Frazier, E. Franklin. The Negro in the United States. New York: Macmillan, 1949.

Freund, Ernst. Standards of American Legislation. Chicago: The University of Chicago Press, 1917.

Friedman, Lawrence M.

(1) Contract Law in America: A Social and Economic Case Study. Madison: The University of Wisconsin Press, 1965.

(2) "Legal Rules and the Process of Social Change," 19 Stanford Law Review 786 (1967).

(3) A History of American Law: New York: Simon & Schuster, 1973.

Friedman, Lawrence M., and Stewart Macaulay. Law and the Behavioral Sciences. Indianapolis: Bobbs-Merrill, 1969.

Fuller, Lon L. "American Legal Realism," 82 University of Pennsylvania Law Review 429 (1934).

Galanter, Marc. "Why the 'Haves' Come Out Ahead: Speculations on
the Limits of Legal Change," 9 Law and Society Review 95 (1974).

Galbraith, John Kenneth. The New Industrial State. Boston: Houghton
Mifflin, 1967.

Galloway, George B. The Legislative Process in Congress. New York:
Thomas Y. Crowell, 1953.

Gellhorn, Walter.
  (1) Security and Science. Ithaca: Cornell University Press, 1950.
  (2) Individual Freedom and Governmental Restraints. Baton
Rouge: Louisiana State University Press, 1956.

Georgetown Law Journal. Media and the First Amendment in a Free
Society. Amherst: The University of Massachusetts Press, 1973.

Ginsburg, Ruth Bader. See Davidson, Ginsburg, and Kay.

Glenn, John M., Lillian Brandt, and F. Emerson Andrews. Russell Sage
Foundation, 1907–1946. 2 vols. New York: Russell Sage Foundation,
1947.

Goodrich, Carter. Government Promotion of American Canals and
Railroads, 1800–1890. New York: Columbia University Press, 1960.

Gotting, Karl L. See Feller and Gotting.

Graham, George A. Morality in American Politics. New York: Random
House, 1952.

Graham, Howard Jay. Everyman's Constitution. Madison: The State
Historical Society of Wisconsin, 1968.

Gray, Horace M. See Adams and Gray.

Green, Mark J. The Closed Enterprise System. New York: Grossman,
1972.

Griswold, Erwin N. The Fifth Amendment Today. Cambridge, Mass.:
Harvard University Press, 1955.

Grodzins, Morton. The Loyal and the Disloyal: Social Boundaries of
Patriotism and Treason. Chicago: The University of Chicago Press,
1956.

Gross, Bertram M. The Legislative Struggle. New York: McGraw-
Hill, 1953.

Groves, Harold M. Financing Government. New York: Henry Holt,
1939.

Gulick, Luther Halsey.
  (1) American Forest Policy: A Study of Government Administra-

tion and Economic Control. New York: Duell, Sloan & Pearce, 1951.
(2) Metropolitan Political Developments. In The Metropolis in Modern Life, edited by Ernest M. Fisher, p. 66. Garden City, N.Y.: Doubleday, 1955.

Hacker, Louis M.
(1) The Triumph of American Capitalism. New York: Simon & Schuster, 1940.
(2) The World of Andrew Carnegie, 1865–1901. Philadelphia: J. B. Lippincott, 1968.

Hacker, Louis M., and Helene S. Zahler.
(1) The Shaping of the American Tradition. 2 vols. New York: Columbia University Press, 1947.
(2) The United States in the 20th Century. New York: Appleton-Century-Crofts, 1952.

Hale, Robert L. Freedom Through Law: Public Control of Private Governing Power. New York: Columbia University Press, 1952.

Hamilton, Alexander. The Works of Alexander Hamilton, edited by Henry Cabot Lodge. 12 vols. New York: G. P. Putnam's Sons, 1904.

Hamilton, Walton. The Politics of Industry. New York: Alfred A. Knopf, 1957.

Hamilton, Walton, and Irene Till. Anti-Trust in Action. TNEC Monograph No. 16. Washington, D.C.: U.S. Government Printing Office, 1940.

Handlin, Oscar.
(1) Race and Nationality in American Life. Boston: Little, Brown, 1948.
(2) The Uprooted: The Epic Story of the Great Migrations That Made the American People. Boston: Atlantic Monthly Press Book, Little, Brown, 1951.

Harbison, Winfred A. See Kelly and Harbison.

Hardwicke, Robert E. "The Rule of Capture and Its Implications as Applied to Oil and Gas," 13 Texas Law Review 391 (1935).

Harris, Joseph P. Congressional Control of Administration. Washington, D.C.: The Brookings Institution, 1964.

Harris, Marshall. Origin of the Land Tenure System in the United States. Ames: The Iowa State College Press, 1953.

Harris, Seymour E. See Sutton et al.

Hartz, Louis. The Liberal Tradition in America: An Interpretation of American Political Thought Since the Revolution. New York: Harcourt, Brace, 1955.

Harvard Law Review. Note: "Impoundment of Funds," 86 Harvard Law Review 1505 (1973).

Hawley, Ellis W. The New Deal and the Problem of Monopoly: A Study in Economic Ambivalence. Princeton, N.J.: Princeton University Press, 1966.

Haynes, Evan. The Selection and Tenure of Judges. Newark, N.J.: The National Conference of Judicial Councils, 1944.

Hays, Samuel P. Conservation and the Gospel of Efficiency: The Progressive Conservation Movement, 1890–1920. Cambridge, Mass.: Harvard University Press, 1959.

Heilbroner, Robert L.
  (1) The Limits of American Capitalism. New York: Harper Torchbooks, 1967.
  (2) The Roots of Social Neglect in the United States. In Is Law Dead? edited by Eugene V. Rostow, p. 288. New York: Simon & Schuster, 1971.

Held, Burnell. See Clawson and Held.

Heller, Walter W. New Dimensions of Political Economy. Cambridge, Mass.: Harvard University Press, 1966.

Herberg, Will. Protestant-Catholic-Jew: An Essay in American Religious Sociology. Garden City, N.Y.: Doubleday, 1955.

Hicks, Granville. Small Town. New York: Macmillan, 1946.

Hill, Christopher. The Century of Revolution, 1603–1714. New York: W. W. Norton, 1966.

Hofstadter, Richard. "What Happened to the Antitrust Movement?" In The Paranoid Style in American Politics and Other Essays, p. 188. New York: Vintage Books, 1967.

Hofstadter, Richard, and Wallace, Michael, eds. American Violence: A Documentary History. New York: Alfred A. Knopf, 1970.

Horack, Frank L., Jr. "The Common Law of Legislation," 21 Iowa Law Review 41 (1937).

Howe, Mark DeWolfe. The Garden and the Wilderness: Religion and Government in American Constitutional History. Chicago: Phoenix Books, The University of Chicago Press, 1965.

Hunt, Freeman. Lives of American Merchants. 2 vols. New York: Derby and Jackson, 1858.

Hunter, Louis C. The Heroic Theory of Invention. In Technology and Social Change in America, edited by Edwin T. Layton, Jr., p. 25. New York: Harper & Row, 1973.

Huntington, Samuel P. The Soldier and the State: The Theory and

Politics of Civil-Military Relations. Cambridge, Mass.: The Belknap Press of Harvard University Press, 1957.

Hurst, James Willard.

(1) The Growth of American Law: The Law Makers. Boston: Little, Brown, 1950.

(2) Law and the Conditions of Freedom in the Nineteenth-Century United States. Madison: The University of Wisconsin Press, 1965.

(3) Law and Social Process in United States History. Ann Arbor: University of Michigan Law School, 1960.

(4) Law and Economic Growth: The Legal History of the Lumber Industry in Wisconsin, 1836–1915. Cambridge, Mass.: The Belknap Press of Harvard University Press, 1964.

(5) The Legitimacy of the Business Corporation in the Law of the United States, 1780–1970. Charlottesville: University Press of Virginia, 1970.

(6) The Law of Treason in the United States. Westport, Conn.: Greenwood, 1971.

(7) A Legal History of Money in the United States, 1774–1970. Lincoln: University of Nebraska Press, 1973.

Huxley, T. H. and Julian Huxley. Touchstone for Ethics. New York: Harper & Brothers, 1947.

Jacob, Herbert. Justice in America. Boston: Little, 1965.

Jacobsson, Per. The Market Economy in the World of Today. Philadelphia: The American Philosophical Society, 1961.

Jewkes, John, David Sawers, and Richard Stillerman. The Sources of Invention. New York: St. Martin's Press, 1958.

Jones, Harry W.

(1) Introduction to The Courts, the Public and the Law Explosion, p. 1. Englewood Cliffs, N.J.: Prentice-Hall, 1965.

(2) The Trial Judge—Role Analysis and Profile. Id., p. 124.

(3) Legal Inquiry and the Methods of Science. In Law and the Social Role of Science, edited by Harry W. Jones, p. 120. New York: The Rockefeller University Press, 1966.

Jones, Jesse H., and Edward Angly. Fifty Billion Dollars: My Thirteen Years with the RFC (1932–1945). New York: Macmillan, 1951.

Johnson, E. A. J., and Herman E. Krooss. The Origins and Development of the American Economy. New York: Prentice-Hall, 1953.

Johnson, George M. Education Law. East Lansing: Michigan State University Press, 1969.

Kalachek, Edward D. See Nelson et al.

Kallenbach, Joseph E. The American Chief Executive: The Presidency and the Governorship. New York: Harper & Row, 1966.

Kalven, Harry, Jr. See Blum and Kalven.

Kanowitz, Leo. Women and the Law. Albuquerque: University of New Mexico Press, 1969.

Kapp, K. William. The Social Costs of Private Enterprise. Cambridge, Mass.: Harvard University Press, 1950.

Kardiner, Abraham. The Psychological Frontiers of Society. New York: Columbia University Press, 1945.

Kay, Herma Hill. See Davidson, Ginsburg, and Kay.

Kaysen, Carl. See Sutton et al.

Kaysen, Carl, and Donald F. Turner. Antitrust Policy: An Economic and Legal Analysis. Cambridge, Mass.: Harvard University Press, 1965.

Keeton, Robert E., and Jeffrey O'Connell. "Basic Protection—A Proposal for Improving Automobile Claims Systems," 78 Harvard Law Review 329 (1964).

Kelly, Alfred H., and Winfred A. Harbison. The American Constitution, Its Origins and Development. 3d edition. New York: W. W. Norton, 1963.

Key, V. O., Jr. Politics, Parties and Pressure Groups. New York: Thomas Y. Crowell, 1942.

Kimmel, Lewis H. Federal Budget and Fiscal Policy, 1789–1958. Washington, D.C.: The Brookings Institution, 1959.

Kirkland, Edward Chase.
(1) Men, Cities and Transportation: A Study in New England History, 1820–1900. 2 vols. Cambridge, Mass.: Harvard University Press, 1948.
(2) Business in the Gilded Age. Madison: The University of Wisconsin Press, 1952.
(3) Charles Francis Adams, Jr., 1835–1915. Cambridge, Mass.: Harvard University Press, 1965.

Knight, Frank H. Intelligence and Democratic Action. Cambridge, Mass.: Harvard University Press, 1960.

Koenig, Louis W. The Chief Executive. New York: Harcourt, Brace & World, 1964.

Kohlmeier, Louis M., Jr. The Regulators. New York: Harper & Row, 1969.

Kolko, Gabriel.
(1) The Triumph of Conservatism: A Reinterpretation of American History, 1900–1916. Glencoe, Ill.: The Free Press, 1963.

(2) Railroads and Regulation, 1877–1916. Princeton, N.J.: Princeton University Press, 1965.

Konvitz, Milton R. The Alien and the Asiatic in American Law. Ithaca, N.Y.: Cornell University Press, 1946.

Kouwenhoven, John A. Made in America: The Arts in Modern Civilization. Garden City, N.Y.: Doubleday, 1948.

Kuehnl, George J. The Wisconsin Business Corporation. Madison: The University of Wisconsin Press, 1959.

Kutler, Stanley I. Privilege and Creative Destruction: The Charles River Bridge Case. Philadelphia: J. B. Lippincott, 1971.

Lake, James A. Law and Mineral Wealth: The Legal Profile of the Wisconsin Mining Industry. Madison: The University of Wisconsin Press, 1962.

Lampard, Eric E. Industrial Revolution. Washington, D.C.: Publication No. 4, Service Center for Teachers of History, American Historical Association, 1957.

Lampman, Robert J. The Share of Top Wealth Holders in National Wealth, 1922–56. Princeton, N.J.: Princeton University Press, 1962.

Landis, James M.
  (1) "Congressional Power of Investigation," 40 Harvard Law Review 153 (1926).
  (2) "A Note on Statutory Interpretation," 43 Harvard Law Review 886 (1930).
  (3) The Administrative Process. New Haven: Yale University Press, 1938.

Lapp, Ralph E. Atoms and People. New York: Harper & Brothers, 1956.

Larkin, Oliver W. Art and Life in America. New York: Rinehart, 1949.

Laurent, Francis W. The Business of a Trial Court: 100 Years of Cases. Madison: The University of Wisconsin Press, 1959.

Layton, Edwin T., Jr. Introduction, in Technology and Social Change in America, edited by Edwin T. Layton, Jr., p. 1. New York: Harper & Row, 1973.

Lederberg, Joshua P. "The Freedoms and Controls of Science," 45 Southern California Law Review 595 (1972).

Lerner, Max. America as a Civilization. New York: Simon & Schuster, 1957.

Letwin, William. Law and Economic Policy in America. New York: Random House, 1965.

Levy, Leonard W.
  (1) The Law of the Commonwealth and Chief Justice Shaw. New

York: Harper Torchbooks, 1967.

(2) Origins of the Fifth Amendment: The Right Against Self In-crimination. New York: Oxford University Press, 1968.

Lewis, Ovid C. Restriction on the Use of Animals and Persons in Scientific Research. In Law and the Social Role of Science, edited by Harry W. Jones, p. 53. New York: The Rockefeller University Press, 1966.

Lindblom, Charles E. See Dahl and Lindblom.

Link, Arthur S. Wilson: The New Freedom. Princeton, N.J.: Princeton University Press, 1956.

Livingston, J. A. The American Stockholder. New York: Collier Books, 1963.

Llewellyn, Karl N. The Common Law Tradition: Deciding Appeals. Boston: Little, Brown, 1960.

Lowi, Theodore J. The End of Liberalism. New York: W. W. Norton, 1969.

Luce, Robert. Legislative Procedure. Boston. Houghton Mifflin, 1922.

Lynch, David. The Concentration of Economic Power. New York: Columbia University Press, 1946.

Lynd, Robert S., and Helen Merrell Lynd.

(1) Middletown. New York: Harcourt, Brace, 1929.

(2) Middletown in Transition. New York: Harcourt Brace, 1937.

McAllister, Breck P. "Public Purpose in Taxation," 38 California Law Review 136, 241 (1930).

Macaulay, Stewart. "Non-Contractual Relations in Business: A Pre-liminary Study," 28 American Sociological Review 55 (1963). See also Friedman and Macaulay.

McCamy, James L. Science and Public Administration. University, Ala.: University of Alabama Press, 1960.

McCloskey, Robert G. The American Supreme Court. Chicago: The University of Chicago Press, 1960.

McCraw, Thomas K. "Regulation in America," 49 Business History Review 159 (1975).

MacDonald, John W. See Read et al.

McDougal, Myres S. The Impact of the Metropolis Upon Land Law. In the Metropolis in Modern Life, edited by Ernest M. Fisher, p. 212. Garden City, N.Y.: Doubleday, 1955.

McKelvey, Blake. The Urbanization of America, 1860–1915. New Brunswick, N.J.: Rutgers University Press, 1963.

McKenzie, R. D. The Rise of Metropolitan Communities. In President's Research Committee on Social Trends, Recent Social Trends in the

United States, p. 443. One-volume edition. New York: Whittlesey House, 1934.

McLaughlin, Andrew C. A Constitutional History of the United States. New York: D. Appleton-Century, 1936.

Malone, Dumas. Jefferson the President: Second Term, 1805–1809. Boston: Little, Brown, 1974.

Mann, Horace. The Importance of Universal, Free Public Education. In The People Shall Judge, edited by The Staff, Social Sciences, 1:589. 2 vols. Chicago: The University of Chicago Press, 1949.

Mansfield, Harvey C. See Millis et al.

Maritain, Jacques. On Science and Faith. In Mid-Century: The Social Implications of Scientific Progress, edited by John Ely Burchard, p. 218. Cambridge, Mass.: The Technology Press of M.I.T., 1950.

Mason, Alpheus T. Brandeis: A Free Man's Life. New York: The Viking Press, 1946.

Mayer, Andre, and Jean Mayer. "Agriculture, The Island Empire," 103 Daedalus 83 (1974).

Meier, Hugo A. The Ideology of Technology. In Technology and Social Change in America, edited by Edwin T. Layton, Jr., p. 79. New York: Harper & Row, 1973.

Mermin, Samuel. Law and the Legal System. Boston: Little, Brown, 1973.

Merriam, C. E. Government and Society. In President's Research Committee on Social Trends, Recent Social Trends in the United States, p. 1489. One-volume edition. New York: Whittlesey House, 1934.

Meyers, Marvin. The Jacksonian Persuasion: Politics and Belief. Stanford, Calif.: Stanford University Press, 1957.

Mill, John Stuart. Utilitarianism, Liberty, and Representative Government. 2 vols. London: J. M. Dent & Sons, 1929.

Miller, Byron S. See Newman and Miller.

Miller, Warren E. See Campbell et al.

Miller, William. See Cochran and Miller.

Milliman, J. W. Can People Be Trusted with Natural Resources. In The New Argument in Economics: The Public Versus the Private Sector, edited by Helmut Shoeck and James W. Wiggins, p. 72. Princeton, N.J.: D. Van Nostrand, 1963.

Millis, Walter, Harvey C. Mansfield, and Harold Stein. Arms and the State: Civil-Military Elements in National Policy. New York: The Twentieth Century Fund, 1958.

Mills, Lewis R. "The Public Purpose Doctrine in Wisconsin," 1957 Wisconsin Law Review 40, 282.

Morison, Elting R.
(1) Turmoil and Tradition. Boston: Houghton Mifflin, 1960.
(2) Men, Machines, and Modern Times. Cambridge, Mass.: The M.I.T. Press, 1966.
(3) From Know-How to Nowhere: The Development of American Technology. New York: Basic Books, 1974.

Morison, Samuel Eliot, and Henry Steele Commager. The Growth of the American Republic. 2 vols. New York: Oxford University Press, 1942.

Morris, Lloyd. Not So Long Ago. New York: Random House, 1949.

Mosher, Frederick C., and Orville F. Poland. The Costs of American Governments. New York: Dodd, Mead, 1964.

Mueller, Willard F. A Primer on Monopoly and Competition. New York: Random House, 1970.

Munster, Joe H., Jr., and Justin C. Smith. Project Research and the Universities. In Law and the Social Role of Science, edited by Harry W. Jones, p. 40. New York: The Rockefeller University Press, 1966.

Murphy, Arthur W. Law and Research Supported by Government. In Law and the Social Role of Science, edited by Harry W. Jones, p. 16. New York: The Rockefeller University Press, 1966.

Murphy, Earl Finbar.
(1) Governing Nature. Chicago: Quadrangle Books, 1967.
(2) Man and His Environment: Law. New York: Harper & Row, 1971.

Myrdal, Gunnar.
(1) An American Dilemma: The Negro Problem and Modern Democracy. 2 vols. New York: Harper & Brothers, 1944.
(2) An International Economy. New York: Harper & Brothers, 1956.

National Academy of Sciences. Technology: Processes of Assessment and Choice. Washington, D.C.: Committee on Science and Astronautics, U.S. House of Representatives, 1969.

National Commission on the Causes and Prevention of Violence. Report: To Establish Justice, To Insure Domestic Tranquility. New York: Award Books, 1969.

Nelson, Richard E., Morton J. Peck, and Edward D. Kalachek. Technology, Economic Growth, and Public Policy. Washington, D.C.: The Brookings Institution, 1967.

Nesbit, Robert C. Wisconsin, A History. Madison: The University of Wisconsin Press, 1973.

Neustadt, Richard E. Presidential Power. New York: The New American Library, Signet, 1964.

Nevins, Allan. John D. Rockefeller: The Heroic Age of American Enterprise. 2 vols. New York: Charles Scribner's Sons, 1940.

Newman, James R., and Byron S. Miller. The Control of Atomic Energy: A Study of Its Social, Economic, and Political Implications. New York: McGraw-Hill, 1948.

New York: Reports of the Proceedings and Debates of the Convention of 1821 Assembled for the Purpose of Amending the Constitution of the State of New York. Albany, 1821. Reprinted in Louis M. Hacker and Helene S. Zahler, The Shaping of the American Tradition, 1:515. 2 vols. New York: Columbia University Press, 1947.

Nunn, Clyde. See Etzioni and Nunn.

Nye, Russel Blaine. Society and Culture in America, 1830–1860. New York: Harper Torchbooks, 1974.

O'Connell. See Keeton and O'Connell.

Ogburn, William F., and Clark Tibbitts. The Family and Its Functions. In President's Research Committee on Social Trends, Recent Social Trends in the United States, p. 661. One-volume edition. New York: Whittlesey House, 1934.

Oppenheim, S. Chesterfield. Cases on Trade Regulation. St. Paul, Minn.: West, 1936.

Padover, Saul. The Complete Jefferson. New York: Duell, Sloan & Pearce, 1943.

Palfrey, John Gorham. Colleagueship in Law and Science. In Law and the Social Role of Science, edited by Harry W. Jones, p. 69. New York: The Rockefeller University Press, 1966.

Panitch, Ronald L. See Seidel and Panitch.

Patterson, Edwin M.
  (1) Jurisprudence: Men and Ideas of the Law. Brooklyn: The Foundation Press, 1953.
  (2) Law in a Scientific Age. New York: Columbia University Press, 1963.

Paul, Randolph E. Taxation in the United States. Boston: Little, Brown, 1954.

Peck, Merton J. See Nelson et al.

Penick, James L., Carroll W. Pursell, Jr., Morgan B. Sherwood, and Donald C. Swain. The Politics of American Sciences 1939 to the Present. Revised edition. Cambridge, Mass.: The M.I.T. Press, 1972.

Perlman, Selig. A Theory of the Labor Movement. New York: August M. Kelley, 1949.

Perry, John. The Story of Standards. New York: Funk and Wagnalls, 1955.

Pierce, William J. See Read et al.

Poland, Orville P. See Mosher and Poland.

Polanyi, Karl. The Great Transformation. New York: Farrar and Rinehart, 1944.

Posner, Richard A. Economic Analysis of Law. Boston: Little, Brown, 1972.

Pound, Roscoe.

(1) "Liberty of Contract," 18 Yale Law Journal 454 (1909).

(2) The Formative Era of American Law. Boston: Little, Brown, 1938.

(3) Jurisprudence. 5 vols. St. Paul, Minn.: West, 1959.

Price, Don K.

(1) Government and Science: Their Dynamic Relation in American Democracy. New York: New York University Press, 1954.

(2) The Scientific Estate. Cambridge, Mass.: The Belknap Press of Harvard University Press, 1965.

(3) "Money and Influence: The Links of Science to Public Policy," 103 Daedalus 97 (1974).

Pursell, Carroll W., Jr. See Penick et al.

Radin, Max.

(1) Handbook of Anglo-American Legal History. St. Paul, Minn.: West, 1936.

(2) Manners and Morals of Business. Indianapolis: Bobbs-Merrill, 1939.

Raney, William Francis. Wisconsin, A Story of Progress. New York: Prentice-Hall, 1940.

Ratner, Sidney. American Taxation: Its History as a Social Force in Democracy. New York: W. W. Norton, 1942.

Read, Horace E., John W. MacDonald, Jefferson B. Fordham, and William J. Pierce. Materials on Legislation. 3d edition. Mineola, N.Y.: The Foundation Press, 1973.

Redman, Eric. The Dance of Legislation. New York: Simon & Schuster, 1973.

Reedy, George E. The Presidency in Flux. New York: Columbia University Press, 1973.

Reeve, Harold L. Recent Developments in the Law of Property. In The Metropolis in Modern Life, edited by Ernest M. Fisher, p. 165. Garden City, N.Y.: Doubleday, 1955.

Rice, Stuart A. See Willey and Rice.

Robbins, Sidney. The Securities Markets. New York: The Free Press, 1966.

Roberts, Chalmers McGeach. The Nuclear Years: The Arms Race and Arms Control, 1945–1970. New York: Praeger, 1970.

Robinson, Richard R. "Interests and Institutions Reflected in Wisconsin Penal Statutes," 1966 Wisconsin Law Review 154.

Roosevelt, Theodore. An Autobiography. New York: Charles Scribner's Sons, 1925.

Rose, Arnold, and Caroline Rose. America Divided. New York: Alfred A. Knopf, 1953.

Rosenberg, Charles E. The Cholera Years. Chicago: The University of Chicago Press, 1962.

Rosenberg, Maurice. Court Congestion: Status, Causes, and Proposed Remedies. In The Courts, the Public and the Law Explosion, edited by Harry W. Jones, p. 29. Englewood Cliffs, N.J.: Prentice-Hall, 1965.

Rostow, Eugene V.
(1) Planning for Freedom: The Public Law of American Capitalism. New Haven: Yale University Press, 1959.
(2) To Whom and For What Ends Is Corporate Management Responsible? In The Corporation in Modern Society, edited by Edward S. Mason, p. 46. Cambridge, Mass.: Harvard University Press, 1960.

Rottschaefer, Henry. Handbook of American Constitutional Law. St. Paul, Minn.: West, 1939.

Ruebhausen, Oscar M., and Orville G. Brim, Jr. Privacy and Behavioral Research. In Law and the Social Role of Science, edited by Harry W. Jones, p. 80. New York: The Rockefeller University Press, 1966.

Sawers, David. See Jewkes et al.

Sayre, Francis Bowes. "Criminal Conspiracy," 35 Harvard Law Review 393 (1922).

Schaffter, Dorothy. The National Science Foundation. New York: Praeger, 1969.

Schattschneider, E. E. Politics, Pressures and the Tariff. New York: Prentice-Hall, 1935.

Scheiber, Harry N. Ohio Canal Era: A Case Study of Government and the Economy, 1820–1861. Athens, Ohio: The Ohio University Press, 1969.

Schlesinger, Arthur M., Jr. The Imperial Presidency. Boston: Houghton Mifflin, 1973.

Schmookler, Jacob. Technological Progress and the Modern American Corporation. In The Corporation in Modern Society, edited by Edward S. Mason, p. 141. Cambridge, Mass.: Harvard University Press, 1960.

Schonfield, Andrew. Modern Capitalism: The Changing Balance of Public and Private Power. New York: Oxford University Press, 1965.

Scott, Austin Wakeman. The Law of Trusts. 3d edition. 6 vols. Boston: Little, Brown, 1967.

Seidel, Arthur H., and Ronald L. Panitch. What the General Practitioner Should Know About Trade Secrets and Employment Agreements. Philadelphia: Joint Committee on Continuing Legal Education, 1973.

Sharkansky, Ira. Spending in the American States. Chicago: Rand McNally, 1968.

Sherwood, Morgan B. See Penick et al.

Sinclair, Bruce. The Direction of Technology. In Technology and Social Change in America, edited by Edwin T. Layton, Jr., p. 65. New York: Harper & Row, 1973.

Skilton, Robert H.
(1) "Field Warehousing as a Financing Device," 1961 Wisconsin Law Review 221, 403.
(2) "Tradition and Change: The Law of Mortgages on Merchandise," 1963 Wisconsin Law Review 359.

Smelser, Neil. Social Change in the Industrial Revolution. Chicago: The University of Chicago Press, 1959.

Smith, Henry Nash. Virgin Land: The American West As Symbol and Myth. Cambridge, Mass.: Harvard University Press, 1950.

Smith, James Morton. Freedom's Fetters: The Alien and Sedition Laws and American Liberties. Ithaca, N.Y.: Cornell University Press, 1956.

Smith, Justin C. See Munster and Smith.

Smith, Louis. American Democracy and Military Power: A Study of Civil Control of the Military Power in the United States. Chicago: The University of Chicago Press, 1951.

Smithies, Arthur. The Budgetary Process in the United States. New York: McGraw-Hill, 1955.

Snow, C. P. Science and Government. Cambridge, Mass.: Harvard University Press, 1961.

Sobel, Robert. The Big Board: A History of the New York Stock Market. New York: The Free Press, 1965.

Solo, Robert A. Economic Organizations and Social Systems. Indianapolis: Bobbs-Merrill, 1967.

Stein, Harold. See Millis et al.

Stein, Herbert. The Fiscal Revolution in America. Chicago: The University of Chicago Press, 1969.

Stern, Robert L. "That Commerce Which Concerns More States Than One," 47 Harvard Law Review 1335 (1934).

Stetson, Francis Lynde. Preparation of Corporate Bonds, Mortgages, Collateral Trusts, and Debenture Indentures. In Association of the Bar of the City of New York, Some Legal Phases of Corporate Financing, Reorganization and Regulation, p. 1. New York: Macmillan, 1930.

Stillerman, Richard. See Jewkes et al.

Stimson, Frederic J. American Statute Law. 2 vols. Boston: C. C. Soule, 1886–1892.

Stocking, George W., and Myron W. Watkins. Monopoly and Free Enterprise. New York: The Twentieth Century Fund, 1951.

Stokes, Donald E. See Campbell et al.

Stone, Christopher D.
    (1) "Should Trees Have Standing?—Toward Legal Rights for Natural Objects," 45 Southern California Law Review 450 (1972).
    (2) Where the Law Ends: The Social Control of Corporate Behavior. New York: Harper & Row, 1975.

Stone, Julius.
    (1) Social Dimensions of Law and Justice. Stanford, Calif.: Stanford University Press, 1966.
    (2) "Knowledge, Survival, and the Duties of Science," 23 American University Law Review 231 (1973).

Struik, Dirk J. Yankee Science in the Making. Boston: Little, Brown, 1948.

Summer, William Graham. What Social Classes Owe to Each Other. Reprinted in Louis M. Hacker and Helene S. Zahler, The Shaping of the American Tradition, 2:718. 2 vols. New York: Columbia University Press, 1947.

Sutherland, J. G. Statutes and Statutory Construction, edited by C. Dallas Sands. 4th edition. 3 vols. Chicago: Callaghan, 1972.

Sutton, Francis X., Seymour E. Harris, Carl Kaysen, and James Tobin. The American Business Creed. Cambridge, Mass.: Harvard University Press, 1956.

Swain, Donald C. See Penick et al.

Sydenstricker, Edgar. The Vitality of the American People. In President's Research Committee on Social Trends, Recent Social Trends in the United States, p. 602. One-volume edition. New York: Whittlesey House, 1934.

Taft, Philip. Rights of Union Members and the Government. Westport, Conn.: Greenwood Press, 1975.

Tannenbaum, Frank. A Philosophy of Labor. New York: Alfred A. Knopf, 1951.

Taylor, Telford. Grand Inquest. New York: Simon & Schuster, 1955.

Thayer, J. B. "The Origin and Scope of the American Doctrine of Constitutional Law," 7 Harvard Law Review 129 (1893).

Thorelli, Hans B. The Federal Antitrust Policy. Baltimore: The Johns Hopkins Press, 1955.

Tibbitts, Clark. See Ogburn and Tibbitts.

Till, Irene. See Hamilton and Till.

Tobin, James. See Sutton et al.

Tocqueville, Alexis de. Democracy in America, edited by Phillips Bradley. 2 vols. New York: Alfred A. Knopf, 1951.

Tribe, Laurence H. Channeling Technology Through Law. Chicago: The Bracton Press, 1973.

Truman, David P. The Governmental Process: Political Interests and Public Opinion. New York: Alfred A. Knopf, 1951.

Tullock, Gordon. See Buchanan and Tullock.

Turner, Donald F. See Kaysen and Turner.

Turner, James S. The Chemical Feast. New York: Grossman, 1970.

Urofsky, Melvin J. A Mind of One Piece: Brandeis and American Reform. New York: Charles Scribner's Sons, 1971.

Walker, Harvey. Law Making in the United States. New York: Ronald, 1934.

Wall, Joseph Frazier. Andrew Carnegie. New York: Oxford University Press, 1970.

Wallace, Michael. See Hofstadter and Wallace.

Wanner, Craig. "The Public Ordering of Private Relations," 8 Law and Society Review 421 (1974), 9 id., 293 (1975).

Ware, Norman. The Industrial Worker, 1840–1860. Chicago: Quadrangle Paperbacks, 1964.

Warren, Charles. The Supreme Court in United States History. Revised edition. 2 vols. Boston: Little, Brown, 1935.

Watkins, Myron W. See Stocking and Watkins.

Weaver, Warren. U.S. Philanthropic Foundations: Their History, Structure, Management, and Record. New York: Harper & Row, 1967.

Weinberg, Steven. "Reflections of a Working Scientist," 103 Daedalus 33 (1974).

Wellington, Harry H. Labor and the Legal Process. New Haven: Yale University Press, 1968.

Wharton's Criminal Law, J. C. Ruppenthal, ed. 12th edition. 3 vols. Rochester, N.Y.: The Lawyers Co-operative Publishing Co., 1932.

White, Leonard D. Public Administration. In President's Research Committee on Social Trends, Recent Social Trends in the United States, p. 1391. One-volume edition. New York: Whittlesey House, 1934.

Whitehead, Alfred North. Science and the Modern World. New York: New American Library, Mentor Books, 1948.

Wiebe, Robert H. Businessmen and Reform: A Study of the Progressive Movement. Cambridge, Mass.: Harvard University Press, 1962.

Wiesner, Jerome B. Where Science and Politics Meet. New York: McGraw-Hill, 1965.

Wigmore, John Henry. Evidence. 3d edition. 10 vols. Boston: Little, Brown, 1940.

Wildavsky, Aaron. The Politics of the Budgetary Process. Boston: Little, Brown, 1964. See also Davis et al.

Willey, Malcolm M., and Stuart A. Rice. The Agencies of Communication. In President's Research Committee on Social Trends, Recent Social Trends in the United States, p. 167. One-volume edition. New York: Whittlesey House, 1934.

Williams, Robin M., Jr. American Society: A Sociological Interpretation. New York: Alfred A. Knopf, 1951.

Wilson, Joan Hoff. Herbert Hoover: Forgotten Progressive. Boston: Little, Brown, 1975.

Wilson, Woodrow. Congressional Government. 9th edition. Boston: Houghton Mifflin, 1894.

Winters, Glenn R., and Robert E. Allard. Judicial Selection and Tenure in the United States. In The Courts, the Public and the Law Explosion, edited by Harry W. Jones, p. 146. Englewood Cliffs, N.J.: Prentice-Hall, 1965.

Wisconsin Legislative Reference Library. Debt Limitations and the State Building Program in Wisconsin. Bulletin No. 152. Madison, 1956.

Withey, Stephen B. See Fisher and Withey.

Wolfman, Bernard. Federal Tax Policy and the Support of Science. In Law and the Social Role of Science, edited by Harry W. Jones, p. 25. New York: The Rockefeller University Press, 1966.

Woodbury, Robert S. The "American System" of Manufacturing. In Technology and Social Change in America, edited by Edwin T. Layton, Jr., p. 47. New York: Harper & Row, 1973.

Wooddy, Carroll H. The Growth of Governmental Functions. In President's Research Committee on Social Trends, Recent Social Trends in the United States, p. 1274. One-volume edition. New York: Whittlesey House, 1934.

Wright, Benjamin F., Jr. The Contract Clause of the Constitution. Cambridge, Mass.: Harvard University Press, 1938.

Zahler, Helene S. See Hacker and Zahler.

Zeitlin, Maurice. "Corporate Ownership and Control: The Large Corporation and the Capitalist Class," 79 American Journal of Sociology 1073 (1974).

Zimmerman, Joseph F. State and Local Government. New York: Barnes & Noble, 1962.

Zimring, Frank. "Is Gun Control Likely to Reduce Violent Killings?" 35 University of Chicago Law Review 721 (1968).

Zollman, Carl. American Civil Church Law. New York: Columbia University, 1917.

Index

Abolitionists, 90

Academies, 50, 86, 150; *see also* Education

Accidents, industrial, 33, 197; *see also* Factories *and* Safety

Adams, John Quincy, 182

Adkins v. *Children's Hospital,* 230

Administration, corporate, 244

Administrative arm of government, 143-154; and committees of legislature, 33; conflict of interests, 151-152; consumers protected by, 236; corporate charters issued by, 87; delegation of powers to, 270, 271; detail handled by, 140, 150, 151, 152; distrust of, 143, 145, 151; expertise, 35, 147; failures, 217-218, 222, 229, 236, 269; fragmenting of policy, 150; incrementalism and budgets, 112; investigations by legislature as check, 123-124; judicial review of, 152; legislative power limited by, 95, 96-97, 104-105, 116-117; 1905-1915 a critical decade for, 33, 36, 40, 87, 96, 137, 141, 145-146; nineteenth-century neglect of, 40, 167; practical construction of statutes by, 142, 152; preventive law and, 254, 255; separation of powers and, 25, 26, 35, 40, 41, 139-140, 144-145, 271; special interests and, 70, 72, 218; specialization as mark of, 140, 150, 151, 152; timing of growth in twentieth-century, 145, 167

Administrative Procedure Act, federal, 153

Advertising, 160, 218, 245

Age, as basis of legal classification, 68, 75, 79

Agency, law of, 188

Agrarianism, *see* Farmers

Agricultural Adjustment Act, Thomas Amendment to, 234

Agricultural Economics, Bureau of, 258

Agriculture: commercial, 29; second chambers as representing, 29; waterpower subordinated to, 23

Agriculture, U.S. Department of, 175

Aliens; Act Concerning, 63; discrimination against, 77; occupations, 76; vote, 27

Allison Commission, 182

Allocation of resources by government, 266-269; *see also* Fiscal power; Legislatures: Congress: purse power; *and* Legislatures: State legislatures: purse power

American Academy of Arts and Sciences, 168

American Philosophical Society, 168, 190

American Telephone & Telegraph Co., 51, 169

Anomie, *see* Associations, private *and* City

Antitrust law, 138, 146, 162, 218, 222, 242, 246-266; administered prices, 257-258; affirmative action the duty of government, 251; Antitrust Division, U.S. Department of Justice, 258, 259; bigness not destroyed by, 264, 265; civil actions, 252; concentration and balance of power, 49, 51, 80-81, 264, 265, 273; corporations as